Put 'em Up!

Pickled 'Shrooms

CORN SALSA

GRAPE SYRUP

PICKLED Spring RAMPS

Tomato Aspic

CHARRED CHILI BBQ SAUCE

DRIED MUSH-ROOMS

TARRAGON VINEGAR

FIGS preserved in Honey

Dilly Beans

Pickled Sweet Peppers

PUT 'EM UP!

A COMPREHENSIVE
HOME PRESERVING GUIDE
FOR THE CREATIVE COOK
FROM DRYING AND FREEZING
TO CANNING AND PICKLING

SHERRI BROOKS VINTON

Chili Tomato Jam

SWEET & SOUR PICKLED ONION

Storey Publishing

*The mission of Storey Publishing is to serve our customers by
publishing practical information that encourages
personal independence in harmony with the environment.*

Edited by Margaret Sutherland and Rebecca Springer
Art direction and book design by Dan O. Williams
Text production by Liseann Karandisecky

Photography by © Kevin Kennefick
Author photo by Lindsay France
Illustrations by © Elara Tanguy

Indexed by Christine Lindemer, Boston Road Communications

Storey Publishing
210 MASS MoCA Way
North Adams, MA 01247
www.storey.com

Printed in the United States by Quad/Graphics
10 9 8 7 6 5 4

Library of Congress Cataloging-in-Publication Data

Vinton, Sherri Brooks, 1968–
 Put 'em up! / by Sherri Brooks Vinton.
   p. cm.
 Includes index.
 ISBN 978-1-60342-546-9 (paper with flaps : alk. paper)
 1. Vegetables—Preservation 2. Fruit—Preservation. 3. Cookery (Vegetables)
4. Cookery (Fruit)
 I. Title.
TX612.V4V56 2010
641.6′51—dc22
              2010009609

For all of the home cooks
who nourish family and friends,
culture, and tradition

Contents

Part One: Techniques

Part Two: Recipes

CORN SALSA

page 179

SWEET & SOUR PICKLED ONION

page 220

Pickled 'Shrooms

page 216

Chili Tomato Jam

page 169

CHARRED CHILI BBQ SAUCE

page 167

CURRIED cauliflower

page 151

page 209

Orange MAR-MA-LADE

page 173

Dilly Beans

page 118

DRIED CORN

page 177

FIGS preserved in Honey

page 196

PICKLED CHILI PEPPERS

page 164

GRAPE SYRUP

page 202

Introduction

"*Why on earth would you do that?*" That's what people want to know when they see me moving through the hardware store balancing five cases of Mason jars on my way to the cash register. It's often followed by *"Aren't you afraid you'll kill someone?"* I guess these questions pretty much sum up the most widely held beliefs about home food preservation: 1) that it's hugely time-consuming and not worth the effort, and 2) that it's mysterious, difficult, and wickedly dangerous. Well, I say, not true and not true. Home food preservation is simple and delicious, and no one was harmed in the making of this book.

Preserving your own food doesn't have to be complicated. Some procedures, like stringing a chili ristra (see page 164), take no more than 10 minutes and require nothing more than a length of string to accomplish. In fact, I'd say that I would probably spend more time running back and forth to the grocery store acquiring the food I've put up than I do preserving it (and no checkout line!).

The results of putting up your own food are phenomenal for many reasons, which I will discuss in detail in the chapters to come. In short, home preserved foods are much better than anything you could find on a store shelf anywhere, ever. The jams are fruitier, the pickles are more flavorful, and the chutneys and relishes will trick out your dinner table like nothing else. Your friends will be beating down the door for a taste.

And fear not: It's no more dangerous than cooking dinner. A few simple rules to follow and you're on your way. If you still have a case of the canning jitters, there are plenty of recipes here that show you how to put up a pile of food without going near a canner. I promise you, though, that once you start preserving your own food, you'll be hooked and find yourself deep in the ferment in no time.

IF I WERE THE ONLY ONE bouncing around with the home-preserving pom-poms, you might just be able to write me off as an isolated food fanatic. But I'm far from the only cheerleader for putting up your own food. Preserving is hot! People are rediscovering the pleasure of the process: the delight of squirreling away locally grown corn, the joy of putting by some of those treasured summer strawberries, the kinky thrill of opening up our own jarred tomatoes in the middle of February. We get together for canning parties, attend pickle tastings, and trade jam recipes.

CHERRY AND BLACK PEPPER PRESERVES, PAGE 160

Why? Well, obviously because we're hedonists. This stuff tastes great! But also because home food preservation is a natural progression of the Real Food Revival — our increasing demand for food that is grown the way it should and used to be. We want food that's good for the farmer, the environment, and ourselves. Putting up food is part of this passion. It's part of coveting the harvest so much that you can't let it slip through your fingers so fleetingly. It's part of cherishing the work of local growers or your own toil in the backyard and wanting to hold on to some aspect of that even when fields lie fallow.

Putting up food is also about nourishing cultural and culinary traditions that should be enjoyed and preserved. Even though there was no one in the kitchen dictating recipes, I have rich memories of my granny Toni putting by her own garden — her tomatoes and cucumbers, her cherries and peaches. Even though she never gave me the measurements that went into the crock, I carry the memory of what a good homemade pickle tastes like. My grandmother Lucille never sat me down and explained how to make jam, but I remember tasting the good stuff on a biscuit hot from the oven on one of our trips to the family farm in South Carolina. I want my kids to have memories like these, too.

For many, the tradition of preserving food has skipped a generation. Our grandparents put up food but their children did not. I've heard this from a number of cooks my age — we're about 40 — who have fond memories of our grandparents' pickles or a great-aunt's jelly but didn't have it going on in our parents' homes. If my generation doesn't pick up the thread, we'll lose these techniques.

This stuff is just too tasty and the tradition too rich to let it go. So that's why on earth I do it.

Why Preserve Your Own Food?

Home-preserved foods are . . .

DELICIOUS. The number one reason to do this? Taste! The flavors of foods you preserve yourself are terrifically fresh. Best of all, they reflect your palate. Like your salsa spicy, mild, or off-the-charts hot? Make it the way you take it.

HIGH QUALITY. When you preserve your own food, you control its quality. You know your food is coming from local growers you can trust. Everything is farm fresh and wholesome. These recipes don't use any artificial preservatives, colorings, or additives.

ECONOMICAL. Home preserving will save you money in a number of ways. When you preserve food, you're often purchasing produce in bulk — by the flat or bushel — quantities that farmers sometimes sell at a reduced price. Home-canned goods make great gifts; just think of all the shopping time and money you'll save! And now you have a way to use up all that zucchini that would otherwise go to waste.

GREEN. Home food preservation is planet-friendly. Preserving locally grown food reduces reliance on imported produce, so it minimizes energy-intensive shipping. Locally sourced foods are more likely to come from small, biodiverse farms that do not require the chemical applications that are commonplace in large monocultures. Supporting local agriculture protects open space. Canned and dried foods are shelf-stable, so they don't require the energy for storage that frozen foods do. Even home-frozen foods don't require the energy-intensive industrial processing, refrigerated shipping, and storage of their commercial counterparts.

TRADITIONAL. Putting food by preserves cultural and social traditions. For many of us, home food preservation is part of our family heritage, with recipes that have passed down through generations. Many of these recipes reflect the culinary traditions of ancient cultures, some dating from ancient Persia, medieval Europe, and even the days before the Lower East Side was hip. Canning is the new knitting circle: get together with friends, open a bottle of wine, put up a case of tomatoes, and preserve the art of preserving.

Sourcing Food

For home food preservation, sourcing local food really is the only choice. Of course, as someone who eats a mostly local diet, I would say that sustainably produced, local food is always the best way to fly. Simply put, enjoying the bounty of local agriculture — even if it's just a small patch in your backyard — is the single best thing you can do for our natural resources, the community, and yourself. Acres of sustainably farmed land purify the air, enrich the soil, and reduce fuel-intensive food shipping. Local farms also boost the regional economy by keeping grocery dollars in the community and creating a variety of jobs both on and off the farm.

Supporting your foodshed is also important because, as Wendell Berry says, eating locally produced foods keeps agriculture in our culture. It protects our vital food chain from the changing tides of foreign policy, it ensures that our kids will grow up with an understanding of and respect for well-produced food, and it deepens our commitment to protecting our natural resources.

Some of the reasons that the food you put by should come from nearby:

LOCAL FOOD IS FRESHEST. Produce typically takes about 6 days to make the journey from the fields to store shelves. Food that you preserve should be no more than a day or two old, so that you capture the produce at its peak of flavor. More important, fresher produce is more likely to be free of the molds that threaten the success and safety of preserving.

LOCAL FOOD IS MORE FLAVORFUL. Fruits and vegetables sold in grocery stores are often picked unripe so they can withstand the rigor of the journey to the produce department. Locally grown food ripens in the field or on the vine, providing you with that much more flavor.

LOCALLY PRODUCED FOOD IS LESS LIKELY TO BE TREATED. Produce sold in grocery stores is often coated with edible waxes and fungicides to prolong shelf life. These applications can come between you and good results by hampering the food's ability to soak up brines and syrups.

YOU WILL BE PUTTING BY MEMORIES. Harvest a flat of blueberries from your area pick-your-own and you will be not only canning jam but also storing away the memory of a sunny afternoon with your friends or family.

How to Use This Book

I have organized this book by produce item. In doing so, I hope to help answer the question "What do I do with . . . ?" Because, if you're like me, sometimes — maybe many times — throughout the season you find yourself with a little too much of a good thing. Perhaps you've been seduced by the ruby red strawberries that just came into season and returned home with all you could carry. Or maybe you have a garden blessed with the too many varieties of tomatoes that looked so good in the catalog and are now overrunning the kitchen. Or you're the neighbor of a gardener who is on the surplus side of zucchini that just kept coming. However you come by it, sometimes abundance finds you looking for something — anything — to keep these fresh-from-the-farm goodies from going to waste. Here's the plan.

Within each produce item there are a number of recipes that vary in time commitment, from the very quick and easy to what one might consider "project cooking." Pick the one that suits your schedule or energy level. The recipes also offer a range of preservation methods that can be used with that produce item. Among ideas for getting the most out of your harvest are options for *fresh storage*, extended preservation in the *refrigerator* and *freezer*, using *infusions* to extract or preserve flavor, *drying* techniques, and *canning*, with step-by-step instructions for creating shelf-stable foods using the *boiling-water method*.

The recipes are designed so that no experience is required to ensure safe and delicious results. If you're an old hat at putting up the harvest, I hope you'll find some fresh ideas and flavor combinations that take you in new directions. But you don't have to have a culinary degree to turn out these goods. Granted, some recipes are simpler than others. But even the more detailed recipes will get you from start to finish if this is your first time cranking up a canner.

I have tried to limit the amount of special equipment or ingredients you'll need to accomplish these recipes. After you've come back from the market, the U-pick, or the garden, you may not have the time or energy to go shopping for complicated gadgets or things. Plus, home food preservation is an exercise in economy, not consumerism, so you shouldn't have to invest a lot of money in new, single-use gadgets to get the job done.

It's the same with your kitchen. I had a gifted art professor, Daniel Kazimierski, who once said, "People take pictures, not cameras." Meaning, of course, that you don't need a high-end Leica to get a good shot. I have canned on an electric stovetop. I have friends who turn out great pantries from their little two-burner, Barbie-sized apartment ranges. You don't need state-of-the-art, top-of-the-line anything to accomplish these recipes. Human-scale BTUs will do just fine.

Above all, relax and enjoy. Good food is for everyone. Cooking is easy and fun, so get into that kitchen and put 'em up!

SWEET-AND-SOUR PICKLED ONIONS, PAGE 220

Part One: Techniques

page 182

page 280

page 127

page 211

page 215

page 188

page 246

page 151

page 196

page 140

TOMATO ASPIC

FROZEN BLUE-BERRIES

TARRAGON VINEGAR

DRIED MUSH-ROOMS

Classic CROCK PICKLES

PICKLED

CURRIED cauliflower

FIGS preserved in Honey

MASON

Techniques

*P*reserving food is really a two-step process: preparing the food and choosing a preservation method to make it last longer. Sometimes a preparation method can be used for different methods of preserving. For example, you can prepare green beans by blanching them and then preserve them by freezing or drying. Prepare tomatoes by turning them into a ketchup, and then preserve them for a brief time by storing that ketchup in the refrigerator or for a longer time by making it shelf-stable using the boiling-water method. I have broken down the techniques into two sections — *Food Preparation Methods* and *Food Preservation Methods*. These reflect the two aspects of putting up food. For each technique, I outline any extra equipment or special ingredients you need to make it work, the steps to follow, and recommendations for storage.

For all of these techniques, I think you will also find handy:

PLENTY OF TEA TOWELS

Preserving is wet work. You might not expect it, but even drying produce, which often calls for the very wet step of blanching, has its sopping moments. It's very helpful indeed to have plenty of material to mop up the damp, even if it's just a pile of cut-up old T-shirts. Don't use scented laundry detergent, and steer clear of dryer sheets, which will leave your produce smelling "April fresh." That scent might be a good quality in a bath towel; not so much in a pickle.

A KITCHEN SCALE FOR WEIGHING PRODUCE

This is not a critical piece of equipment, but boy is it a time-saver. If you don't have a kitchen scale, you can always ask the grower at the farmers' market to weigh the produce to suit your recipe, but make sure to label the bags. I've spent my share of time in the middle of the kitchen with my arms stretched out like the hands of justice, trying to determine if it was the onions that weighed two pounds or the apples.

Food Preparation Methods

It all started innocently enough. I didn't really have a focused plan to start preserving my own food. I just had a few strawberries lying around that were starting to pout from being off the vine for a day. Sad. So, in the middle of making dinner, I just plucked off their stems and tossed them into a pot with a little sugar and cooked them until they broke down a bit. Voila! — Back-Burner Strawberry Sauce was born. My kids loved it, it was so easy to do, and I was so turned on by the prospect of being able to stop the hands of time on fading food that I began to dabble some more in this kind of alchemy. Refrigerator pickles were next — just boil up some brine, add it to the vegetables and — ta-da — lovely, lively, refrigerator pickles. And from there I've just kept going.

You can just jump in, too. If you feel a bit daunted at the prospect of making these recipes, it helps to think of putting up food as having two separate components — food preparation and food preservation. In this chapter I talk about all of the techniques — blanching and making agua fresca, granita, jams and jellies, vinegar pickles, fermented pickles, salsas and chutneys, relishes, butters, sauces, and ketchups — you will need to essentially stop your food's aging process. In fact, even if you go no further than this chapter you will be able to save piles of fresh food from a date with the compost (and loads of grocery dollars in perishable food).

Whether you have a little extra produce or a lot — six extra apples or a freshly picked bushel — this section will help you prep them before you lose them. You'll be able to put together some jam while dinner simmers, or whip up some tomato sauce while you watch a movie, not your stove. It's all you need to buy yourself some time before good food goes bad. So let's get started.

BLANCHING

Blanching is often called for in food preservation recipes. It's a simple process: you drop small batches of produce into a pot of boiling water, boil them briefly, then scoop them out and plunge them into ice water. Why go through this extra step? Well, blanching serves a number of purposes:

- Most important, blanching deactivates natural enzymes in food that would hasten its decay.

- It helps to set the color of foods.

- It makes it easier to remove the skins of fruits such as tomatoes and peaches.

- It coaxes liquid out of produce so that it won't dilute a pickling brine.

- It softens foods so they're easier to pack into canning jars and freezer containers.

- It softens skins, such as grape skins, so they dry more readily.

EQUIPMENT

▶ LARGE POT (FOR BOILING WATER)

If you have a canning kit, by all means use the canner. But, you can use any large stock, soup, or lobster pot you have. A cover helps the water reach and return to a boil more quickly, so you'll need a lid, too.

▶ SLOTTED SPOON OR SPIDER (TO REMOVE THE PRODUCE)

I prefer the mesh spiders you can buy in Asian groceries or at restaurant supply stores to scoop produce out of the blanching water. Their open weave picks up just the produce, not the hot water. You can also use a slotted spoon, but try to find a large one so you don't need to make too many scoops.

▶ LARGE BOWL OR COOLER (FOR SHOCKING PRODUCE)

You're going to need something large enough to hold the produce you're work- ing with plus enough ice and water to chill it. If you're doing only a small batch of produce — 2 pounds or so — a large bowl will be fine. For really substantial quantities of produce, an insulated cooler is handy. Just scrub it so it's nice and clean. If you haven't got a cooler, the freshly scrubbed kitchen sink will hold the ice bath.

KEY INGREDIENTS

▶ ICE, AND PLENTY OF IT

I've tried using reusable freezer packs, thinking they would chill the water and save my supply of ice, but they aren't nearly as effective. Either freeze extra trays the night before (you'll need six to eight trays for a typical 25-pound case of produce) or pick up a 5-pound bag and stash it in the freezer until you're ready to use it.

BLANCHING STEP-BY-STEP

1. ▶ Wash all produce.

2. ▶ Fill a large bowl, cooler, or the sink halfway with water. Add enough ice to chill the water without melting all of the ice (six to eight trays or 3 to 5 pounds).

3. ▶ Bring a large pot of water to a rolling boil.

4. ▶ Using a slotted spoon, place about a pound of produce in the pot. It's important to keep the batches small so that the water can regain its boil quickly without cooking the food through.

Give produce a quick dip
in boiling water.

5. ▶ Begin timing after the water has returned to a boil. Blanch the produce for the length of time indicated in the recipe.

6. ▶ Using a spider or slotted spoon, scoop the produce from the boiling water and plunge it directly into the ice bath.

Shock the produce in ice water
to stop the cooking.

7. ▶ Let the food chill in the ice bath while you repeat the process in small batches with the remaining produce.

8. ▶ When all of the produce has been blanched and then chilled, drain and proceed with the recipe.

MAKING AGUA FRESCA AND GRANITA

Agua fresca is a delicious, refreshing beverage from Mexico. Fresh fruit juice is lightly sweetened and spiked with citrus. It's the perfect complement to the grilled foods of summer, a cooling beverage when paired with spicy foods, and a terrific base for a cocktail. It's quick and easy to make; you'll want to have some on hand all summer long. Make a little extra for the freezer and you can enjoy it year-round. Don't want to fuss with straining? Then just combine the puréed fruit with a little simple syrup, pour into a shallow pan, and freeze for granita.

EQUIPMENT

▶ A BLENDER OR FOOD PROCESSOR

Okay, I'm really not crazy about gadgets, particularly the kind you have to plug in, but it really helps to release the juice for this recipe quickly if you grind the fruit. Unlike rendering juice for jelly, you don't have to concern yourself with clarity here, so you can pulverize the pulp as much as you like. I've grated produce on a box grater and then squeezed the pulp by the handful to release the juice. It's possible and an alternative if you need it, but absolutely no fun at all.

▶ A STRAINING RIG

You have to drain the ground-up pulp. Use either a fine-mesh sieve or a colander lined with a single layer of cheesecloth set over a bowl. Agua fresca, unlike jelly, doesn't require the tight weave that would yield a clear juice, so you don't have to be too careful about the setup. Any kind of small-weave strainer is fine.

KEY INGREDIENTS

▶ FRESH-ISH PRODUCE

This agua fresca will be stored in the fridge or the freezer, so it's fine to cut away any bumped-up sections of the produce and use the rest without compromising the integrity of the recipe. Feel free to use the half melon left over from the weekend party that isn't going to get eaten during the week, or the cucumbers you picked on Wednesday for a refreshing Sunday-brunch eye-opener. Of course, truly sad produce belongs in the compost, not in your belly.

▶ SWEETENER

I don't mind sugar, but if you do, substitute something else. I think honey's strong taste overpowers in this beverage (apologies to my beekeeping friends), but stevia or agave nectar are good choices.

▶ LIME JUICE

A tangy little spark will brighten the flavor of the strained juice. If you don't have lime, any other citrus will do.

STORAGE

Refrigerate for up to 3 days or freeze in small freezable containers for up to 6 months.

AGUA FRESCA AND GRANITA STEP-BY-STEP

1. ▶ Set a fine-mesh sieve or colander lined with dampened cheesecloth over a bowl.

2. ▶ Purée the produce in a blender or food processor, working in batches as necessary.

3. ▶ Transfer the puréed produce to the sieve or colander as you go.

4. ▶ Let the mixture drain fully.

Strain puréed fruit for agua fresca.

5. ▶ Compost the solids and pour the juice into a pitcher.

6. ▶ Add water and sugar to the juice, as instructed in the recipe, and stir to dissolve the sugar.

With a bit more sugar to taste and some citrus, agua fresca is ready to serve.

7. ▶ Serve over ice, with a splash of seltzer (optional).

MAKING JAMS AND JELLIES

My friend and editor Gabrielle Langholtz knows a great little French rhyme she shared with me: "La vie est dure sans confiture" (Life is hard without jam). Indeed it is. You should always have some little sweet thing in the pantry.

Jam is often a cook's canning debut. It's tasty and pretty and fun to give to friends. With all of the acid from the fruit and the added sugar, it's also relatively stable from a foodborne illness perspective — a big plus for anyone with first-time canning jitters.

I have to say, though, that jam can be tricky, particularly if you expect the homemade jam to be just like the store-bought kind. Some of the most experienced canning pros hit a jam hurdle every once in a while. They've come up with the batch that wouldn't set, the pot that turned rubbery as it cooled, the fruit that bobbed to the top of the jar rather than dispersing equally throughout. And double that for jelly, which, being made mostly from clear fruit juice, mercilessly shows its flaws.

I say, "So what." We're not out to win any blue ribbons here. We're in this to feed our families, our friends, and ourselves. Sometimes the careful balance of fruit and sugar, acid, and pectin goes a little haywire. No matter. If it's real food, it will be real good. A jam or jelly that's a little loose is still a gorgeous, delicious sauce for ice cream or waffles. One that's a little stiff is still a shockingly good thing to whiz into a smoothie or, dare I say it, downright decadent blended into a margarita. And if you've got bobbing fruit in your jam (also called fruit float), well, that's jam on the top and jelly on the bottom. Tell everyone you meant to do it that way and no one will know you didn't.

EQUIPMENT

▶ **A HEAVY-BOTTOMED POT**

High heat and sugar are a recipe for scorching. A heavy-bottomed pot reduces the chance that the jam or jelly will burn during cooking. It can be a Dutch oven with high sides or a skillet with relatively low sides, as long as there is enough height for the spread to boil without bubbling over (you don't want that mess on the stove). But thicker is definitely better.

▸ JELLY BAG OR CHEESECLOTH

Whereas jam is made from the whole fruit, jelly is made from the juice alone. To extract the juice, you need to strain the fruit gently through a jelly bag or a colander lined with a double layer of cheesecloth set over a bowl. A jelly bag renders the clearest juice, but you need a special stand for it and the whole thing stacks up quite tall. So, if you plan to strain pulp overnight, as is often required in jelly recipes, you may have to do a bit of rearranging in the fridge. A cheesecloth-lined strainer doesn't have the fine mesh of a jelly bag, so it may not give you the same level of clarity, but I find it much easier to use. I always have cheesecloth on hand and the lined colander and bowl fit easily into the fridge, so for me it's the more user-friendly option.

▸ CANDY THERMOMETER (OPTIONAL)

There are several ways to test whether a spread has reached the gelling stage. One is to watch its temperature on a candy thermometer (220°F is the magic number here). If you have one, time to bust it out. If you haven't, we'll talk about alternative tests you can run in the "Testing for Gel" section (see page 38).

KEY INGREDIENTS

▸ PECTIN

Pectin is the natural thickening agent found in fruits. Some fruits have more pectin than others (see the chart at right). Underripe fruit always has more pectin than fully ripened fruit. To make jam or jelly out of lower-pectin fruits or even vegetables (such as the Sweet Pepper Jam on page 264), you'll have to incorporate some additional pectin to get it to gel.

I use Pomona's Universal Pectin for all of the recipes in this book that require additional pectin. Pomona's is very versatile; it doesn't require a large quantity of sugar to set and can be used for both refrigerator and shelf-stable preparations. Pomona's comes as a two-part kit that contains pectin powder and calcium powder, which act together to gel your spread. The quantities to use are outlined in each recipe.

▸ GORGEOUS FRUIT

The fruit should look good and be free of rot and mold. I've heard that many economically minded cooks buy seconds for jams and jellies, but I don't recommend it. The spot on the peach is really just the tip of the bacterial iceberg. Even if you

Fruit Pectin Levels

HIGH-PECTIN FRUITS

tart cooking apples
blackberries
boysenberries
citrus skins (oranges, tangerines, grape-
    fruit, lemons, limes; the pectin is high
    in the skin but low in the fruit)
cranberries
currants
gooseberries
wild grapes (Eastern Concord variety)
plums
quince

MEDIUM-PECTIN FRUITS

ripe apples
sour cherries
figs
grapes (California)
rhubarb

LOW-PECTIN FRUITS

apricots
blueberries
sweet cherries
melons
pears
raspberries
strawberries

VERY LOW–PECTIN FRUITS

nectarines
peaches

cut away that section, there are colonies of bacteria that reach deep into the fruit — too much for the home canning process to compensate for. You could wind up with moldy jelly — or worse — on the shelf. Start with fresh, wholesome fruits.

Berries are particularly fragile, so that can mean processing on the same day the berries are picked. If you can't manage the double-header of picking and putting up, just freeze the berries and process them into jam and jelly when you have ample time to do so (see Freezing, page 61).

Fresh does not have to mean perfectly ripe, however. In fact, the ripeness of the fruit will play an important role in the setting ability of the jam and jelly. Unripened fruits have much more firming pectin than do fully ripened ones. It's a good idea to use at least one-third underripe fruit (peaches that are a bit hard, for example, or strawberries with white shoulders) to guarantee a good set.

▶ SUGAR

Sugar plays a number of roles in jam and jelly making:

- It helps the gel to set.

- It preserves the color of the spread on the shelf.

- It increases shelf life once the spread is opened.

- It gives jam and jelly an unctuous, satiny texture and a glossy sheen.

The jam and jelly recipes in this book use an amount of sugar that I think lets the flavor of the fruit shine through without overburdening it. It is often significantly less sugar than in other spread recipes. This is perfectly safe. Just like their high-sugar counterparts, these spreads will stay shelf-stable for up to a year if processed using the boiling-water method. For a sweeter jam or jelly, you can increase, up to double, the amount of sugar recommended here.

▶ ACID

Most fruits are naturally acidic to some degree. Some require a little additional acid, most commonly bottled lemon juice, to make a successful jam or jelly. Although fresh lemon juice tastes great, it's not the one to use for shelf-stable recipes. The acidity of lemons varies, so your citrus might not pack the power necessary to get the job done. Unless otherwise noted, use bottled lemon juice, which has a more reliable level of acidity. The acid performs a number of duties in the jelly and jam business:

- Most important, acid is the key to safety. *Never eliminate or reduce the amount of acid (lemon juice or vinegar) called for in any recipe* — even jams and jellies. Likewise, make sure you measure the fruit and use the quantity detailed in the recipe to ensure enough acid in the mix to keep things safe.

- Acid works with pectin to help the jam or jelly set.

- Acid brightens the flavor of jams and jellies, particularly long-cooking spreads. It revives the fruit flavor and makes the spread taste fresh.

PROCESS

▶ CLASSIC JAM, LONG-COOKED

Long cooking is the traditional method of making jams. These jams use no additional pectin to reach their gel stage, which affects the results in a number of ways. They have a deeper flavor, with the notes of caramel that some cherish, from the long cooking process. The longer simmer also means you'll have a more concentrated flavor but less jam volume. Because the jam cooks a long time, air that might be trapped in the fruit during a quick cooking will be released, so you have less chance of fruit float. The texture is tender and succulent. Worth the extra cooking time, if you ask me.

▶ QUICK-COOK JAMS

Quick-cook jams use added pectin, rather than long cooking, to help them set. There are some advantages to this. You spend less time at the stove, which is crucial when food is coming from the field almost faster than you can process it. The jam also has a lighter, fruitier flavor that some find appealing. And because you aren't cooking it down, you retain a greater volume of jam.

For my quick-cook jams, I use Pomona's Universal Pectin because it allows me to control the amount of sugar I use in my recipes. I like the taste of a not-so-sweet jam or jelly. You can really taste the fruit. Sometimes this results in fruit float: the finished product will have a layer of jam at the top of the jar and a layer of jelly at the bottom. This is because there isn't enough sugar saturating the fruit to weigh it down in the suspension. It won't win you any blue ribbons at the county fair, but this aesthetic trade-off is fine with me if it results in bright, full-of-fruit flavor. When you open a jar, just stir the fruit back into suspension. If you find fruit float unappealing or if you simply prefer a sweeter spread, feel free to double the sugar quantity listed in any recipe.

▶ JELLY

Jellies are the jewels of the pantry — gorgeous little gems in sparkling colors. They are made by gelling fruit juice. Because you strain out the solids, it takes a large volume of fruit to yield the pure juice you need for the recipe. I don't make a lot of jellies — I prefer a more varied texture most of the time. But for fruits such as watermelon and raspberries that have more seeds than I'm willing to put up with, jelly is the way to go.

There are two main challenges when making jelly. The first is getting it to set properly. When you remove all of the rinds, skins, and pips, you take away a good deal of the natural pectin that makes spreads firm up. Keep in mind that jellies can take a week or more — even after processing — to reach their full gelling potential, so a jelly that seems a bit loose right after cooling may well be perfect in the coming days. Give it time and don't fret. If in the end it's still not right, try to make it over by reheating it and adding a little more pectin to tighten it up, or thin it with a little extra juice or water to loosen the jelly a touch. Or just love it as it is and pour it over pancakes!

Another hurdle to clear when making jelly is clarity. A crystal-clear product is the goal of the serious jelly maker. There are several steps to achieving a clear jelly. Heat the fruit gently before you strain it to avoid clouding. Make sure you use a jelly strainer or several layers of dampened cheesecloth lining a colander to ensure a fine-enough mesh to strain out all the pulp. Never, ever press on the solids or you'll have a cloudy spread. If you achieve crystal perfection, that's great, but I encourage you to enjoy your less-than-perfect jellies as well. Cloudy still tastes great.

CLASSIC JAM STEP-BY-STEP

 1. Combine fruit and a splash of water, as indicated in your recipe, in a medium saucepan.

 2. Bring to a boil, stirring and crushing the fruit to release its juice.

Crush the fruit.

2

3. Add sugar as directed in the recipe, stirring constantly to dissolve it.

4. Add lemon juice, if using.

5. Continue to cook, stirring frequently, until the jam reaches the desired gel (see Testing for Gel, page 38).

3 4

Whisk in sugar and lemon juice.

6. Turn off the heat.

 7. Let the jam rest for 5 minutes, stirring occasionally to release air bubbles and prevent fruit float.

A 5-minute rest-and-stir period releases air trapped in the hot jam.

 8. Skim any foam from the top of the jam.

7

9. Proceed with directions for refrigerating or using the boiling-water method.

QUICK-COOK JAM STEP-BY-STEP

1. Combine the sugar and pectin powder in a small bowl and set aside.

Combine the sugar and pectin powder.

2. Place the produce in a medium saucepan and crush with a potato masher to release its juice and break up the fruit.

3. Slowly bring to a boil.

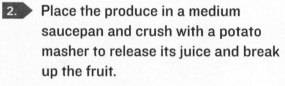

Crush the fruit.

4. Stir in the calcium water (included in the Pomona's Universal Pectin Kit) and lemon juice, if using.

Add lemon juice and calcium water to the hot fruit.

5. ▶ Slowly pour in the sugar-pectin mixture and stir to dissolve.

Add the sugar-pectin mixture to the jam.

6. ▶ Return to a boil, and then remove from the heat and let rest for 5 minutes, stirring occasionally to release air bubbles from the jam.

A 5-minute rest-and-stir period releases air trapped in the hot jam.

7. ▶ Skim off any foam.

Skim foam from the jam.

8. ▶ Proceed with the recipe directions for refrigerating or processing using the boiling-water method.

JELLY STEP-BY-STEP

1. Bring the prepped produce and a splash of water to a boil in a medium saucepan.

2. Reduce the heat and mash the fruit gently with a potato masher or wooden spoon to release its juices.

Gently mashing the fruit helps to release its juices.

3. Simmer as directed in the recipe.

4. Transfer the fruit pulp to a dampened jelly bag hung over a bowl or to a sieve or colander lined with several thicknesses of dampened cheesecloth (so the cloth doesn't wick up the juice) and set over a bowl to collect the juice.

Draining fruit pulp yields juice for jelly.

5. Allow to drain as directed in the recipe, from 2 hours to overnight. Never push on the pulp, as doing so will cloud the jelly.

6. Measure the strained juice and transfer it to a medium saucepan. (Compost the solids or reserve for another use, such as a base for a delicious smoothie.) Bring the juice to a boil.

7. Combine the sugar and pectin, if using, in a small bowl and set aside.

8. To the strained juice, add lemon juice, if using, and calcium water (included in the Pomona's Universal Pectin Kit), if your recipe calls for it, and bring to a boil.

Add calcium water and lemon juice to the fruit juice.

9. Whisk the sugar-pectin mixture into the hot juice and stir to dissolve. Return to a boil.

Add the sugar-pectin mixture to the boiling juice.

10. Turn off the heat and let settle, stirring gently for several minutes to allow any air bubbles to rise.

11. Skim any foam from the surface of the jelly.

Skim foam from the jelly.

12. Proceed with the recipe directions for refrigerating or processing the jelly using the boiling-water method.

Testing for Gel

I don't want to sound like a grandma here, so I won't say cook it until it's done. But jam made without any added pectin can be like that — it's a process that combines art and science. There are some tests you can perform that will help you make the call about when a jam or jelly is ready, and I'll outline them here. But after a few jam sessions, you'll get a feel for it. You'll start to know when it's about there, test or no. And if you misjudge, don't despair. Gel stage is not related to spoilage. If it's too soft, just label it sauce and enjoy it as such.

▸ BUBBLE

Before you run any jam test, just watch the bubbles: they get bigger as the jam approaches its gel stage. You'll notice them turn from small and profuse to bigger, lazier, and less numerous as the jam gets further along. Then you can do any of these other tests to make sure the jam is just right.

Small bubbles mean the jam needs
more time on the stove.

Large bubbles indicate that the gel
stage is approaching.

▶ THERMOMETER

There is a "magic number" for gelling, and that number is 220°F, the temperature at which a jam or jelly technically reaches its gel stage. If you have a candy thermometer, clip it to the side of the pot and keep an eye on the rising mercury (or benign red liquid these days). It's a good guide, but I back it up with visual and taste tests, partly because I just need to get my taste buds into the action. Because I prefer my spreads a little on the loose side, which I find more succulent and inviting, I always wind up taking it off the heat a few degrees under 220°F.

Spreads gel at about 220°F.

▶ SHEETING

When two drops become one — that's the happy moment called sheeting. To check for it, stir the spread with a wooden spoon. Lift the spoon out of the bubbling liquid so it's parallel to the floor and tilt it to face you. The spread will run off the spoon in a stream at first and then in individual drops. When two drops lean into each other on the edge of the spoon and join into one big sloppy drop before dripping off the edge of the spoon, you have sheeting. It reminds me of the way tandem parachuters join hands before leaping out of a plane. It's one of those cooking things that are difficult to picture but once you see them in action, they make perfect sense. Just remember to look for the two drops that hook up before they drip back into the jam pot.

Two drops that become one is a sign that jam or jelly has reached the gel stage.

▶ CHILL

I think this is the easiest test. Put a plate in the freezer. When you think the jam or jelly is nearly ready, drip a few drops onto the cold plate and let cool, then push the smudge with your finger. If it wrinkles when you push it, your jam or jelly is ready. If you push it with your finger and it looks like you're parting a mini Red Sea but there are no wrinkles, cook a few minutes longer and try again. (To be perfectly honest, I love this test, but I always forget to put a plate in the freezer. I just drizzle a few drops onto the bottom of an ice-cream container, which works just as well.)

A drop of jam or jelly that wrinkles when pushed on a cold plate has reached the gel stage.

MAKING VINEGAR PICKLES

Cucumbers may be the vegetable that comes to mind when you think of pickled produce, but the sour, salty, and often sweet flavors of the brines you find in these pages will have you pickling all manner of produce, vegetables, and fruits. Pickled asparagus? Elegant. Pickled cauliflower? A great garnish for a cheese plate. Pickled watermelon rind? A splendid transformation of trash to treasure. After testing recipes for this book, I'm pretty much convinced that if you can grow it, you can pickle it.

Vinegar pickles are often called fresh pickles or quick pickles because they're made without a long fermentation process. They rely on a vinegar brine for the acidity necessary to preserve them safely.

If you've never canned before, vinegar pickles might be the place to start; the recipes are quite straightforward. Unlike jams and jellies, there is no nuanced gel stage to reach. They don't require the chopping and dicing of salsas, chutneys, and relishes. In fact, you can make the easiest vinegar pickles — refrigerator pickles — in minutes and store them in the icebox without any additional processing. Quick and simple: Just follow the recipe for guaranteed delicious results.

Just because they're easy to make, that's not to say that vinegar pickles aren't without merit — they're wondrously delectable, indeed. I love the classic Bread-and-Butter Chips (page 184). But the pickles I adore the most (and that my friends are happiest to share) are the funky combinations. They're no more challenging to accomplish than the standard Dill Spears (page 185), yet the unique flavor combinations make them seem like much more work than they actually entail. Spicy Carrots (page 148), Pickled Beets with Cumin and Cloves (page 121), and Sweet-and-Sour Pickled Onions (page 220) seem exotic, but even the most modestly provisioned kitchen has everything necessary to make them. Do give them a go.

EQUIPMENT

There are no special gadgets required to make vinegar pickles.

KEY INGREDIENTS

▶ ACID

To process pickles safely using the boiling-water method, you must add acid, namely vinegar, to the brine. Some of the recipes call for quantities of vinegar that may sound excessive, perhaps as much as an entire quart. Never reduce the quantity of vinegar called for in a recipe; doing so risks the safety of your food. If you want a less tart pickle, increase the sugar to taste. The vinegar called for most frequently in shelf-stable pickles is distilled vinegar, either white or cider (this is the kind sold in jugs in the supermarket). These vinegars have been standardized to a consistent 5 percent acidity and are labeled as such. This standardization guarantees consistent results when canning. You can use the white and cider vinegars interchangeably in the recipes in this book. Keep in mind, however, that cider vinegar will darken pickles slightly and carries with it a flavor of its own that may or may not please your palate.

There are a lot of delicious vinegars on the market — lovely ones made from wines or infused with herbs. Save them for salads, where the delicate nuances of their flavors can be appreciated. Ditto for gorgeous organic vinegars that come with a living mother on the bottom of the jar. These are terrific and great for you, but the high temperature of the boiling-water method will destroy their probiotic benefits, so you'll be wasting the vinegars — and the money spent on them.

Caution: Do not substitute other vinegars for the ones called for in pickle recipes using the boiling-water method; that could throw off the pH balance and risk the safety of the pickles.

Refrigerator pickles, on the other hand, rely on cold temperatures for preservation, not a critical pH level. If you want to experiment with pickle flavors by varying the amount of vinegar or using different kinds of vinegars, you can safely do so by popping them in the fridge and eating them within a few weeks instead of trying to process them into shelf-stable pickles.

PROCESS

The key to success in making vinegar pickles is simply to follow the recipe. It's also important to prep the produce as indicated in the directions. When following a recipe for pickle chips, for example, make sure to cut the cucumbers into coins as directed. This ensures that the brine you've made will have the time and strength to penetrate the food. Larger pieces might not process sufficiently and, conversely, smaller pieces might overprocess.

Many pickle recipes call for salting or soaking the produce in a brine solution before cooking. This step flavors the produce and also crisps it. The salt in vinegar pickles is not the key to safe food preservation, however; the vinegar is. Vinegar raises the acidity of the recipe so that it is safe for boiling-water processing. Thus, you can reduce the amount of salt you use in the recipe, but *never* alter the quantity of produce or vinegar. That would certainly throw off the pH balance critical for safe pickle production.

▶ HOT-PACK METHOD

There are two ways to fill canning jars: hot pack and cold pack. The hot-pack method — in which food is heated in the preserving liquid — is the more common. Heating softens the produce, giving you a better pack. It also releases air from the cell walls of the produce, so you get less fruit float (produce rising to the top of the liquid after processing).

▶ COLD-PACK METHOD

The cold-pack method — in which you fill the jars with raw food and pour a hot preserving solution over it — gives you a chance to better organize food in the jar. Items such as asparagus and long beans are often cold-packed so that you can stand them all up. Large fruits such as tomatoes and peaches are sometimes cold-packed so that you can better dispel large air pockets or empty spaces around their spherical shapes. Cold-packed items may require additional processing time to enable the heat to penetrate all the way through to the center of the food.

STORAGE

Most of the vinegar pickles in this book can be safely stored in the refrigerator for a short time or made shelf-stable by processing with the boiling-water method. The exceptions are cold-packed pickles that need the heat of the boiling-water method to sufficiently soften the texture of the produce; low-acid pickles that cannot be safely processed using the boiling-water method; and delicately textured pickles that cannot withstand the heat of the boiling-water method. Follow individual recipes for specific storage recommendations.

HOT-PACK VINEGAR PICKLES STEP-BY-STEP

1. ▶ Prep the produce according to the recipe.

2. ▶ Soak or salt as directed.

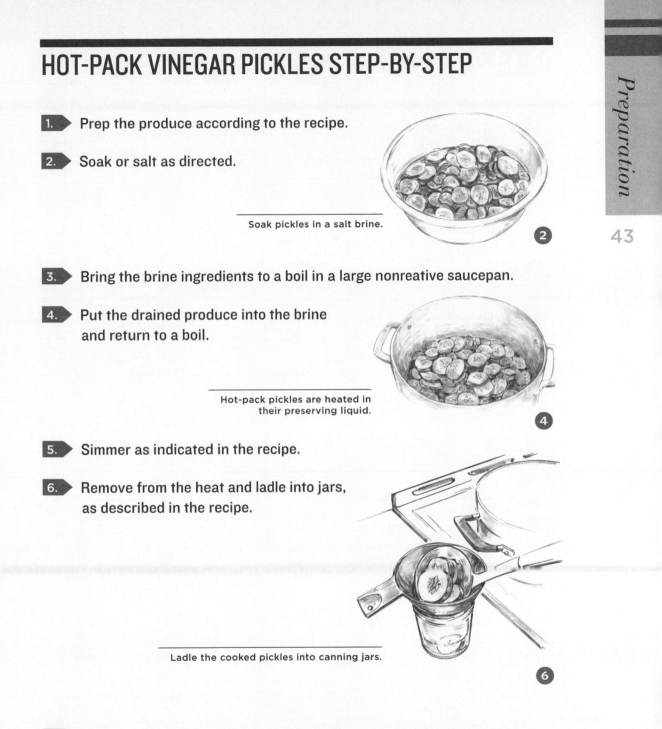

Soak pickles in a salt brine.

2

3. ▶ Bring the brine ingredients to a boil in a large nonreative saucepan.

4. ▶ Put the drained produce into the brine and return to a boil.

Hot-pack pickles are heated in their preserving liquid.

4

5. ▶ Simmer as indicated in the recipe.

6. ▶ Remove from the heat and ladle into jars, as described in the recipe.

Ladle the cooked pickles into canning jars.

6

7. ▶ Follow the recipe instructions for refrigerator or shelf-stable storage.

COLD-PACK VINEGAR PICKLES STEP-BY-STEP

 1. Prep the produce according to the recipe.

 2. Divide the produce among clean, hot canning jars.

Cold-pack pickles are packed raw
in canning jars.

 3. Bring the brine to a boil in a nonreative
saucepan.

4. Ladle the hot brine over the produce.

Hot brine is ladled over the raw
produce to pickle it.

5. Process as directed in the recipe.

MAKING FERMENTED PICKLES

Fermenting your own foods is an amazing process — part science, part art, part ancient tradition. Its alchemical nature makes fermentation a little "dark-arts" creepy for some, but you needn't fear it. Here's the science: fermentation generates lactic acid, which destroys pathogens and gives the brine the acidic pH necessary to make pickles safe (and scrumptious!).

There are two methods for kicking off the fermentation process. One is to make a brine and submerge the produce in it, as you do with Classic Crock Pickles (page 188). The other is to layer the produce with salt, as with Classic Fermented Sauerkraut (page 136), and let the moisture that leaches out of the plant material create its own brine. No matter which method you choose to get the brine, it's the salt in the mix that discourages pathogenic bacteria from growing and encourages beneficial bacteria, like those found in yogurt, to proliferate. This probiotic action is great for digestion — like getting a little tonic with your gherkin. Here's how to make your own.

EQUIPMENT

▶ **LARGE, CLEAN CROCK**

The key piece of equipment for fermenting food is a good clean crock. This can be made of glass, food-grade ceramic, or food-grade plastic. Never use crystal or decorative pottery, as it might contain lead, or metal which may react with the acid or salt. Use only food-grade plastic containers; others may carry residues that could leach into your recipe.

▶ **A PLATE JUST A BIT SMALLER THAN THE CROCK**

The plate is going to keep the vegetables submerged, so it needs to fit inside the crock but not be so small that the produce bobs up in the liquid around it.

Plastics and Preserving

Many recipes call for a plastic bag filled with brine to weigh down the plate. I'm not a fan. I try to keep the amount of plastic in my life, particularly around acidic foods, to a minimum. Additionally, you have to observe the liquid during the fermentation process to check for the formation of scum (some call it bloom), and I find the folds of the plastic make this difficult to do. You also have to dip off this bloom and wash the plate and the weight throughout the process. For me the wrinkles in the plastic make it difficult to remove the bloom efficiently and are really tough to clean.

▶ A WEIGHT TO HOLD DOWN THE PLATE

I use a quart-size canning jar full of water as a weight. It's heavy enough to get the job done, it lifts neatly out of the brine without disturbing the bloom, and it has a nice, smooth surface that is easy to clean.

▶ A CLEAN TEA TOWEL

You want to prevent dust from settling on the brine and curious bugs from flying into it. A nice big clean tea towel serves as an effective tent over the whole thing.

KEY INGREDIENTS

▶ IMPECCABLY FRESH PRODUCE

Fermentation is a war among microorganisms, battling it out right there in the crock. Give the good bacteria the advantage by making sure that contaminants — such as molds and fungi, which develop quickly in decaying produce — are at their smallest possible numbers. For that, you want produce that is straight out of the field and thoroughly washed. Produce that is a few days old may be fine for other recipes, but do not use it here if you want to reach pickle perfection.

▶ SALT

In most of the recipes in this book, salt is used for taste alone. In fermented recipes however, proper salinity is necessary to create safe and tasty results. For these recipes, salt is important to keep detrimental bacteria from crowding out the good bacteria that give these pickles their characteristic flavor. Using more salt than what's called for slows down the fermentation; too much can bring it to a halt. Too little salt and produce will rot rather than ferment.

In all cases I use kosher salt. It's readily available — much more so than pickling salt — so much so that it's becoming the "house salt" for many families, and then it's one less thing to buy. You can also use sea salt, if that's your preference, but highly mineralized salts, such as red and black varieties, may discolor the food and affect their flavors. Don't use table salt that has added iodine; it doesn't dissolve well and will give recipes an off taste.

▶ WATER

Regular tap water is fine for most of the recipes in this book. Fermented recipes, however, are the most sensitive to trace amounts of chlorine and other minerals, so if you're on the borderline, you might want to take some precautions to guarantee the success of your ferment. If you know you have heavily chlorinated water, boil it for a few minutes and then let it come to room temperature before proceeding with the recipe. If you have a high mineral content in your water (faucets tend to have a white or green ring under them) use filtered or distilled water in these recipes.

PROCESS

Fermented pickles, such as Classic Crock Pickles, are submerged in a salty bath that encourages fermentation and discourages the growth of contaminants such as molds and fungi.

Recipes such as Kimchi (page 137) and Classic Fermented Sauerkraut (page 136) can be made without added brine. The salted produce provides all of the moisture needed to create its own pickling liquid

STORAGE

Fermented pickles are a living food, full of natural, beneficial bacteria. I protect this vibrancy by storing pickles in the refrigerator once they're fully fermented. Fermented pickles keep well in the chill of the icebox if you make sure they're submerged under their brine. I love dipping into the pickle pot for a cold, crunchy dill whenever I want one. Subjecting them to the boiling-water method would make them shelf-stable — and a lot of people do it — but the heat kills off all of the beneficial bacteria that are such an important part of our diets.

FERMENTED PICKLES WITH ADDED BRINE STEP-BY-STEP

 1. Thoroughly wash the crock.

 **2.** In the crock, combine the brine ingredients, according to the recipe, and stir to dissolve.

Make the brine for the ferment right in the crock.

3. Add any texture preservatives (such as clean oak leaves), if using.

4. Wash and prep the produce.

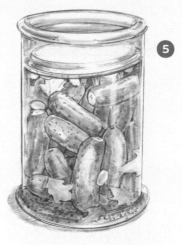 **5.** Add the produce to the crock and submerge under the brine.

Pack cucumbers for pickles into a crock of brine.

6. Press a dish into the solution to keep the produce submerged at least an inch under the brine.

7. If you need more liquid, mix up a solution of 1 tablespoon of salt to 1 cup of water and add it to the pickling liquid to reach the desired volume.

8. ▶ Place a weight on the dish to keep it submerged.

Use a weighted dish to keep the produce submerged.

9. ▶ Cover the top of the container with a tea towel and set aside.

A tea towel keeps contaminants out of the pickles.

10. ▶ Check the ferment every day. You'll see bubbles rising, sometimes ferrying seeds up and down the pickling liquid. That's a good sign.

11. ▶ Skim off any foam or bloom. If you see mold forming on the top of the liquid, dip it out too. Remove the plate and the weight, then wash and replace them.

Check and skim the ferment daily.

12. ▶ When the bubbles stop rising, remove the plate and test a pickle. Slice it in half; it should be uniformly pickled to its center. Take a bite. It should be pleasantly sour and salty. If it isn't uniform in texture or sour enough, let it sit for a day or two to complete the ferment.

FERMENTED PICKLES WITHOUT ADDED BRINE STEP-BY-STEP

1. Thoroughly wash the crock.

2. Prep the produce following the recipe directions.

3. Toss the produce with salt in amounts indicated in the recipe.

Toss the produce with salt.

4. Pack the salted produce into the crock.

Pack the salted produce into the crock.

5. Let rest for an hour.

6. Press the produce further to encourage the brine to rise over the top of the produce.

Press on salted vegetables to create a brine.

7. Press a dish into the solution to keep the produce submerged at least an inch under the brine.

8. If you need more liquid, mix up a solution of I tablespoon of salt to I cup of water and add it to the pickling liquid to reach the desired volume.

9. Place a weight on the dish to keep it submerged.

10. Cover the top of the container with a tea towel and set aside.

Weight down the dish to keep it submerged. A tea towel keeps contaminants out of the pickles.

11. Check the ferment every day. You'll see bubbles rising, sometimes ferrying seeds up and down the pickling liquid. That's a good sign.

12. Skim off any foam. If you see mold forming on the top of the liquid, dip it out, remove the plate and the weight, wash them, and replace them.

Check and skim the ferment daily.

13. When the bubbles stop rising, remove the plate and test a bite. It should be pleasantly sour and salty. If it isn't uniform in texture or sour enough, let it sit for a day or two to complete the ferment.

MAKING SALSAS, CHUTNEYS, AND RELISHES

Salsas, chutneys, and relishes can energize any meal. They're a lifesaver midwinter when low and slow braises and stews leave the palate aching for something tangy and bright. Because they need a good amount of liquid to process properly, these recipes might be a little looser than you're used to. If you don't want as much liquid in the finished product, just drain off a little before serving.

EQUIPMENT

▸ EDWARD SCISSORHANDS

It doesn't take any special equipment to makes salsas, chutneys, and relishes. There is a lot of chopping involved, however, so I recommend a sharp chef's knife, a food processor, a friend with some knife skills, or a combination of the three to help out.

KEY INGREDIENTS

▸ ACID

These condiments are basically a chopped vinegar pickle, the key ingredient for which is plenty of acid. Acid preserves the vegetables, which make up the body of these concoctions, and is necessary, certainly, for any recipe that you want to make shelf-stable. To fill this role significant amounts of vinegar are often required. Sugar is then added to balance out the flavor of the recipe. As with any other preserving recipe that calls for additional acid, never reduce the amount recommended, as you will compromise the quality and therefore the safety of the final product. If the flavor is too tart, increase the amount of sugar to suit your taste. Also, be sure to prep the produce as directed in the recipe so that proper texture and adequate processing will be achieved.

SALSAS, CHUTNEYS, AND RELISHES STEP-BY-STEP

1. Prep the produce according to the recipe.

2. In a large nonreactive pot, bring the brine ingredients to a boil.

Boil the brine.

3. Add the remaining ingredients and simmer, following the recipe.

Simmer to combine flavors and reach the desired texture.

4. Remove from the heat.

5. Package the condiments for the refrigerator or process using the boiling-water method.

MAKING BUTTERS, SAUCES, AND KETCHUPS

These smooth-textured condiments are great tricks to have up your culinary sleeve. They are super-simple to make, requiring in most cases just some boiling and blending. Their surprising flavors and silky texture are a cut above anything you'll find on grocery-store shelves.

Ketchup is a condiment tray staple, but make it yourself and it becomes a richly spiced, tangy dip that will impart an elegant touch to any meal (it will turn fries into *pommes frites* instantly). The exceptional flavor of these homemade condiments will have you using them in unexpected, creative ways. Think Apple Butter (page 110) on a roasted turkey sandwich, or Back-Burner Strawberry Sauce

Using a Food Mill

1. Set the food mill over a bowl and fill halfway with food to be puréed.

2. Turn the crank to purée the food.

3. Turn the crank in the opposite direction and scrape down the sides periodically.

4. Continue to crank until only the seeds and skins remain.

5. Empty and repeat.

Cranking food through the mill purées it.

(page 255) as a base for a cocktail. Something new and tasty from the kitchen: what better reason to bust out the pots and pans?

EQUIPMENT

▶ FOOD MILL

A food mill is a very low-tech but useful tool. It's terrific for taking the pips out of grapes and for removing seeds and skins from tomatoes. There are a number of models, but they all work essentially the same way (see Using a Food Mill at left).

▶ IMMERSION BLENDER

Another appliance I find particularly helpful for these blended recipes — one that frankly I use almost every day — is a stick blender, also called an immersion blender. This tool has a blender blade mounted on a handle that lets you purée recipes directly in their pot. No single-tasker in the kitchen, it's also a boon to making vinaigrettes, smoothies, pestos, and dips.

If you haven't a food mill or an immersion blender, you can always mash ingredients with a potato masher and force them through a sieve. This is time-consuming, but I've done it in a pinch. If you do a lot of food processing, one of these tools will save you oodles of time.

▶ HEAVY-BOTTOMED POT

These recipes often call for an extended cooking time, so, as with jams, it helps to use a heavy-bottomed pot to keep spreads from scorching. In fact, these recipes often cook longer than jams — some for nearly 2 hours — making a heavy-bottomed pot even more of a necessity. Use a nonreactive pot to avoid discoloration and minerals leaching into the food. Because you'll be boiling down a large volume of produce, be sure to have a deep pot that can accommodate the goods. I find that an enamel-coated cast-iron pot does a really great job of retaining a consistently low, even heat. I have also used a pasta pot. Mind the sides of the pot, which tend to scorch, and stir frequently.

KEY INGREDIENTS

▶ GOOD PRODUCE

If you plan to store homemade sauce in the refrigerator for a brief time or to put it in the freezer, you can use slightly damaged produce. Just cut away the bruise or insect damage. Produce that is about to fade is also acceptable for the storage methods that employ cool temperatures to arrest bacterial development. If you plan to use the boiling-water method to make the sauce shelf-stable, however, you must start with fresh, perfect produce. This guarantees that you won't be overwhelming the process with more bacteria than it can handle.

STORAGE

Store homemade butters, sauces, and ketchups in the refrigerator or freezer. For those that are sufficiently acidic, such as Homemade Applesauce (page 104), the boiling-water method will make them shelf-stable. See individual recipes for specific storage recommendations.

BUTTERS, SAUCES, AND KETCHUPS STEP-BY-STEP

 1. Combine all the ingredients in a large nonreactive pot, as detailed in the recipe.

2. Heat until the produce begins to break down.

Simmer ingredients for a blended sauce.

3. Cool slightly, and then purée with a stick blender or run through a food mill (see Using a Food Mill, page 54).

Stick blenders purée spreads directly in the pot.

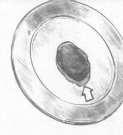

 4. Simmer the purée over medium-low heat until thickened.

 5. The sauce is ready when a dollop on a plate does not weep juice around its perimeter.

A weeping dollop needs more cooking time.

6. Remove from heat.

When a dollop no longer weeps, the spread is ready for processing.

Food Preservation Methods

There are a number of methods you can use to preserve the harvest. Some will take only a few minutes, while others are more involved, project-cooking endeavors. Choose the one that works for you.

After you've prepped your recipe, you need to find a way to preserve it. Say the words "home food preservation," however, and you can almost see someone's shoulders wilt under the weight of such a daunting prospect. That's too bad, because the process is really quite easy. If you've ever popped some leftovers into the fridge or wrapped up some bread for the freezer, you have preserved food. I find it loads of fun and peculiarly satisfying — like I've tapped into some inner hunter/gatherer who has successfully put away stores for the winter.

Each method described in this chapter — whether it uses the refrigerator, freezer, alcohol or vinegar, drying, or the boiling-water method — will extend the shelf life of seasonal produce for a specific length of time. Some will preserve the flavors of the harvest for a few days, others for up to one year. Generally, refrigerated preparations are the most short-lived, followed by dried and frozen items, those preserved in alcohol and vinegar and, at the far end of the spectrum, the boiling-water method, which will make items shelf-stable.

Food preservation does not have to be time-consuming or difficult. Some techniques will take only a few minutes, while others, such as mastering the boiling-water method, are a bit more time-intensive but simpler than you might think. All of the preserving techniques are fairly straightforward and doable — there is nothing in this book that requires culinary training or even significant kitchen experience.

In the peak of the season, I often have multiple processes going on at any given time. Once you get the hang of preserving, you may find your kitchen looks part science lab, with crocks of fermenting foods bubbling away and strings of produce desiccating on the line. It's the perfect time to host a dinner party — very impressive in a Victorian mad scientist kind of way. So get in there and put 'em up!

REFRIGERATION

Using the fridge to delay spoilage is an excellent way to squeeze some extra life out of the harvest. Refrigerator jams and pickles can extend the shelf life of delicate items such as berries and quick-to-shrivel cukes for up to three weeks without additional processing.

EQUIPMENT

You don't need any special equipment to store things in the refrigerator — even recycled jelly, mayo, and pickle jars will do. Just make sure they're good and clean so you don't transfer that yummy dill flavor to the lemon curd.

KEY INGREDIENTS

The only special ingredient in refrigerator storage is the cold. The cool temperature of the fridge slows down the enzymes in food that lead to decomposition.

Adding acid or sugar will delay spoilage even further. Refrigerated foods, however, don't need to be as acidic as shelf-stable products to remain safe to eat, so you can experiment more freely with recipes for chilled foods. Because you don't have to rely on the standardized acidity of distilled vinegars, try delicately flavored wine, rice, and other vinegars. And because you won't be heating the brine, take advantage of unpasteurized vinegars that have a living mother without damaging the probiotic nature of these products.

Refrigeration also slows down the action of fermented foods so they last longer, but unlike foods preserved with the boiling-water method — which relies on heat to stabilize the product — their natural beneficial bacteria remain intact. I just transfer the whole crock of pickles or kraut, for example, directly to the fridge. Cover it loosely, as the fermentation will continue, albeit slowly, and the resulting gases must be able to escape.

Fermenting foods can perfume the fridge. I find the smell very pleasant, but there have been only a couple of times in my life when the combination of pickles and ice cream sounded like a good idea. Consider putting a small dish of baking soda in the fridge if you're going to store fermenting things in there, to keep everything from tasting too pickle-y or kraut-y.

PROCESS

You can modify many of the recipes here that are designed to be canned into refrigerated foods simply by skipping the boiling-water bath that makes them shelf-stable. You can make a jam or jelly, a salsa or relish and keep it in the refrigerator for up to three weeks. Recipes for which this treatment is appropriate are noted as such. It's a great way to have these products on hand without the added step of canning them. It also allows you to experiment a bit with the flavors in a recipe because the balance of acid isn't as critical.

Refrigeration is particularly useful for protecting the integrity of probiotics in fermented foods, for gentle handling of delicate foods that couldn't withstand the heat and processing of the boiling-water method, or simply to save time.

STORAGE

It's a sad thing to find a half-eaten jar of refrigerator jam or pickles hidden in the back of the fridge. You can't quite remember when you packed it, and you have no idea whether it's still good to eat or if you should heave it into the bin. Often I've stood in front of the fridge, jar in one hand, fork in the other, caught in a dilemma: to taste or to toss? To avoid this decision, jot a "made on" date on the jar of the refrigerator concoction or on a piece of masking tape affixed to the jar, and remove it once you've emptied the container. Then you can rest assured your food is wholesome and fresh.

Ditto with jars of food that have been processed by the boiling-water method. They must be refrigerated once they are opened. Jot the "opened" date on their lids with a marker so you can keep track of their freshness. These products will last a few weeks once you open a jar, but they do have a limited shelf life, even when they're kept cold.

Label your refrigerator pickles and jams with "made on" dates to track shelf life.

Label your canned goods with "opened on" dates and enjoy them within several weeks of breaking the airtight seal.

FREEZING

With all due respect to Ms. Monroe, I don't think it's diamonds that are a girl's best friend — it's an extra energy-efficient freezer, one dedicated to putting up frozen foods. I never thought I could get so bothered over an appliance, but a freezer is my treasure chest in the barren months of the year. I pack mine full of local flavor — quarts of frozen berries that I'll use in recipes or make into jam when I have some extra time in the fall, fresh peas that will brighten a winter stew, corn cut from the cob to turn into a comforting chowder. And I make sure I have some prepared items, such as Caramelized Onion Confit (page 218), Easy-Bake Tomato Paste (page 275), and Mushroom Confit (page 214), that add depth of flavor to winter dishes. They're great as a base for soups, in risotto, and as a topping for pizza. Whether you're storing whole or prepared foods, freezing is almost like a time machine — a quick, easy way to stop the clock on a bountiful harvest.

EQUIPMENT

▶ FREEZER

Well, a freezer is certainly helpful here. Any one will work. If you're shopping for one, however, there are a few choices to consider. Side-by-sides and door freezers provide ready access to food. They usually come with an array of bins and shelves that make them easy to organize. Either is fine for everyday needs and food storage.

Chest freezers, on the other hand, are more energy-efficient, so they're economical to run. Their depth makes food retrieval a challenge, so it's important to "file" filled containers in freezable trays and crates. Use these to sort food by category, and simply lift out to uncover items on the bottom of the chest.

No matter how much you think you'll remember what's in those frosty little containers, you won't, so it takes a lot of frustration out of the equation when you keep yourself organized. Label everything: write directly on each container or on a piece of masking tape that you affix to the container.

▶ CONTAINERS

Any freezer-safe container will do. Here are the pros and cons of several choices.

Freezer bags are inexpensive and stack up very well. There is some concern that plastic can leach chemicals into foods that it touches, particularly acidic foods. If you do choose to use plastic bags, you can wash them out with a little soap and water and dry them on a rack to reuse them.

You can use canning jars for the freezer. If you're trying to reduce the amount of plastic in your life, this is one way to do it. Their multipurpose nature makes them good to have on hand. And you can reuse them again and again and they won't stain or warp. On the other hand, because they're round, they're space hogs in the freezer. The glass is fragile and a nice coating of frost doesn't make it any easier to grip, so breakage is a real hazard. If you freeze in jars, be sure to allow plenty of room for expansion — 1 inch for pints and 2 inches for quarts — or the freezing liquids can shatter the glass.

Reusable plastic containers are another option. Flats and squares stack up most efficiently. I've never been particularly good about holding on to the tops and bottoms, so I wind up with a mishmash of container parts. Their ability to go from fridge to freezer is a plus, as is the availability of various shapes and sizes.

My "old reliable" for freezing small portions of sauces and reductions is an ice-cube tray dedicated to the cause. Once the cubes are frozen, transfer them to another container or simply cover the tray and store as is.

KEY INGREDIENTS

▶ GOOD-QUALITY PRODUCE

The only essential ingredient in freezing most produce is good-quality food. Foods that come out of the freezer are only as good as those that go in. Freeze foods when they're at or close to their peak of ripeness. Freezing is not a sanitizing process — it does not destroy bacteria, so any foods that aren't safe going into the freezer won't be improved by the cold. However, unlike canned foods, it's okay to freeze foods that are less than perfect. A bruise, a little soft spot, a field bug making itself cozy — all these can be cut away. Remove any imperfections in the food before you freeze it so it can go straight into the pot when you take it out.

PROCESS

There are a number of ways to stock up a freezer, outlined below. Each recipe in this book will indicate the most appropriate method for that food.

▶ BLANCHING

Many foods can go directly into the freezer raw. The cold temperature slows down the enzymes in produce that cause it to deteriorate. Fruit, in particular, which has natural acids that further stagger this enzymatic activity, can usually hit the deep freeze without any additional preparation. Many low-acid vegetables, however, benefit from a quick blanching to deactivate those enzymes that would hasten their deterioration even in the low temperature of a freezer (see page 21 for more on blanching).

▶ INDIVIDUALLY FREEZING

Individually freezing foods before you package them keeps them loose and separate so you can defrost just the amount you need. It's useful when you want a few berries for your oatmeal or a handful of peas for your pasta. Freeze individually and you won't be stuck with half a quart of defrosted fruit lingering in the fridge.

Individually freezing fruits and veggies also means you don't have to first blanch them to remove the skins. A tomato, for example, easily gives up its skin when you run the fully frozen fruit under warm water for a few seconds.

▶ ROASTING/CHARRING

Like reducing and caramelizing, roasting or charring foods brings out their sugars and decreases their volume. Roasted foods freeze well and are a treasure to have on hand. Charring is also a nifty trick for removing the skin from foods such as peppers without blanching.

▶ REDUCING AND CARAMELIZING

My favorite things to freeze — and those that I find make the best use of the space and energy it takes to store foods in this manner — are heavily reduced sauces, confits, and concentrates. Foods that are cooked way, way down pack a punch without eating up deep-freeze real estate. Their versatility, too, makes them an invaluable player in the pantry.

STORAGE

Freezing foods is a great way to preserve flavor quickly and easily. Here are a few things to keep in mind.

▶ FILL HEIGHT

When you're freezing foods, it's important to leave adequate room for expansion. When packing food into a container, never fill all the way to the top or the frozen food will heave off the lid and could break a glass vessel. When packing tall containers, I leave about 1 inch for pints and about 2 inches for quarts, particularly if I'm using jars. For bowl- or dish-shaped containers, 1 inch of expansion room is sufficient.

▶ PACKING THE FREEZER

A well-stocked freezer is great, but don't overdo it. You don't want the freezer to be so jammed that you don't get good cold air circulating around all of the containers. Also, when you introduce unfrozen goods, make sure you don't overwhelm the appliance. Try not to put in more unfrozen food than the equivalent of 25 percent of the freezer's capacity at a time. Never put hot foods in the freezer, as the residual heat can defrost what's already in there.

INDIVIDUALLY FREEZING STEP-BY-STEP

 1. Arrange clean, dry produce on a baking sheet or pan that will fit, lying flat, in the freezer.

2. To freeze more than one sheet at a time, position four teacups or small canning jars on the corners of the tray to use as pillars on which to stack another sheet.

Stack trays for the freezer.

3. Let produce freeze fully, at least overnight but not more than 2 days or you risk freezer burn.

4. Once the food is frozen, repackage it — quickly, so it doesn't defrost — into airtight, freezer-ready containers.

Package individually frozen produce in airtight containers, pressing out as much air as possible.

ROASTING/CHARRING STEP-BY-STEP

 Preheat a gas or charcoal grill or broiler.

 Lightly coat clean, dry produce with olive oil or a flavorless oil such as canola or grapeseed.

 Set the produce close to the heating element, either 3 to 4 inches under the broiler or over the hottest part of the fire.

 Allow the produce to char to black in spots, turning as necessary to char all surfaces.

Charred peppers, fresh from the broiler.

 Remove the produce to a heatproof bowl and cover with a plate or lid for 5 minutes. (Do not leave covered for longer or the food will cook in its own steam and become unmanageably soft.)

 Remove the bowl cover and allow the produce to cool to room temperature.

7. Slip off the skins and remove any seeds and stems.

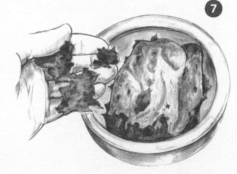

Charred peppers easily give up their skins.

8. Package for the refrigerator or freezer.

REDUCING AND CARAMELIZING STEP-BY-STEP

 Set a large, heavy-bottomed skillet over medium heat.

2. Add fat (olive oil, butter, lard, or a combination).

3. Add the prepped produce and a sprinkle of salt, then cover to coax out the juices.

A skillet full of produce ready to cook down.

4. Once the vegetables are tender, 5 to 7 minutes, remove the lid and reduce the heat to low. (Once you get it going, you can move the pan to a back burner and let it simmer away while you cook dinner.)

 Stir occasionally, scraping the bottom of the pan to prevent food from sticking.

After spending some time on low heat, produce packs a lot of flavor into a little space.

6. When the vegetables are caramelized (follow recipes for timing), add a splash of liquid (such as wine, stock, or water) to deglaze the pan. Remove from the heat, let cool, and package for the refrigerator or freezer.

INFUSE

I come from a long line of white lightning makers and speakeasy owners, so my friends were really expecting some nitty-gritty how-to in a section that includes alcohol. Maybe that's version 2.0. The alcohol and vinegar recipes in this book are infusions. Infusions are a simple way to capture all the great flavors of food before it's gone and to enjoy it in a different way.

The alcohol-based infusions make terrific tipples either straight or mixed into a cocktail, but don't stop there. They're also wonderful for deglazing the skillet after searing a steak or piece of chicken, or you can drizzle them on ice cream for a grown-up dessert.

The vinegars are wonderful in salad dressings. They also add a whole new zing to homemade mayonnaise and bring a boost to long-simmered soups and stews — just stir in a tablespoon or so at the end of the cooking time.

Unlike many of the other preservation methods in this book, you don't need perfect produce to make infused alcohols and vinegars. You can cut off a bruised section of a cucumber or use a piece of a leftover watermelon and still have safe and delicious results. Berries that are going a little soft will be okay. Of course, any moldy or rotten food needs to head to the compost, but less-than-perfect food is just fine here.

EQUIPMENT

No specialized equipment is necessary to make alcohol and vinegar infusions. You probably already have what it takes on hand.

▶ CLEAN GLASS JARS OR CONTAINERS

These don't have to be anything special; just make sure they're food grade. Crystal may look gorgeous, but the lead can leach. I use canning jars that are quart-sized or larger, and they work quite well.

▶ A BLENDER

Some recipes call for puréeing the fruit. You can use an immersion blender, a standard blender, or a food processor. Don't have one of those? A potato masher is a good low-tech stand-in.

KEY INGREDIENTS

The flavor of the produce will dominate, so for these recipes, don't waste your best bourbon or the vinegar you brought home from that great shop in France. Standard bar booze will do, and distilled white vinegar is a nice blank canvas.

STORAGE

I store alcohol infusions as I would their base liquid: sake and white wine in the fridge, bourbon on the bar, vodka in the freezer. Infused vinegar keeps in a cool, dark place for up to one year. If you like, decant the strained infusions back into the original bottles. You could also put them in something decorative — as long as it's food grade — if you prefer. Even when strained, the liquids may have some precipitates that settle in the bottles. Carefully decant your infusion into another bottle, leaving the precipitate behind.

DRUNKEN CHERRIES, PAGE 157

TARRAGON VINEGAR, PAGE 211

INFUSING ALCOHOLS AND VINEGARS STEP-BY-STEP

1. ▶ Thoroughly wash the jars or bottles that will hold your infusion and place them, top side up, in a large pot or canner fitted with a rack. Fill the pot with water to cover the vessels by 2 inches. Bring water to a boil and reduce to a simmer for 10 minutes. Using canning tongs, carefully remove jars or bottles, pour out the boiling water, and invert on a clean dish towel.

2. ▶ In a nonreactive pot, heat vinegar until it is just about to boil. While the vinegar is heating, wash the produce thoroughly.

3. ▶ Combine the produce and alcohol/vinegar according to the recipe.

4. ▶ Cover and set aside in a cool, dark place to enable flavors to infuse.

5. ▶ Shake every day to encourage infusion.

6. ▶ After you've reached the level of infusion you seek, strain out the produce, if you prefer. I find that when an infusion is done, the fruits tend to become sad-looking, so I strain them out. It looks nicer and takes up less storage space. The only exception is stone fruits, which hold their shape and make a delicious garnish (or yummy snack) scooped straight out of the jar.

Fresh fruit infuses liquor or vinegar with flavor.

DRYING

Drying is one of the most accessible methods of home food preservation. It's economical and low-tech, and it results in foods that are easy to store, light to ship as gifts, and delicious to eat. No wonder cooks have relied on dehydration to preserve the harvest for so long. Since the beginning of farming, growers have dried a part of their harvest to carry them over to the next season. Even before the dawn of agriculture, ancient hunters and gatherers would dry meat between expeditions. We use the method today on both small and large scales. I was surprised to hear from a modern grape grower that his family still makes raisins by laying the harvested fruit on sheets between the rows. They let the sun do all of the work, turning the juicy grapes into succulent raisins.

Drying works to preserve food in a number of ways. It removes all of the moisture from food, making the environment inhospitable for bacterial growth. Drying also slows down the natural enzymes in food that lead to its decomposition. That's not to say that dried food lasts forever. It will deteriorate over time — because of their low sugar content, vegetables expire more quickly than fruits — and must be protected from infestation by hungry pests and airborne contaminants. It also needs to be kept in a sealed container so it won't absorb moisture from the air, which will shorten its shelf life. That said, if you're new to home food preservation or short on time, drying is an easy, quick way to put up some food.

For this book, I use two methods of food drying: air-drying and oven-drying. If you live in a hot, arid climate, you can dehydrate foods outdoors, under the sun. But for those of us who live in the sometimes damp and often humid Northeast or the frequently muggy South, the less weather-dependent indoor air-drying and oven-drying methods are more approachable.

AIR-DRYING EQUIPMENT

▸ **NEEDLE AND THREAD**
For small, easy-to-dry foods such as chili peppers and green beans, all that's necessary to get started is a darning needle and some thick upholstery thread or fishing line. In a pinch I've used baling cord left over from a recycling project. You're just

looking for something sturdy enough to hold the weight of about half a pound of food as it dries.

AIR-DRYING PROCESSES

There are a number of ways to string food.

▶ DRIED BOUQUETS

Perhaps the simplest and easiest method of drying, whether you're working with flowers or herbs, is to make little bouquets. Bundles of chamomile, lavender, lemon verbena, mint, and other fragrant edible posies make gorgeous "tea bouquets."

▶ LEATHER BRITCHES OR LAUNDRY LINES

"Leather britches" is the descriptive name given to green beans whose tops have been run through with needle and thread and are allowed to dangle, equally spaced, like clothes drying on a line. This is a good method for beans, which need to be blanched before they're strung and greatly benefit from the air circulation provided by the wide spacing between them. This method is also good for drying chilies.

Because of their high moisture content, it's best to give beans a quick pasteurization in the oven before you store them, just to make sure that any lingering molds are destroyed. Simply arrange the beans on a baking sheet and pop it into a 170°F oven for 15 minutes. Cool completely, then store in an airtight container.

▶ RISTRAS

Ristras are the braided garlands of dried chilies you see in the Southwest. They're easy to make, handy to have in the kitchen, and cute. This method works for all kinds of chilies, and for cured garlic as well. There are traditional methods for braiding the stems or for sort of crocheting the stems together with thread. This simpler method requires much less technique and yields fine results.

DRIED BOUQUETS STEP-BY-STEP

1. Gather the stalks of the herbs or flowers in one hand.

2. Use the other hand to tightly bind them with a piece of twine or cord.

3. Hang them, upside down, in a well-ventilated area until they're brittle.

4. Store them as they are, or crush the petals or leaves off the stems and store in a sealed container.

Herbs and flowers
drying in "bouquets."

LEATHER BRITCHES STEP-BY-STEP

1. Prep your produce as indicated in the recipe.

2. Thread a needle through the top of a chili or bean, just under the stem. Do not pull your string all the way through; leave about 6 inches for hanging.

3. Tie a knot around the stem.

4. Thread another vegetable in the same manner, leaving about an inch of space between the first and second, and knot again.

5. Repeat until you have about a 3-foot length of strung beans or chilies plus another 6 inches of string for hanging.

6. Choose a location that gets a lot of air circulation and is relatively dry — the kitchen or an attic or the garage.

7. Tie the ends of the string to two nails spaced about 3 feet apart, or two cupboard handles that you won't need to use for the next few days.

8. Let the produce dry until it's leathery.

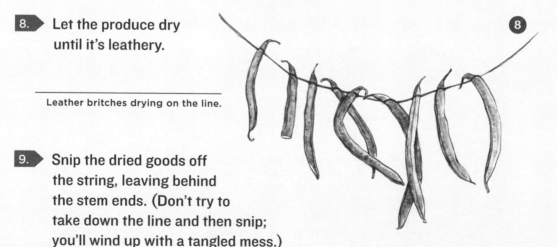

Leather britches drying on the line.

9. Snip the dried goods off the string, leaving behind the stem ends. (Don't try to take down the line and then snip; you'll wind up with a tangled mess.)

RISTRAS STEP-BY-STEP

 1. Thread a needle and run it through the stem of a chili.

 2. Wrap the string around the stem several times, and then run it through again. This will be the bottom chili.

3. Continue to string chilies by running the needle through the bottom of the stems, stacking the chilies as you go.

4. Hang the ristra in a well-ventilated area and dry until the pods are brittle — a week or two, depending on the weather.

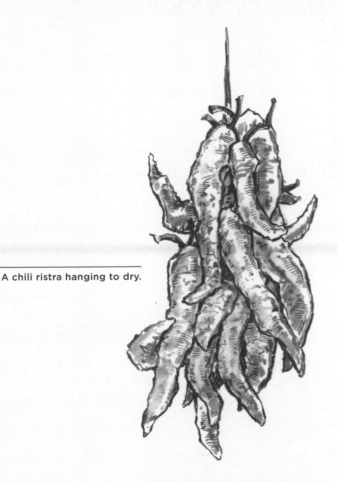

A chili ristra hanging to dry.

OVEN-DRYING EQUIPMENT

I say oven, instead of dehydrator, because everyone has an oven — not everyone has a food dehydrator. If you do, by all means crank it up. If you're new to home food preservation, though, or just don't like to have a lot of gadgets in the *cucina*, the oven is the way to go. If you use your space wisely, you can dry a sizable quantity of food at once, so it makes firing up the oven on a summer day worth the effort.

▸ CAKE COOLING RACKS OR OTHER GRATES

Of course the key piece of equipment is the oven. It's also handy to have a number of cake cooling racks, barbecue grates, or something similar that will hold the food but allow air to circulate around it, too. Small foods, such as grapes, can be dried directly on baking sheets.

OVEN-DRYING KEY INGREDIENTS

▸ VITAMIN C TABLETS

Some foods, such as apples, peaches, and pears, which would discolor, benefit from a quick dip in an acid bath before drying. To make an acid bath, crush vitamin C tablets and dissolve them in water, as directed in your recipe. Soak the sliced fruit for about 10 minutes to prevent discoloration.

OVEN-DRYING PROCESSES

▸ WHOLE OR CUT PRODUCE

This is a great way to use up little bits of extra produce. You can put several different kinds on a rack and remove them as they are ready.

▸ FRUIT LEATHERS

Fruit leather is easy to make and tastes delicious. Sure, kids love it, but you will, too. The fruit flavor really comes through in this homemade treat.

OVEN DRYING STEP-BY-STEP

 1. Preheat the oven to 170°F, which is low enough to dehydrate without roasting and high enough to simultaneously pasteurize.

2. Prep the produce as indicated in the recipe.

3. Arrange the food on racks and set them in the oven.

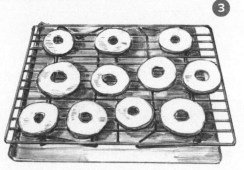

Dry food on racks to ensure proper air circulation.

4. Prop open the oven door a bit with a wooden spoon to enable steam to escape.

5. If you have a convection feature, all the better; the circulating air will speed the dehydration process.

6. When food has dried to the specifications in the recipe, let it cool to room temperature.

7. Pack the dried food into an airtight container, such as a clean, dry canning jar.

8. Let the food rest for a few days to redistribute any remaining moisture in the produce.

9. If droplets form on the sides of the container, there is too much moisture to guarantee long-term storage. Return the food to the oven and dry it a bit more. Cool, transfer it to an airtight container, and check again in a few days.

10. If the container stays dry, you can safely store the food as indicated in the recipe.

FRUIT LEATHERS STEP-BY-STEP

 1. Prepare a fruit purée following the recipe's directions.

 2. Line a rimmed baking sheet or jelly-roll pan with parchment paper or a Silpat.

 3. Spread the sweetened purée onto the baking sheet, tilting it to create an even layer about ⅛ inch thick.

4. Dry in a 170°F oven until the fruit is tacky to the touch, about 2 hours.

5. Cool to room temperature.

6. Slide the fruit leather onto a cutting board and roll it up into a tube.

7. Slice the tube into 2-inch segments and store in a covered jar.

fruit leather 9/12

BOILING-WATER METHOD

When people say they "can," they usually mean they use the boiling-water method or a pressure canner to preserve food. Confusing, indeed, as food is packed into jars, not cans, in both cases. In this book, we'll be using the boiling-water method to make delicious foods that are shelf-stable for up to one year, and yes, sometimes we'll refer to it as canning.

The boiling-water method is the standard technique for safely preserving acidic foods such as salsas, chutneys, relishes, jams, jellies, pickles, tomatoes, and many fruits. It's not at all dangerous or complicated if you follow a few basic rules and stick to the recipe. The process involves packing prepared foods into specially designed jars with two-part lids. When the jars are heated in boiling water, vapor vents through the special lid. Once removed from the water, the cooling food contracts and the resulting negative pressure sucks down the lid onto the jar, creating an airproof (and contamination-proof) seal.

EQUIPMENT

▶ CANNING TONGS

Canning tongs are not cooking tongs. They have a unique shape that enables them to grip the hot jars so you can safely lift them out of the boiling-water bath. *Caution:* Don't try to substitute regular tongs — that can be dangerous. You're going to be lifting glass jars full of boiling contents in and out of boiling water: you need the special shape and rubberized nonslip grips of the canning tongs to keep you and your delicious concoctions safe.

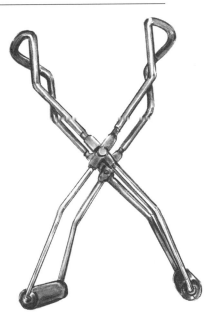

Canning tongs are specially designed to safely lift jars in and out of the boiling-water bath.

▶ CANNING JARS

There is just no substitute for canning jars. Jars made specifically for home canning are thicker than the typical store-bought mayonnaise or pickle jar, so they can withstand the boiling temperatures of the process. Don't use anything else.

There are a variety of shapes and sizes from which to choose — everything from quarts, for whole fruits and tomatoes, to pints, half-pints, and tiny 4-ounce jam pots. Some have interesting prints embossed on the glass. Most commonly, there are regular and widemouthed versions. I find the wide mouth easier to use but the regular mouth is handy for keeping foods that may float submerged under the brine. You can use all of the shapes interchangeably, but make sure you're using the size indicated in the recipe to ensure sufficient processing.

You may reuse canning jars time and time again as long as they stay in good condition: that is, the glass remains scratch- and chip-free.

▶ CANNING LIDS

Canning lids have two parts — a flat lid that is rimmed with a soft rubberized gasket that provides an airtight seal after the jars cool and a ring that holds the lid in place during processing. This unique design allows vapor to vent during processing and creates a vacuum seal as the jars cool. The rings can be used many times as long as they aren't damaged.

Canning jars have a special two-part lid and thick glass that
make them safe for the boiling-water method.

BPA in Canning Lids

Canning lids have been shown to contain a small amount of BPA, bisphenol A, a compound used in manufacturing that is suspected to have detrimental health impacts. While the amount of BPA in the lids is reported to be well within FDA regulation, it is a cause for concern for many eaters. To limit your exposure to BPA, always store your jars right side up and allow the proper headspace between the top of the food and the lid.

Caution: The lids can be used only once, as their gaskets will not provide a reliable seal the second time around.

▶ CANNER OR BIG STOCKPOT

You'll need a big pot that is at least 3 inches taller than the jars you plan to fill and a lid to cover it. You can get a canner if you think you'll be in this for the long haul, but it's essentially just a big pot, so if you're a beginner or you see yourself doing only small batches, just take out that big lobster, stock, or pasta pot from the back of a cupboard.

Any pot that is 3 inches taller than your jars is fine for the boiling-water method.

▶ CANNING RACK OR EXTRA JAR RINGS

You're going to need to raise the canning jars off the bottom of the pot so that boiling water can circulate around them. Canning kits come with a canning rack that does this. If you don't have a rack, that's okay: use a cake cooling rack that fits in the pot or simply put down a layer of extra rings from canning jars, top-side up, and set the jars on top of those.

Use a canning rack or a layer of jar rings, shown here, to elevate your jars.

▶ CANNING FUNNEL

A canning funnel is a useful bit of equipment. It makes filling jars an easy, clean process. If you haven't got one, though, substitute a regular funnel with the spout and a piece of the base sawed off, or simply pour very carefully from a small ladle.

A canning funnel reduces mess.

▶ BUBBLE TOOL, PLASTIC KNIFE, OR CHOPSTICK

A bubble tool comes with every canning kit. It's certainly helpful, but I lost mine a long time ago. Instead, I use a plastic knife or sometimes a chopstick or skewer. I dip it into the boiling water to give it a quick scald before running it around the inside of the jars to release any trapped air.

A bubble tool, plastic knife, or chopstick releases trapped air.

▶ LID LIFTER

A lid lifter is another handy little thing that comes in a canning kit. It looks like a pencil with a round magnet on the end instead of an eraser. The magnet is used to fetch lids, one at a time, from the hot water in which they're immersed. If you have the "asbestos fingers" that many home cooks and certainly chefs develop after handling hot foods for years, gingerly reach in and grab a lid bare-handed. Or use some regular cooking tongs — preferably the silicone-tipped ones — to grab one lid at a time. However you retrieve them, be sure to avoid scratching the food side of the lids, which invites rust during storage.

A lid lifter is handy for retrieving hot lids.

KEY INGREDIENTS

▶ ACID

Having the proper amount of acid in a recipe is the key to safe use of the boiling-water method. Recipes that call for this method of preservation are developed to achieve a proper acidic pH: 4.6 or lower. (Recipes with a higher pH must be processed using other methods.) An acidic pH is reached in one of three ways:

- By canning acidic ingredients, such as some berries.

- By adding enough acid — in the form of bottled lemon juice or vinegar — to lower the pH to a safe level.

- By fermenting the food in a salt brine so that it creates its own lactic acid.

You don't need to concern yourself with the 4.6 number. Just follow the recipe and rest assured that you're well within the bounds of safety. Use the ingredients indicated, in the amounts indicated, and cut or chop to the size indicated. This will ensure that you have the right proportion of acid to alkaline ingredients and that the acid can fully penetrate the ingredients.

Caution: It's important *never* to reduce the amount of acid called for in the recipe. Doing so jeopardizes the quality of the results. Also, don't boil your recipe for longer than indicated. Extended boiling reduces the acidity in the recipe, making it less effective at maintaining a proper pH.

Acid can react with some metals, such as aluminum, resulting in an off taste in your final recipe. Be sure to use only nonreactive pots and pans when preparing your recipes to ensure consistent results.

▸ TIME

You must process your jars for the full amount of time indicated. Even though the acid will protect against a variety of contaminants, the food you're canning needs

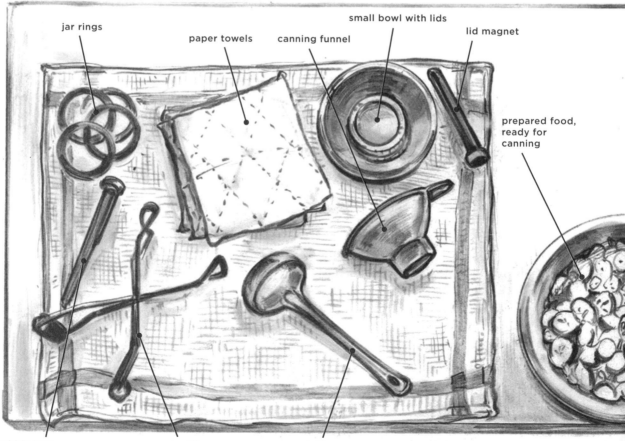

jar rings

paper towels

small bowl with lids

canning funnel

lid magnet

prepared food, ready for canning

bubble tool

jar lifter

ladle

time to reach a temperature high enough to finish the job. This ensures that the heat penetrates to the center of the food and doesn't heat just the outside layer. Processing kills any lingering bacteria that may have gotten into the jars while you were packing them and also helps to deactivate the natural enzymes in raw food that cause it to decompose. Insufficient processing will result in a cool or raw core in the center of the jar that can lead to spoilage. Conversely, don't overprocess foods either. Doing so will yield less-than-great results — for example, foods may become mushy or disintegrate, or pectins will break down in spreads and cause separation.

PROCESS

This schematic shows the basic arrangement for all of the equipment you will need for canning with the boiling-water method. Wash and lay out everything before you start a recipe so you can move smoothly through the process from start to finish. You don't want jelly to set up in the pot while you scratch around for a canning funnel.

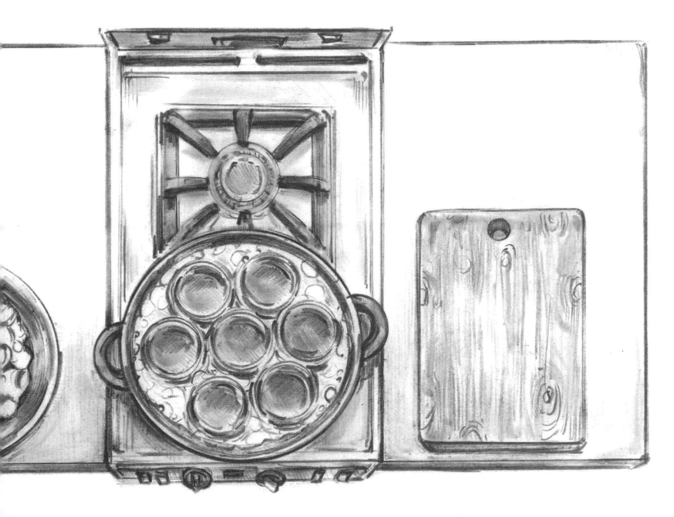

BOILING-WATER METHOD STEP-BY-STEP

WASH AND LAY OUT YOUR EQUIPMENT

1. Put the canning rack in the bottom of the canner. If you don't have a canning rack, substitute a layer of jar rings, placed thread-side down on the bottom of the pot.

2. Wash all the jars and equipment. You're not trying to sterilize them at this point; you just want to get them clean. Harsh chemicals (such as bleach) are not necessary, just regular dish soap and a soft cloth or sponge. Don't use abrasive cleansers or scouring pads, as these will scratch canning jars.

3. As you wash them, set aside the rings, place lids bottom-side down in a small heat-proof bowl, and load the clean jars into the canner.

4. Arrange all the other equipment on a clean kitchen towel as detailed in the equipment map on pages 84–85.

PREPARE THE CANNER

Canners can take a good while to come to a full boil. Begin heating your water before you begin your recipe so your completed concoction doesn't linger, losing heat and jeopardizing your processing time while you wait for the canner. If your canner comes to a boil well before you're done cooking, just turn it off and cover it, then return it to a boil when you're ready to fill and begin processing your jars.

The canner or pot uses a canning rack or layer of jar rings to ensure that boiling water can circulate.

Load the canner to capacity with empty jars, regardless of expected yield, to keep jars from tipping during processing.

 Fill the canner with enough water to fill and cover the jars.

3. Set the canner over high heat.

4. Cover the canner and bring the water to a boil. The goal is to heat the jars so you won't be adding hot food to cold jars, which could cause them to crack. Again, you're not sterilizing the jars at this point.

Bring the loaded canner to a boil.

PREPARE YOUR RECIPE

Prepped produce deteriorates rapidly, so you want to make sure that you have everything on hand before you begin and move steadily through your recipe. You don't need to rush, but it's not a good idea to stop and run an errand or dash to the store for more lids.

CONTINUED ON NEXT PAGE ⟶

Packing Fruit

Halved fruits, such as peaches, plums, and pears, easily trap air bubbles among their large pieces and particularly in the divot left from removing the stone or seeds. It's important to release this air to ensure proper headspace. It's tricky to release the trapped air with a bubble tool without puncturing or breaking up the fruit, so here's what I do. After I pack the fruit and ladle the preserving liquid over it, I screw on a lid temporarily. I gently twirl, or even invert, the jar to release the bubbles and enable them to float to the top of the jar. I remove the lid, add more liquid if necessary to achieve the proper headspace, clean the rim, and proceed with boiling-water processing.

BOILING-WATER METHOD STEP-BY-STEP (CONTINUED)

FILL THE JARS

1. Using canning tongs, remove a jar from the canner. Carefully tip the hot water into the bowl with the jar lids so that their sealing rings begin to soften. Place the empty jar, open-side up, on a towel-covered work surface.

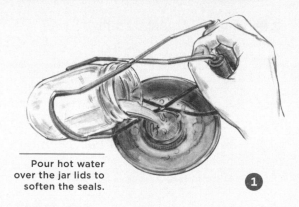

Pour hot water over the jar lids to soften the seals.

①

2. Using canning tongs, remove three additional jars from the canner, emptying their water directly back into canner and placing them, open-side up, on the towel.

3. **For cold-pack recipes,** where the raw food is put in the jars and the hot preserving liquid is poured over it, fill the jars snugly with food, then pour over enough liquid to leave the headspace indicated in the recipe. (See page 44 for more about the cold-pack method.)

For hot-pack recipes, use the canning funnel to fill jars with the hot, prepared food, leaving the headspace indicated in the recipe. (See page 43 for more information about the hot-pack method.)

For hot-pack preparations, use a canning funnel to fill jars.

③

4. One jar at a time, run the bubble tool, chopstick, or plastic knife around the inside of the jar to release air bubbles. (See Packing Fruit, page 87)

Use the bubble tool to release trapped air.

5. Run a damp paper towel around the rim to clean it thoroughly.

Carefully wipe the rim.

6. Using the magnet tool, tongs, or your fingers, grab a lid from the bowl and center it on the nearest jar.

Use a magnet tool to center the lid on the jar.

7. Gently screw a lid ring onto the jar until it's *just fingertip-tight.* You don't want to screw the band so tightly that there's no room for gases to escape during processing. Use your fingertips — no knuckles — to turn the ring, and when the jar begins to spin on the towel, you know it's tight enough.

Fingertip-tight means screwing the band on a jar using just your fingertips.

8. Repeat with the remaining jars.

CONTINUED ON NEXT PAGE ⟶

PROCESS THE JARS

1. Using canning tongs, lift the filled jars and lower them into the canner, being sure that they are covered by 2 inches of water.

Using canning tongs to return the jars to the canner.

2. Cover the pot and bring the water to a rolling boil. Lower the heat a bit, so the water isn't boiling out of the pot but still maintains a lot of rolling action. Start timing only after the full boil is reached and process according to the recipe.

3. When the processing time is achieved, turn off the heat and remove the lid from the canner.

4. Let the jars cool in the canner for 5 minutes. The contents of the jars will still be simmering, and if you remove them from the canner prematurely, they might spurt.

5. After 5 minutes, use the canning tongs to lift the jars straight out of the canner. There will be a small pool of water on top of each jar. *Resist the temptation to tip the jars.* They have yet to seal and you might spill some of the contents if you tip them. Instead, lift them straight out and set them on a dish-towel-covered counter. If you must move them before they are done resting, set the dish towel on a tray before transferring the jars to it.

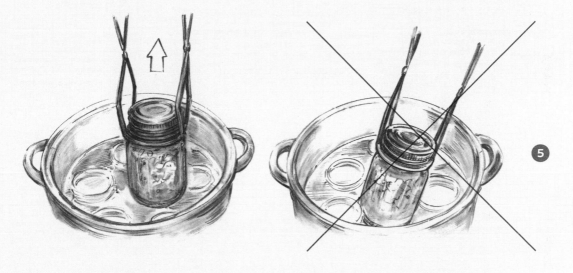

Using canning tongs, lift the jars straight out of the canner without tipping them.

6. Let cool overnight.

STORAGE

Remove a jar ring and push gently on the lid. If it stays in place, you have a good seal.

Do this with each jar. Some say if the jar isn't sealed you can reprocess, but I don't recommend it. Double processing often diminishes the quality of canned items, making them softer and dulling flavor. If a jar isn't sealed, refrigerate it and use within a week.

Wipe all your jars with a damp cloth. If you're storing them in the house, in a place where they won't be jostled, it's best to remove the rings, which may trap moisture that would corrode the lids. You can always put on a ring if you give away the jar or want to ship it.

Store jars in a cool, dark place for up to 1 year.

Push gently on the lid to ascertain a seal.

Processing Time Altitude Adjustments

If you live at a high altitude, it's important to adjust processing times to account for the lower boiling point.

ALTITUDE ADJUSTMENTS FOR BOILING-WATER PROCESSING

If your altitude in feet is	Increase processing time by
1,001–3,000	5 minutes
3,001–6,000	10 minutes
Over 6,000	15 minutes

Working in Groups

Canning parties are great fun. By dividing the work, assembly line style or in shifts, you can put by a lot of food. Canning is also a terrific project to do with friends, one that will nurture you every time you dip into your stash.

It's tempting, with all those hands at the ready, to double and triple a recipe. I don't recommend it. A too-large batch will need more time to cook through properly and may leave some of the food undercooked, a danger for safe processing. Large batches of jam may not set properly. Stick to the quantities recommended. You'll have better success cooking more batches, not bigger ones. Here are some ideas for sharing the workload. (I don't recommend group work for jellies, which hang in the jelly bag for so long.)

FOR MAKING JAMS, SALSAS, RELISHES

- 2 or 3 people prepping produce
- 1 person doing the cooking
- 1 person washing jars, loading the canner, and watching the processing clock
- 1 or 2 people packing jars

FOR PROCESSING WHOLE TOMATOES

Because of the extended processing time, two canners will keep things moving along. Load one canner and start the timing while you prep for and load the second.

- 2 or 3 people prepping tomatoes
- 1 or 2 people packing jars
- 1 person washing jars, loading the canners, and watching the processing clock

FOR FREEZING

It helps to have two pots of water boiling in order to blanch a lot of produce. Drop the produce into pot #1; while it's coming to a boil, drop produce into pot #2. Scoop #1 and reload. Scoop #2 and reload. Repeat.

- 2 or 3 people prepping vegetables (shelling peas, topping beans, shucking corn)

- 1 person blanching

- 1 or 2 people drying

- 2 or 3 people post-blanch processing (such as corn kerneling or tomato peeling)

- 1 person packing

FROZEN BLUE- BERRIES

Things That Will Surely Get You into Trouble

You'll kill someone. That's what it's all about, isn't it? Many home cooks I know — dedicated, accomplished cooks — have told me they're afraid to preserve their own food because they could kill someone. Let's set the record straight. Yes, you will follow some commonsense rules about cleanliness and you will be asked to follow a recipe without a lot of improvisation. But hey, raw chicken has its hazards if not handled properly. Unless you think it's okay to swab kitchen counters with raw poultry, I can pretty much guarantee that you can handle home food preservation. After all, home cooks have been doing so for generations and we've managed to survive as a species. And now, with more foolproof methods than ever before, the process is even safer. To demystify the demons, here are the big no-nos.

THE BIG "B": BOTULISM

Botulism is a foodborne illness that can result from consuming improperly canned foods. It is indeed deadly and deserves the respect of our attention, but let's put it in perspective. Botulism spores are a natural part of the environment. The bacteria themselves are not harmful: it's the botulism toxin, created when the bacteria reproduce, that's hazardous. Botulism toxin forms only in a low-acid, airtight environment. Follow these two simple steps and you eliminate the conditions necessary for food to become tainted with botulism toxin.

- Fully process the food. Heat kills the bacteria that generate the toxin. If you process canned food as directed, you will kill off any *Clostridium botulinum* present and eliminate the threat of botulism toxin.

- Maintain the proper pH. *Clostridium botulinum* bacteria need a low-acid environment in order to grow. If you use the amount of acid indicated in a recipe and don't add more produce than is called for, your canned goods will have the necessary acidity to guard against botulism.

PLAYING FAST AND LOOSE WITH A RECIPE

The recipes in this book are based on USDA standards for safe home food preservation. Careful attention has been paid to the kind and amounts of ingredients that will yield successful (read: safe) results. Unless a recipe indicates an area where you can adjust "to taste," do not alter it at all.

Signs of Good Food Gone Bad

Chances are everything will go smoothly, but it's always a good idea to know what to look for when something isn't quite right. The following signs indicate processed food that has taken a turn for the worse. Don't take a chance — throw it out!

FIZZING OR BUBBLING Food spoilage causes gases to form. Discard canned goods that look carbonated, with bubbles rising in the liquid, or that spurt when opened.

SWELLING Lids that bulge or pop off are signs of bacterial growth or fermentation.

ODOR A foul or boozy smell is a sign of decay or fermentation.

MOLD Speckles or fuzz on the top of food or throughout the food is most likely mold.

TEXTURE Slimy or dramatically changed texture is a sign of decay or age.

PLAYING WITH FATHER TIME

Many of the methods described in the book rely on time as a major ingredient. Foods will transform before your very eyes: sweets will become savory, savory will taste sweet, vegetables will turn into pickles, and jams morph into a treat — but not always instantly. Give the alchemy time to do its "magic" if you want food that's tasty and safe, too. Never process foods for less than the amount of time indicated — heat needs time to fully penetrate the food and make it shelf-stable. Conversely, over-processing can also have a negative impact on your results — food may have a softer texture and duller flavors, and the pectin will separate from fruit preparations.

NOT USING MODERN METHODS

You may have family recipes that conflict with those in this book and even with the USDA guidelines. Your grandmother may swear by her method for putting up her garden because it has been used for generations even though it flies in the face of any local health department's recommendations. I would never dream of pulling you away from those time-tested culinary traditions. But if you don't have a Nona (or a Memaw or a Bubbe or an Abuela) who taught you and you're learning from books, stick to the script.

Things That Look Bad but Aren't Dangerous

FRUIT FLOAT

A separation of solids and liquids after processing is called fruit float. Most commonly it refers to jams that have divided so that you have a thick layer of fruit solidified at the top of the jar and a band of clear jelly at the bottom. Fruit float may also refer to whole or halved fruits, such as tomatoes and pears, that bob up to the top of the jar after processing. And it can be used to describe a thick sauce, such as barbecue sauce, that has a thin band of clear liquid that settles at the bottom of the jar after processing.

Fruit float is nothing more than an aesthetic problem. You can reblend a jam by stirring the contents after a jar is opened. Whole fruits will often settle back into suspension after the air bubbles in the fruits' cell structure — which are making it buoyant — have a chance to escape and rise to the surface. Shake sauces before use to redistribute their ingredients. If you have extensive fruit float that doesn't settle after a week and leaves produce bobbing up out of the liquid, turn the jars periodically so that the food remains properly saturated with preserving liquid.

BUBBLES ON RECENTLY PROCESSED FOODS

Whereas bubbles and fizzing throughout a jar are signs of spoilage, it's quite normal to see a light covering of bubbles on recently processed produce. These are from the escaping air that was trapped in the cell structure of the produce. Gently swirl the jar to encourage these bubbles to rise to the top. This reduces the fruits' buoyancy and enables them to sink down into the preserving liquid, which will better protect them in storage and reclaim the proper headspace.

MINERAL DEPOSITS ON LIDS

I threw out many quarts of tomatoes before I knew about this one: although black specks that form on food are generally a sign of spoilage, black specks on the lids of tomatoes are harmless mineral deposits that are a by-product of the process. They are perfectly safe.

CLOUDINESS

Fermented vegetables often have a cloudy brine. Unless you also notice a rancid smell, cloudy preserving liquid is harmless. Powdered spices can also cause a preserving liquid to appear a bit cloudy, and that's okay, too.

SCUM OR MOLD ON THE FERMENT

Fermented pickles, which are brined vegetables that generate their own lactic acid (see page 45), will develop a layer of scum — some call it bloom — on the top of the preserving liquid. This is a normal by-product of the fermentation process, and it can be scooped off and discarded.

Part Two: Recipes

HOMEMADE PRUNES

page 238

Recipes

Ah, the delicious part — the recipes! Recipe development for home food preservation is a tricky thing, part creativity and part science. The creative part was truly a group effort — so many friends and family members pitched in.

Home-preserved foods factor large on both sides of my family — Polish and Southern — so a lot of these recipes started there, in my family's roots. While I didn't have the advantage of having recipes that had been passed down from my grandparents, I drew inspiration from a rich treasure of mental pictures and taste memories that they have given me over the years. And many friends shared recipes, came over to help with the chopping and dicing (thank you, Jennifer!), and chipped in with punch-in-the-arm moral support. It was a deeply creative and collaborative process.

At the end of the day, however, safe home food preservation is a matter of science. Recipes have to be sufficiently acidic to be made shelf-stable — and there's no creative way around it. All of these recipes are based on USDA recommendations for safety and have been developed to achieve the proper acid balance necessary for good results. It is because of the special equipment that I use and testing protocol that I went through that I was able to use my kids as taste testers with confidence.

Each recipe indicates the food preservation options that are appropriate for it. Many include multiple options — you could refrigerate your recipe for a number of days or you could use the boiling-water method to make it shelf-stable. Let your time and energy level indicate the preservation method you choose, but never use a method that is not listed in the recipe. Some pickle recipes designed for the refrigerator may not have enough acid to be safely processed otherwise; conversely, some pickles that require the boiling-water method may not reach the desired texture if not subjected to the heat of that process. So be sure to choose only from the options listed in the recipe. I know you'll find them safe, and I hope you'll find them tasty, too.

Apples

There are so many gorgeous heirloom apples available at the farmers' market, each type with a unique flavor and suited to a different job. Some hold their shape during cooking so they work really well in pies or other preparations, such as Spiced Apple Chutney, where you want the fruit to provide some texture. Other apples fall apart easily when cooked and are best suited for recipes such as Homemade Applesauce where you want a nice, smooth result. Still others have a terrific balance of tart and sweet and a crisp texture that make them just right for eating out of hand. Many apples are multi-purpose — ask your farmer for advice on choosing the right apple.

Heirloom apples — those varieties that have been passed down for generations — come in a wide range of tastes and characteristics. These fruits aren't often grown on a commercial scale. You need to ferret them out in farmers' markets and at local, family-owned orchards. Protecting heirloom apples, and all heirlooms, is important: they're a link to our past, have unparalleled flavor, and preserve biodiversity.

My friend Ed Yowell is crazy about an heirloom called the Newtown Pippin. The only apple variety native to New York City, it traces back to an eighteenth-century farm in the borough of Queens (yes, Queens) and was a favorite of Thomas Jefferson's. Ed coordinated with area arborists to graft and plant hundreds of Pippin trees in the city and beyond to ensure the future of this lovely green fruit. You can protect heirlooms, too, just by eating them. Talk to local growers about their offerings. Stock up on the "keepers" — those that last the longest in the root cellar or fridge — and put some of the other good apples to work in these recipes.

FRESH STORAGE RECOMMENDATIONS

STORE APPLES INDIVIDUALLY, WRAPPED IN NEWSPAPER or layered between dry fall leaves or straw. Load them into big barrels or crates and top them with wire mesh, to let air circulate but keep out any pests. Separating apples during storage is critical: as the old adage goes, one bad apple will spoil the whole barrel.

DRIED APPLE RINGS

2 pounds of apples make about 1 cup of rings

Kids love these and I do, too. They have a satisfyingly chewy texture that's a little bit addictive. You can use any variety of apples here.

INGREDIENTS

- **6** (500 mg) tablets vitamin C, crushed
- **2** cups cold water
- **6** apples

PREPARE

1. Preheat the oven to 170°F.

2. To prepare an antibrowning ascorbic-acid bath, dissolve the crushed vitamin C tablets in the water in a large bowl. Peel and core the apples and cut into ¼-inch slices. Add the apple slices to the acid bath as you cut them. Soak for 10 minutes.

PRESERVE

▦ Dry:

1. Pat the slices dry and arrange them on a metal screen or cake cooling rack and place the rack in the oven. Prop open the oven door with a wooden spoon handle to enable moisture to escape. Dry the apples in the oven until leathery, 3 to 4 hours. The slices are fully dry when you can squeeze a handful and they don't stick together.

2. Cool the apple slices, and then condition them by transferring to a covered container and letting sit for 1 week. This allows the dried fruit to redistribute any trapped moisture. If you notice moisture on the sides of the container, repeat the drying process for another hour or so. Fully dried apple rings keep in an airtight container for up to 1 year.

APPLE PRESERVES

Makes about 8 cups

Use these preserves as you would any jam. They're also great spooned into pastry dough and baked as a tart. Ask your farmer for the best baking apples for this recipe — the kind that stay firm when they're heated — or you will wind up with applesauce.

INGREDIENTS

- **2** cups water
- **¼** cup bottled lemon juice
- **4** pounds apples, peeled and cored
- **2** cups sugar
- **1** teaspoon ground cinnamon

PREPARE

Combine the water and lemon juice in a large pot. Dice the apples and add them to the pot as you go to prevent browning. Bring to a boil and stir in the sugar and cinnamon. Simmer until thickened, about 10 minutes.

PRESERVE

⊘ Refrigerate: Transfer to clean bowls or jars. Cool, cover, and refrigerate for up to 3 weeks.

⊙ Can: Use the boiling-water method. Ladle the preserves into clean, hot half-pint canning jars, leaving ¼ inch of headspace. Release trapped air. Wipe the rims clean; center lids on the jars and screw on jar bands. Process for 15 minutes. Turn off heat, remove canner lid, and let jars rest in the water for 5 minutes. Remove jars and set aside for 24 hours. Check seals, then store in a cool, dark place for up to 1 year.

→ See page 27 for more about jams and jellies.

dry (p.71)

infuse (p.68)

can (p.73)

freeze (p.61)

refrigerate (p.59)

HOMEMADE APPLESAUCE

Makes about 4 cups

I cook the apples with their skins and then run the whole lot through a food mill. This cuts down on prep time and gives the sauce a lovely color and much more body than sauce made from peeled fruit. Ask your farmer for his or her best "saucing" apples and feel free to double the recipe if you have extra on hand.

INGREDIENTS

- ½ cup water
- 2 tablespoons bottled lemon juice
- 3 pounds apples, stems removed
- Sugar to taste
- Ground cinnamon (optional)

PREPARE

1. Pour the water and lemon juice into a large nonreactive stockpot. Roughly chop the apples, adding them to the pot with the lemon water as you go to prevent browning. Bring to a boil, and then simmer until the apples are tender, 10 to 20 minutes.

2. Pass the mixture through a food mill. Return the sauce to the heat and add the sugar to taste and the cinnamon, if using. Stir to dissolve the sugar. Remove from the heat.

PRESERVE

Refrigerate: Transfer to nonreactive bowls or jars, cool, and then refrigerate, covered, for up to 5 days.

Freeze: Transfer to freezer containers. Let cool to room temperature, and then cover and freeze for up to 6 months.

Can: Use the boiling-water method. Ladle the applesauce into clean, hot half-pint canning jars, leaving ½ inch of headspace. Release trapped air. Wipe the rims clean; center lids on the jars and screw on jar bands. Process for 10 minutes. Turn off heat, remove canner lid, and let jars rest in the water for 5 minutes. Remove jars and set aside for 24 hours. Check seals, then store in a cool, dark place for up to 1 year.

→ See page 54 for more about butters, sauces, and ketchups.

dry (p.71)

infuse (p.68)

can (p.79)

freeze (p.61)

refrigerate (p.59)

Pierogies with Applesauce

Don't limit applesauce to the kiddie table. It makes a stellar accompaniment to roast meats, but my favorite way to eat it is next to potato and cheese pierogies that have been sautéed in butter and onions.

12 pierogies or large cheese ravioli	**2** tablespoons butter
1 onion, diced	**1** cup Homemade Applesauce (at left)
Salt	½ cup sour cream

1. Bring a large pot of salted water to a boil. Add the pierogies and boil until just tender.

2. Meanwhile, in a medium skillet, sauté the onion, with a pinch of salt, in the butter over medium heat until it is beginning to brown, about 15 minutes. Drain the pierogies and toss them in the pan to combine. Serve with the Homemade Applesauce and sour cream. | **Makes 2 or 3 servings**

APPLED BRANDY

Makes about 4 cups

Infuse some already distilled spirits with sweet apple flavor — you can use any variety that is good for eating out of hand.

INGREDIENTS

- **1** (750 ml) bottle of not-your-best brandy
- **3** apples, cored and cut into 1-inch dice
- **¼** cup sugar
- **1** cinnamon stick (optional)

dry (p.71)

infuse (p.68)

can (p.79)

freeze (p.61)

refrigerate (p.59)

PREPARE AND PRESERVE

Infuse: Pour the brandy into a glass jar large enough to hold the brandy and the fruit. Add the apples, sugar, and cinnamon stick, if using, and cover. Stir daily for 2 weeks. Strain out the fruit and the cinnamon and return the liquid to the bottle. The flavored brandy can be stored at room temperature for up to 1 year.

Pan Sauté with Appled Brandy Cream

Appled Brandy is delicious straight up or on the rocks, but don't save it only for cocktail time. It's also wonderful for deglazing the pan after sautéing steak, pork, or chicken. Don't pour the brandy straight from the bottle into the pan, as the alcohol is flammable. Use a measuring cup or ladle to pour it into the pan.

- **1** tablespoon butter
- **1** tablespoon extra-virgin olive oil
- **2** beef steaks such as strip, porterhouse, or T-bone, or pork medallions or chicken pieces
    Salt

- **4** garlic cloves, with skins on
- **2** cups chopped mushrooms, any variety
- **1** small onion, finely diced
- **¼** cup Appled Brandy (above)
- **½** cup heavy cream
    Freshly ground black pepper

1. Heat the butter and oil in a large skillet over medium heat until sizzling. Generously season the meat with salt and add to the pan with the garlic cloves. Sauté on both sides until the meat is brown and cooked to the desired doneness, turning every 2 minutes to cook evenly. Remove the meat and garlic to a warm plate and set aside while you make the sauce.

2. To make the sauce, add the mushrooms and onion to the pan and sauté until brown, 5 to 7 minutes. Carefully add the brandy and simmer until reduced to a syrup, about 3 minutes. (If the brandy flares, cover the pan with a lid to extinguish flames.) Add the cream and simmer to thicken, about 3 minutes. Add pepper to taste, spoon over steaks, and serve. | **Makes 2 servings**

SPICED APPLE CHUTNEY

Makes about 5 pints

This luscious chutney is a great accompaniment to roast meats and takes a turkey sandwich to a whole new level. My favorite way to serve it is with a huge wedge of a New England cheddar or other sharp, local cheese, and a loaf of bread for an easy nibble with cocktails. Ask your farmer for a good baking apple that will keep its shape when cooked.

INGREDIENTS

- **2** cups apple cider vinegar
- **4** apples, cored and peeled
- **2** cups brown sugar, lightly packed
- **1** cup finely diced onions
- **1** cup dried cranberries or raisins or a combination
- **1** tablespoon freshly grated ginger
- **2** garlic cloves, minced
- **1** tablespoon mustard seed
- **2** teaspoons mild curry powder
- **1** teaspoon ground allspice
- **1** teaspoon salt

PREPARE

1. Pour the vinegar into a large saucepan. Dice the apples, adding them to the pot as you go to prevent browning. Add the brown sugar, onions, cranberries, ginger, and garlic, and bring to a boil, stirring constantly. Reduce the heat to medium-low and simmer for 30 minutes, stirring occasionally.

2. Add the mustard seed, curry powder, allspice, and salt, and simmer 15 minutes longer.

PRESERVE

Refrigerate: Ladle into jars or bowls. Cool, cover, and refrigerate for up to 3 weeks.

Can: Use the boiling-water method. Ladle chutney into clean, hot half-pint or pint canning jars, leaving ½ inch of headspace. Release trapped air. Wipe the rims clean; center lids on the jars and screw on jar bands. Process for 15 minutes. Turn off heat, remove canner lid, and let jars rest in the water for 5 minutes. Remove jars and set aside for 24 hours. Check seals, then store in a cool, dark place for up to 1 year.

→ See page 52 for more about salsas, chutneys, and relishes.

MINCEMEAT

Makes about 5 pints

Mincemeat is a traditional filling for English holiday tarts. It's usually made with suet or stew meat. This recipe is a crowd-pleasing vegetarian version of the traditional meat-laced filling. Mincemeat is a lifesaver to have around the holidays — or anytime — to stuff into pastry shells or tiny turnovers. Baking apples, which retain their shape when cooked, provide some welcome texture to the recipe.

dry (p.71)

infuse (p.68)

can (p.79)

freeze (p.61)

refrigerate (p.59)

INGREDIENTS

- **1** orange
- **3** cups apple cider vinegar
- **1** cup chopped dried figs
- **2** cups golden raisins
- **1** cup dried currants
- **1** cup slivered almonds
- **1** cup sugar
- **1** cup molasses
- **1** tablespoon freshly grated ginger
- **1** teaspoon ground allspice
- **1** teaspoon ground cinnamon
- **1** teaspoon salt
- **½** teaspoon ground cloves
- **¼** teaspoon grated nutmeg
- **3** pounds baking apples (about 9)

PREPARE

1. Wash the orange and, leaving the peel on, roughly chop. Remove any seeds. Combine the orange chunks and 1 cup of the vinegar in a food processor and purée. Add the figs and purée. Pour the puréed mixture into a large saucepan. Stir in the remaining 2 cups vinegar and the raisins, currants, almonds, sugar, molasses, ginger, allspice, cinnamon, salt, cloves, and nutmeg, and set over low heat while you prepare the apples.

2. Peel, core, and dice the apples, adding them to the pot as you go to prevent browning. Increase heat to medium-high and bring the mixture to a boil. Reduce the heat, and simmer until the apples are tender, about 30 minutes. Remove from the heat. If the mixture is dry, add up to ½ cup of water to loosen it and ensure a good pack.

PRESERVE

Refrigerate: Mincemeat keeps in the fridge for 3 weeks.

Can: Use the boiling-water method. Ladle the mincemeat into clean, hot pint canning jars, leaving ½ inch of headspace. Release trapped air. Wipe the rims clean; center lids on the jars and screw on jar bands. Process for 15 minutes. Turn off heat, remove canner lid, and let jars rest in the water for 5 minutes. Remove jars and set aside for 24 hours. Check seals, then store in a cool, dark place for up to 1 year.

→ See page 52 for more about salsas, chutneys, and relishes.

APPLE JELLY

Makes about 5 cups

If you've never made jelly before, this is a great place to start. Use any variety of tart apple, even crab apples. Because apples are naturally high in pectin, the gel sets really nicely. Don't rush — don't be tempted to press the jelly bag — and you'll have a gorgeous, clear jelly.

INGREDIENTS

- **4** pounds apples
  About 4 cups water
- **3** cups sugar
- ½ cup bottled lemon juice

PREPARE

1. Wash and stem the apples but leave the peel and core. Roughly chop and put in a large stockpot. Add enough water to barely cover the apples. Bring to a simmer and cook until tender, about 30 minutes.

2. Pour the mixture into a dampened jelly bag or a colander lined with dampened cheesecloth and let drain in the refrigerator overnight. Do not press or squeeze the bag.

3. Measure 1 quart of the resulting apple juice and add it to a large saucepan over high heat. Stir in the sugar and lemon juice. Bring to a full boil that you cannot stir down. Continue to boil until the gel stage is reached. Remove from the heat.

Note: Apple Jelly sets up quickly, so move swiftly to transfer it to its storage container.

PRESERVE

Refrigerate: Ladle into bowls or jars. Cool, cover, and refrigerate for up to 3 weeks.

Can: Use the boiling-water method. Ladle jelly into clean, hot half-pint or pint canning jars, leaving ¼ inch of headspace. Release trapped air. Wipe the rims clean; center lids on the jars and screw on jar bands. Process for 10 minutes. Turn off heat, remove canner lid, and let jars rest in the water for 5 minutes. Remove jars and set aside for 24 hours. Check seals, then store in a cool, dark place for up to 1 year.

→ See page 27 for more about jams and jellies.

dry (p.71)

infuse (p.68)

can (p.79)

freeze (p.61)

refrigerate (p.59)

APPLE BUTTER

Makes about 3 cups

This condiment is a classic and very easy to make. Essentially, it's an applesauce cooked way, way down, so you want to start with a good saucing apple. The extra cooking gives this spread a bit of a caramelized flavor and a silky texture.

INGREDIENTS

- **3** pounds apples, stems removed
- **2** cups apple cider or water
- **1** cup sugar
- **¼** cup bottled lemon juice
- **1** teaspoon ground cinnamon
- **¼** teaspoon freshly grated nutmeg

PREPARE

1. Quarter the apples but leave the peel and core. Bring the apples and cider to a boil in a large pot. Reduce the heat and simmer until the apples are very soft, 20 to 30 minutes. Cool slightly, and then run through a food mill to remove seeds and skins.

2. Return the apple purée to the pot and stir in the sugar, lemon juice, cinnamon, and nutmeg. Simmer over medium-low heat until the mixture is thickened. The timing will vary, depending on the size and shape of your pot, but you should allow 30 to 45 minutes. Don't try to shorten the cooking time by turning up the heat — as the butter thickens, so does its tendency to burn. Stir and test frequently. The butter is ready when a dollop on a plate does not weep juice around its perimeter.

PRESERVE

Refrigerate: Cool and refrigerate for up to 3 weeks.

Can: Use the boiling-water method. Ladle the butter into clean, hot half-pint canning jars, leaving ¼ inch of headspace. Release trapped air. Wipe the rims clean; center lids on the jars and screw on jar bands. Process for 15 minutes. Turn off heat, remove canner lid, and let jars rest in the water for 5 minutes. Remove jars and set aside for 24 hours. Check seals, then store in a cool, dark place for up to 1 year.

→ See page 54 for more about butters, sauces, and ketchups.

Asparagus

*T*o me, nothing says spring like asparagus. Its grassy green flavor is just what my taste buds are looking for to clear away the cobwebs. It grows with such exuberance that you can imagine the spears bucking under the frost like racehorses at the gate — when they finally do make their debut aboveground, they go great guns. A farmer friend says he can actually see them growing, and I don't think he's exaggerating. In warm temperatures, the spears can grow at a rate of 1 centimeter an hour — inches over the course of a single day.

Perhaps it's this virility that has inspired the belief that asparagus is an aphrodisiac and a health tonic. Since Roman times, the vegetable has been prized by nobles for its, ahem, inspirational qualities. Even in the most proper British circles, the spears are one of the few edibles that diners are invited to eat with their hands — lusty indeed for a culture that insists on eating everything from unpeeled peaches to pizza with knife and fork.

All claims aside, asparagus is an elegant vegetable made even more precious for its brief harvest season. When it's in season I put it in everything I can and then — poof — it's gone. I'm grateful for these recipes, which enable me to have these pretty spears on the table or sautéed in an omelet beyond the vegetable's peekaboo appearance during the spring.

FRESH STORAGE RECOMMENDATIONS

ASPARAGUS IS A THIRSTY VEGETABLE. When buying asparagus, look for ends that are still moist — those are the spears that aren't long from the fields — or are sitting in a pan of clean, fresh water. When you get them home, refrigerate them upright in a shallow pan or bowl with an inch of water at the bottom until you're ready to use them.

ASPARAGUS

...like fresh-from-the-field asparagus, but these quickly frozen spears make ...ies.

Any quantity asparagus, trimmed

PREPARE

1. Line several baking sheets with dish towels and set aside. Prepare an ice-water bath in a large bowl or clean sink.

2. Bring a large pot of water to a boil. Drop the asparagus into the water, no more than 1 pound at a time, and return to a boil. Blanch for 1 minute.

3. Scoop the asparagus out of the water with a spider or slotted spoon and plunge them into the ice-water bath. Continue blanching the asparagus in batches. Remove the asparagus from the ice bath with a slotted spoon and spread on the towel-covered baking sheets. Blot dry.

4. Arrange spears on a baking sheet and freeze solid.

PRESERVE

⊛ **Freeze:** Transfer the asparagus to freezer bags. Keep frozen for up to 6 months.

INGREDIENTS

→ See page 21 for more about blanching.

dry (p.71)

infuse (p.68)

can (p.79)

freeze (p.61)

refrigerate (p.59)

Putting Asparagus Trimmings to Work

Don't throw them out! Asparagus spears must be trimmed to separate the tender part of the stalk from the tough, woody end. Gently bend the stalk from both ends; it will naturally break where tough meets terrific. This point can sometimes be quite a bit farther down the stalk than you would hope. Don't worry about waste, though — you can still use all of that precious produce. Simmer the woody asparagus ends and trimmings with enough chicken stock or water to cover until soft. Purée, force through a sieve, and lace with a little cream for a quick soup. If whittling down the spears to fit the canning jars leaves you with a surplus of tender trimmings, sauté the asparagus bits in a little butter and extra-virgin olive oil and use them to top crostini, or toss with pasta for a delicious lunch.

MARINATED ASPARAGUS

Makes 6 to 8 servings

You'll have a hard time keeping your fingers off these spears, but do try. A little extra time in the marinade turns them into superstars on the antipasto platter, a tasty appetizer topped with a sieved egg, or a welcome addition to a meal-sized salad.

INGREDIENTS

- **2** pounds asparagus, trimmed
- ½ cup lemon juice
- ¼ cup extra-virgin olive oil
- ½ cup water
- **2** tablespoons fresh herbs, such as rosemary, thyme, or sage
- **4** garlic cloves, sliced
- **1** tablespoon salt
  Freshly ground black pepper

PREPARE

1. Line several baking sheets with dish towels and set aside. Prepare an ice-water bath in a large bowl or clean sink.

2. Bring a large pot of water to a boil. Drop the asparagus into the water, no more than 1 pound at a time, and return to a boil. Blanch for 1 minute.

3. Scoop the asparagus out of the water with a spider or slotted spoon and plunge them into the ice-water bath. Continue blanching the asparagus in batches. Remove the asparagus from the ice bath with a slotted spoon and spread on the towel-covered baking sheets. Blot dry.

4. Arrange the asparagus in a shallow bowl just large enough to fit the spears. Whisk together the lemon juice, olive oil, water, herbs, garlic, salt, and pepper to taste in a small bowl. Pour the dressing over the asparagus.

PRESERVE

Refrigerate: Cover and refrigerate for at least 24 hours and up to 1 week, tossing occasionally to blend flavors.

→ See page 21 for more about blanching.

PICKLED ASPARAGUS WITH MUSTARD SEED

Makes about 3 pints

Jars of asparagus are attractive in a chic, European way. They look great on the shelf and taste even better. To safely can asparagus using the boiling-water method, you must add enough acid, so don't skimp on the vinegar.

Note: *The boiling-water method is necessary to tenderize these cold-pack pickles.*

dry (p.71)

infuse (p.68)

can (p.79)

freeze (p.61)

refrigerate (p.59)

- **4** pounds asparagus, washed and dried
- **4** cups cider vinegar
- **1** cup water
- **¼** cup salt
- **2** tablespoons sugar
- **4** garlic cloves, sliced
- **1** tablespoon celery seed
- **1** tablespoon mustard seed
- **1** teaspoon peppercorns

PREPARE

1. Trim the asparagus to lengths 1 inch shorter than your pint jars and pack vertically into the clean, hot jars.

2. Combine the vinegar, water, salt, and sugar in a medium nonreactive saucepan. Bring the brine to a low boil, stirring to dissolve the salt and sugar, and then remove from the heat. Divide the garlic, celery seed, mustard seed, and peppercorns among the jars. Pour the hot brine over the asparagus to cover by ½ inch. Leave ½ inch of headspace between the top of the liquid and the lid.

PRESERVE

Can: Use the boiling-water method. Release trapped air. Wipe the rims clean; center lids on the jars and screw on jar bands. Process for 15 minutes. Turn off heat, remove canner lid, and let jars rest in the water for 5 minutes. Remove jars and set aside for 24 hours. Check seals, then store in a cool, dark place for up to 1 year.

→ See page 40 for more about vinegar pickles.

Beans
(String, Yellow Wax)

*B*eans are magical. You can't *not* grow them. Plunk them into the ground and they will climb any post you provide, shooting up quickly and stretching their tendrils for something to grab on to in a very *Little Shop of Horrors* way. If you're looking for something easy to nurture, beans are it. They grow fast enough to keep the kids entertained and their climbing ways add instant "farm charm" to any patio or backyard garden.

String beans are always available in the supermarket, so many people don't think of them as a seasonal item, but they, too, have their peak. Grab them by the handful when they're fresh from the vine and you'll be surprised by their sweet flavor, so good you can snack on them raw. The typical green beans are fine in these recipes, but don't stop there. Yellow wax and even the striking purple varieties can be used interchangeably here. I often use a combination — the contrasting colors are a "wow" in the jar.

FRESH STORAGE RECOMMENDATIONS

BEANS KEEP FOR A FEW DAYS, wrapped in damp paper towels, in the warmest part of the fridge.

N STRING BEANS

ze is an easy solution to stocking away a surplus of beans.

dry (p.71)

infuse (p.68)

can (p.79)

freeze (p.61)

refrigerate (p.59)

Any quantity fresh beans, washed, topped, and tailed

PREPARE

1. Line several baking sheets with dish towels and set aside. Prepare an ice-water bath in a large bowl or clean sink.

2. Bring a large pot of water to a boil. Drop the beans into the water, no more than 1 pound at a time, and return to a boil. Blanch for 1 minute.

3. Scoop out the beans with a spider or slotted spoon and plunge them into the ice-water bath. Continue blanching the beans in batches. Remove the beans from the ice bath with a slotted spoon and spread on the towel-covered baking sheets. Blot dry.

PRESERVE

⬡ **Freeze:** Transfer blanched beans to freezer bags and press out as much air as possible. Keep frozen for up to 6 months.

→ See page 21 for more about blanching.

DRIED STRING BEANS

Dried string beans are referred to as "leather britches" in old recipe books — how charming is that? Equally endearing, they are as easy to use as they are to make.

INGREDIENTS

Any quantity fresh beans, washed and dried
Darning needle
Heavy thread

PREPARE

1. Line several baking sheets with dish towels and set aside. Prepare an ice-water bath in a large bowl or clean sink.

2. Bring a large pot of water to a boil. Drop the beans into the water, no more than 1 pound at a time, and return to a boil. Blanch for 1 minute.

3. Scoop out the beans with a spider or slotted spoon and plunge them into the ice-water bath. Continue blanching the beans in batches. Remove the beans from the ice bath with a slotted spoon and spread on the towel-covered baking sheets. Blot dry.

PRESERVE

Dry:

1. Line up the beans, parallel to each other, in a 3-foot row with about an inch of space between them. Run the needle and thread through the beans, about ½ inch from the top of each. Suspend the strung beans in a hot, dry area, such as an attic, where there is plenty of air circulation.

2. When the beans are brittle, in 2 to 3 days, clip them from the hanging string, leaving behind the stems and string (don't take down the string first or it will become a tangled mess). Pasteurize the beans in a 170°F oven for 15 minutes. Cool, and then store in an airtight container for up to 6 months.

Putting Leather Britches to Work

Toss leather britches into a simmering pot of soup or stew. They rehydrate as the soup cooks, drawing in moisture from the soup and thickening it.

→ See page 21 for more about blanching.

DILLY BEANS

Makes about 8 pints

My friends go crazy for Dilly Beans. I don't know if it's because they like the way they taste or because they like to say "dilly beans." In either case, here's the recipe. Make a bunch, because everybody wants to get her dilly on in the pickle season.

Note: The boiling-water method is necessary to tenderize these cold-pack pickles.

dry (p.71)

infuse (p.68)

can (p.79)

freeze (p.61)

refrigerate (p.59)

INGREDIENTS

4 pounds green beans, washed, topped, and tailed

6 garlic cloves, peeled and sliced

1 cup fresh dill weed

2 tablespoons dill seed

1 tablespoon black peppercorns

4 cups distilled white vinegar

2 cups water

¼ cup sugar

2 tablespoons salt

PREPARE

1. Cut beans into lengths 1 inch shorter than the pint jars. Pack the beans vertically in eight clean, hot jars, somewhat tightly. Divide the garlic, dill weed, dill seed, and peppercorns among the jars.

2. Combine the vinegar, water, sugar, and salt in a medium nonreactive saucepan, and bring to a boil. Pour the hot brine over the beans to cover by ½ inch. Leave ½ inch of headspace between the top of the liquid and the lid.

PRESERVE

🅒 **Can:** Use the boiling-water method. Release trapped air. Wipe the rims clean; center lids on the jars and screw on jar bands. Process for 15 minutes. Turn off heat, remove canner lid, and let jars rest in the water for 5 minutes. Remove jars and set aside for 24 hours. Check seals, then store in a cool, dark place for up to 1 year.

→ **See page 40 for more about vinegar pickles.**

SZECHUAN BEANS

Makes about 1 quart

Spicy Szechuan green beans are a favorite of mine. This recipe turns their exotic, hot flavors into a quick refrigerator pickle. Chop them and serve on a bed of rice drizzled with some of the pickling liquid for a quick side dish.

INGREDIENTS

- **1** pound green beans, washed, topped, and tailed
- **1** cup cider vinegar
- **½** cup water
- **¼** cup soy sauce
- **¼** cup sugar
- **2** tablespoons dark sesame oil
- **1** tablespoon whole peppercorns, preferably Szechuan
- **1** (1-inch) knob ginger, sliced into coins
- **2** garlic cloves, sliced

PREPARE

1. Line several baking sheets with dish towels and set aside. Prepare an ice-water bath in a large bowl or clean sink.

2. Bring a large pot of water to a boil. Drop the beans into the water, no more than 1 pound at a time, and return to a boil. Blanch for 1 minute.

3. Scoop out the beans with a spider or slotted spoon and plunge them into the ice-water bath. Continue blanching the beans in batches. Remove the beans from the ice bath with a slotted spoon and spread on the towel-covered baking sheets. Blot dry.

4. To make pickles, pack the beans vertically in a quart jar.

5. Combine the vinegar, water, soy sauce, sugar, sesame oil, peppercorns, ginger, and garlic in a medium nonreactive saucepan. Bring to a boil and simmer for 1 minute. Pour the hot brine over the beans to cover by ½ inch. Leave ½ inch of headspace between the top of the liquid and the lid.

PRESERVE

Refrigerate: Cool, cover, and store in the refrigerator for up to 1 month.

→ See page 21 for more about blanching.
→ See page 40 for more about vinegar pickles.

Beets

Is there any vegetable more polarizing than beets? Whenever I use them in a cooking demonstration, they elicit the most powerful responses. "Oh, I adore beets" and "I can't stand the sight of those things" pretty much divide the crowd down the middle, at least at the start. I credit a lot of that disdain to salad-bar beets — those curious, mushy, industrially processed things have given these rustic roots a bad name.

Fresh beets are another animal entirely. I grate them fresh into salads, roast them and layer them with goat cheese, or whir them into borscht. And, of course, I pickle them. No matter how you prepare them, the earthy, sweet flavor of fresh, locally grown beets wins over many a skeptic. And their colors are stunning. Red, gold, candy-cane striped, they're all great. You can use any variety in these recipes.

FRESH STORAGE RECOMMENDATIONS

BEETS ARE PERFECT CANDIDATES FOR YOUR COOL ROOT CELLAR. Fill pest-proof but breathable containers, such as buckets covered with thick-wire mesh, with damp sand and bury the beets — what a treasure hunt! Or you can refrigerate them in a covered bowl or wrapped in a plastic bag to retain moisture — they will keep this way for a week or two.

PICKLED BEETS WITH CUMIN AND CLOVES

Makes about 3 pints

There's something about the combination of the dark, jewel tones of beets and the flavors of cumin and cloves that makes these pickles deliciously redolent of the exotic East.

INGREDIENTS

- **2** pounds beets
- **1** cup distilled white vinegar
- **½** cup water
- **¼** cup sugar
- **½** tablespoon salt
- **1** tablespoon cumin seed
- **¼** teaspoon whole cloves

PREPARE

1. Prep the beets by boiling or roasting them until nearly tender (see page 123). Cut them in half and then into ¼-inch slices.

2. Combine the vinegar, water, sugar, and salt in a medium nonreactive saucepan, and bring to a boil. Stir to dissolve the sugar and salt, and then remove from the heat.

3. Pack the beets into 3 clean, hot pint jars, arranging them snugly but with enough room for brine to circulate. Divide the cumin seed and cloves among the jars. Pour the hot brine over the beets to cover by ½ inch. Leave ½ inch of headspace between the top of the liquid and the lid.

PRESERVE

Refrigerate: Cool, cover, and store in the refrigerator for up to 3 weeks.

Can: Use the boiling-water method. Release trapped air. Wipe the rims clean; center lids on the jars and screw on jar bands. Process for 30 minutes. Turn off heat, remove canner lid, and let jars rest in the water for 5 minutes. Remove jars and set aside for 24 hours. Check seals, then store in a cool, dark place for up to 1 year.

→ See page 40 for more about vinegar pickles.

dry (p.71)

infuse (p.68)

can (p.79)

freeze (p.61)

refrigerate (p.59)

PICKLED BEETS WITH DILL

Makes about 3 pints

Beets and dill are a classic combination. Serve these lovelies with a dollop of sour cream along with potato pancakes. Perfect!

INGREDIENTS

- **2** pounds beets
- **1** cup distilled white vinegar
- ½ cup water
- ½ cup sugar
- ½ tablespoon salt
- ¼ cup fresh dill weed
- **1** tablespoon dill seed

PREPARE

1. Prep the beets by boiling or roasting them until nearly tender (see page 123). Cut them in half and then into ¼-inch slices.

2. Combine the vinegar, water, sugar, and salt in a medium nonreactive saucepan, and bring to a boil. Stir to dissolve the sugar and salt, and then remove from the heat.

3. Pack the beets into three clean, hot pint jars, arranging them snugly but with enough room for brine to circulate. Divide the fresh dill and dill seed among the jars. Pour the hot brine over the beets to cover by ½ inch. Leave ½ inch of headspace between the top of the liquid and the lid.

PRESERVE

Refrigerate: Cool, cover, and store in the refrigerator for up to 3 weeks.

Can: Use the boiling-water method. Release trapped air. Wipe the rims clean; center lids on the jars and screw on jar bands. Process for 30 minutes. Turn off heat, remove canner lid, and let jars rest in the water for 5 minutes. Remove jars and set aside for 24 hours. Check seals, then store in a cool, dark place for up to 1 year.

dry (p.71)

infuse (p.68)

can (p.79)

freeze (p.61)

refrigerate (p.59)

→ See page 40 for more about vinegar pickles.

Prepping Beets

You can either boil or roast your beets to prep them for canning. Both are quite easy but take a bit of unattended time to get the dense roots nice and tender. They are so scrumptious and useful that you might consider cooking up a few extra while you're at it — put them in a covered container in the fridge and slice into a salad or serve sprinkled with some sharp cheese and a drizzle of balsamic vinegar.

Whether you are boiling or roasting, wash beets thoroughly. Cut the greens down to an inch or two from the root, but don't throw the leaves away. Sauté the greens with a little garlic and olive oil or use them in place of mild-flavored sautéing greens such as Swiss chard or spinach in any recipe.

To boil beets, place them in a large pot with enough water to cover by 2 to 3 inches. Bring to a low boil and cook until beets are tender when pierced with a knife, 30 to 40 minutes depending on the size of the beets. Drain and set aside until cool enough to handle.

To roast beets, preheat the oven to 375°F. Wrap the roots individually in foil and arrange in a single layer on baking sheets. Roast until tender when pierced with a knife, 45 minutes to 1 hour. Remove from the oven, open the foil, and set aside until cool enough to handle.

Whichever cooking method you use, skins will slip off cooked beets easily. Pinch the beets with a little pressure and pull the skins away. Use a small paring knife to cut away any stubborn bits or damaged spots.

Red beets will stain everything they touch, including your hands, so wear gloves, or the pink finger badge of a beet lover will be yours for the day.

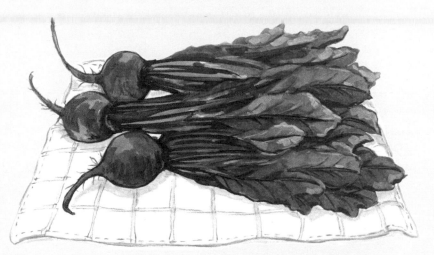

BEET RELISH

Makes about 2 pints

This one is a real shocker. Bright, vibrant color and surprising citrus flavor will turn even the most serious beet-phobe into a beet fanatic.

dry (p.71)

infuse (p.68)

can (p.79)

freeze (p.61)

refrigerate (p.59)

INGREDIENTS

- **2** pounds beets
- **2** oranges
- **2** cups cider vinegar
- **1** cup brown sugar, lightly packed
- **1** cup granulated sugar
- **1** onion, diced
- **2** garlic cloves, minced
- **1** tablespoon salt
- **4** whole cloves
- **1** bay leaf
- **1** cinnamon stick

PREPARE

1. Prep the beets by boiling or roasting them until nearly tender (see page 123). Cut into ½-inch dice and set aside. Remove the zest from the oranges and set aside. Supreme the oranges by cutting away the peel and slicing between membranes to liberate the pulp. Squeeze the juice from the membranes into a small bowl and discard the solids. Set aside the juice and pulp.

2. Combine the vinegar, brown sugar, granulated sugar, onion, garlic, salt, cloves, bay leaf, cinnamon, and zest in a medium nonreactive saucepan, and bring to a boil. Simmer for 15 minutes. Add the beets and the orange juice and pulp and simmer for 10 minutes longer.

3. Divide the mixture between two clean, hot pint-size canning jars, leaving ¼ inch of headspace between the top of the liquid and the lid.

PRESERVE

Refrigerate: Cool, cover, and store in the refrigerator for up to 3 weeks.

Can: Use the boiling-water method. Release trapped air. Wipe the rims clean; center lids on the jars and screw on jar bands. Process for 15 minutes. Turn off heat, remove canner lid, and let jars rest in the water for 5 minutes. Remove jars and set aside for 24 hours. Check seals, then store in a cool, dark place for up to 1 year.

→ See page 52 for more about salsas, chutneys, and relishes.

Berries
Blueberries & Raspberries

I like to move around. Maybe that's one of the reasons I've never seriously committed myself to a garden (besides being the Morticia Addams of horticulture). I seem to have too much wanderlust to put down roots, particularly in crops that take a few years — rhubarb, asparagus, apple trees — to bear edible results. I suppose one day I will. One day I'm going to plant berry bushes and watch them grow. Then I'll know I'm home to stay.

Until then, I rely on area farms for my berry wants and needs. U-pick farms are great fun. With the picking and putting up, you can make a real day of it. Mostly I depend on farmers' markets to get my fix. I do have the hardest time getting berries home, though: my kids tend to gobble them up before we even leave the market. They love them all — blueberries, raspberries, and strawberries, which have a chapter of their own later in the book. If you have the good fortune to make it home with an extra basket or two (or a flat), turn those berries into one of the following treats.

FRESH STORAGE RECOMMENDATIONS

FRESH BERRIES DON'T KEEP LONG AT ALL. Cover them with a damp towel and put them in the warmest part of the fridge to stretch them for a day or so.

ANY-BERRY COULIS

Gorgeous, plump, jewels of the market ... berries are absolutely irresistible. So much so that I sometimes get carried away and wind up with a little too much in my market basket — too few to can, too many to eat fresh. Here's a quick fix for when the berries start to lose their luster.

dry (p.71)

infuse (p.68)

can (p.79)

freeze (p.61)

refrigerate (p.59)

INGREDIENTS

Any quantity berries, stemmed as necessary
Honey or sugar, as desired

PREPARE

1. Combine the berries with a splash of water in a medium saucepan. Cook, stirring, over medium heat until the fruit falls apart, 5 to 10 minutes.

2. Pour the berries into a fine-mesh sieve and strain the juice into a bowl, pressing on the solids to remove the most juice. Discard the solids. Return the juice to the pan and bring to a gentle simmer. Add sweetener to taste, stirring in a tablespoon or two at a time until you reach the flavor that appeals to you. Cook down to desired thickness. Add a little more sugar or honey, to taste.

PRESERVE

Refrigerate: Cool, cover, and store in the refrigerator for up to 3 weeks.

Freeze: Pour the coulis into freezer trays or small freezable containers for easily dispensable portions. Will keep frozen for up to 6 months.

→ See page 54 for more about butters, sauces, and ketchups.

Coulis Sauce for Game

Coulis (pronounced koo-lee) has a lot of uses. Serve it with pancakes, French toast, or waffles; pour it over ice cream; blend it into plain yogurt; or whir it in a blender with rum and ice for a summer-fresh cocktail. For a savory application, you can whisk a tablespoon or two into salad dressings or use it as the base of a sauce for game, as I do here.

2 tablespoons butter
1 onion, finely diced
½ cup red wine

1 cup chicken or beef stock
¼ cup Any-Berry Coulis

Heat the butter in a medium saucepan. Add the onion and sauté until translucent, 3 to 5 minutes. Add the wine, raise the heat to high, and cook until the liquid is reduced by half, 2 to 3 minutes. Add the stock and reduce by half again, about 3 minutes longer. Whisk in the coulis. Spoon over roasted meat. | Makes about 1 cup

FROZEN BERRIES

This is the simplest way to have locally grown berries on hand all the time.

INGREDIENTS

Any quantity berries, stemmed and cleaned

PREPARE

Spread out the berries on a rimmed baking sheet. (Make sure they're not touching one another.) Pop the sheet pan into the freezer and freeze until the berries are solid.

PRESERVE

⊛ **Freeze:** Transfer the frozen berries to airtight containers or bags. Press out as much air as possible, then return to the freezer. Will keep frozen for up to 6 months.

BERRY VINEGAR

Makes about 3 cups

This vinegar has a bright taste and a gorgeous color. Decant it into clean recycled bottles of all shapes and sizes for lovely homemade holiday gifts.

INGREDIENTS

- **2** cups berries
- **2** cups distilled white vinegar

PREPARE AND PRESERVE

⌂ **Infuse:**

1. Purée the berries and vinegar in a blender. Transfer to a quart jar. Let stand 5 to 7 days in a cool, dark place, shaking the jar daily to blend the flavors.

2. Strain through a double thickness of cheese-cloth and discard the solids. Return the strained vinegar to the jar or decant into a decorative bottle. Vinegar keeps at room temperature for up to 1 year.

dry (p.71)

infuse (p.68)

can (p.79)

freeze (p.61)

refrigerate (p.59)

BERRY BOURBON

Makes about 1 pint

The deep flavors of very ripe fruit are a seductive match for the dark caramel flavors of bourbon, making this a great way to use up berries that are too far along for other preserving methods. Squishy, almost-done fruit is fine, but send any moldy berries to the compost.

INGREDIENTS

- **1½** cups crushed very ripe blueberries or blackberries (about 3 cups whole)
- **1½** cups bourbon

PREPARE AND PRESERVE

Infuse: Wash the berries and put them in a clean quart jar. Muddle with a wooden spoon and pour in the bourbon. Shake or stir to combine. Cover with a lid to limit evaporation. Set aside for 5 days, then taste. If it's to your liking, pour through a fine-mesh strainer and discard the solids. If it's not quite ready, try again the next day. Return to a clean jar or the original bourbon bottle and store for up to 1 year.

BERRY LEATHER

One quart of fruit makes about 1 (17-inch) sheet of leather

My kids go nuts for this stuff, and it's fun to do together. Nothing says "yum" like a little kitchen science.

INGREDIENTS

- **4** cups berries, any kind
- **½** cup water
- **¼** cup sugar

PREPARE

1. Wash and dry the berries. Combine them with the water in a large skillet and bring to a boil. Simmer until the berries begin to break down, about 5 minutes. To purée the fruit, mash it with a potato masher or stick blender, or run it through a food mill if you want to remove the pips.

2. Preheat the oven to 170°F. Line a jelly-roll pan or a rimmed baking sheet with parchment paper or a Silpat and set aside.

3. Return the berry purée to the pan and simmer over low heat, stirring frequently, until it thickens to the consistency of baby food. Add the sugar and stir to dissolve.

PRESERVE

Dry:

1. Spread the sweetened purée onto the baking sheet, tilting it to create an even layer about ⅛ inch thick. Dry in the oven until tacky to the touch, about 2 hours.

2. Cool to room temperature. Slide the parchment paper onto a cutting board and roll the leather into a tube. Slice the dried fruit into 2-inch strips and store in a covered jar for up to 1 month.

QUICK BLUEBERRY JAM

Makes about 4 cups

This jam is full of fresh blueberry flavor. Because these berries are easy to stem and have no hulls or noticeable pips, it's a quick project, too.

INGREDIENTS

- **1-2** cups sugar, depending on how sweet you like your jam
- **2** teaspoons Pomona's Universal Pectin
- **8** cups blueberries, stemmed
- ¼ cup bottled lemon juice
- **2** teaspoons calcium water (included in the Pomona box)

PREPARE

1. Combine the sugar and pectin in a small bowl and set aside. Combine the berries with a splash of water in a medium nonreactive saucepan and slowly bring to a boil over low heat. Add the lemon juice and calcium water. Pour in the sugar-pectin mixture and stir to dissolve.

2. Return to a boil, and then immediately remove from the heat and let the jam rest for 5 minutes, stirring occasionally to release air bubbles. Skim off any foam.

PRESERVE

Refrigerate: Ladle into bowls or jars. Cool, cover, and refrigerate for up to 3 weeks.

Can: Use the boiling-water method. Pour into clean, hot 4-ounce or half-pint canning jars, leaving ¼ inch of headspace. Release trapped air. Wipe the rims clean; center lids on the jars and screw on jar bands. Process for 10 minutes. Turn off heat, remove canner lid, and let jars rest in the water for 5 minutes. Remove jars and set aside for 24 hours. Check seals, then store in a cool, dark place for up to 1 year.

→ See page 27 for more about jams and jellies.

CLASSIC BLUEBERRY JAM

Makes about 4 cups

Blueberries have a fair amount of pectin, so with a little time on the stove you can cook them down into a lovely jam without adding a thickener. In a pinch, I warm this jam until it loosens and then ladle it over a pound cake for a nice quick dessert.

INGREDIENTS

- **8** cups blueberries
- **2** cups sugar
- **¼** cup bottled lemon juice

PREPARE

1. Combine the berries with a splash of water in a medium nonreactive saucepan. Bring to a boil, stirring and crushing the berries to release their juice. Add the sugar and stir to dissolve. Stir in the lemon juice. Continue to cook at a steady boil, stirring frequently, until the jam reaches the desired gel.

2. Remove from the heat and let the jam rest for 5 minutes, stirring occasionally to release air bubbles and prevent fruit float. Skim any foam from the top of the jam.

PRESERVE

Refrigerate: Ladle into bowls or jars. Cool, cover, and refrigerate for up to 3 weeks.

Can: Use the boiling-water method. Pour into clean, hot 4-ounce or half-pint canning jars, leaving ¼ inch of headspace. Release trapped air. Wipe the rims clean; center lids on the jars and screw on jar bands. Process for 10 minutes. Turn off heat, remove canner lid, and let jars rest in the water for 5 minutes. Remove jars and set aside for 24 hours. Check seals, then store in a cool, dark place for up to 1 year.

dry (p.71)

infuse (p.68)

can (p.79)

freeze (p.61)

refrigerate (p.59)

Variation: Savory Blueberry and Basil Jam

Blueberry and basil? I found these two at the market one summer day and fell back on my mantra, "What grows together goes together." The tenet proved true — the flavor combination might be unexpected, but it's awesome! Stir in ½ cup fresh basil, cut in chiffonade, after the jam has reached the gel stage. Process as directed above.

→ See page 27 for more about jams and jellies.

QUICK RASPBERRY JAM

Makes about 4 cups

This is a handy little recipe for when you're long on berries and short on time.

INGREDIENTS

- **2** cups sugar
- **1** teaspoon Pomona's Universal Pectin
- **8** cups raspberries
- **1** teaspoon calcium water (included in the Pomona box)

PREPARE

1. Combine the sugar and pectin in a small bowl and set aside. Run 4 cups of the berries through a food mill to remove seeds, if desired. Pour the pulp, the remaining whole berries, and a splash of water into a medium saucepan and bring to a boil over low heat. Stir in the calcium water. Pour in the sugar-pectin mixture and stir to dissolve.

2. Return to a boil, and then immediately remove from the heat and let the jam rest for 5 minutes, stirring occasionally to release air bubbles. Skim off any foam.

PRESERVE

Refrigerate: Ladle into bowls or jars. Cool, cover, and refrigerate for up to 3 weeks.

Can: Use the boiling-water method. Pour into clean, hot 4-ounce or half-pint canning jars, leaving ¼ inch of headspace. Release trapped air. Wipe the rims clean; center lids on the jars and screw on jar bands. Process for 10 minutes. Turn off heat, remove canner lid, and let jars rest in the water for 5 minutes. Remove jars and set aside for 24 hours. Check seals, then store in a cool, dark place for up to 1 year.

→ See page 27 for more about jams and jellies.

RASPBERRY JELLY

Makes about 3 cups

This crystal-clear jelly is beautiful. It uses quite a bit of fruit, so save it for when berries are in full flush. If, on occasion, your set is a little loose, call it berry sauce and use it on ice cream or pour over pancakes.

INGREDIENTS

- **8** cups fresh raspberries
- **3** teaspoons calcium water (included in the Pomona box)
- **3** cups sugar
- **3** teaspoons Pomona's Universal Pectin

PREPARE

1. Combine the berries with a splash of water and bring to a boil in a large pot. Cook, stirring and mashing the berries to release juice, for about 5 minutes. Cool slightly.

2. Transfer to a dampened jelly bag hung over a bowl or to a nonreactive colander lined with several layers of dampened cheesecloth set over a large bowl. Allow the juice to drip into the bowl for 2 hours. Do not press on the bag or fruit.

3. Pour 3 cups of the juice into a large saucepan and bring to a boil. Add the calcium water and return to a boil. Combine the sugar with the pectin powder and add to the boiling juice, stirring to dissolve the sugar. Remove from the heat and let cool for 5 minutes, stirring occasionally to release air bubbles. Skim off any foam.

PRESERVE

Refrigerate: Ladle into bowls or jars. Cool, cover, and refrigerate for up to 3 weeks.

Can: Use the boiling-water method. Pour into clean, hot 4-ounce or half-pint canning jars, leaving ¼ inch of headspace. Release trapped air. Wipe the rims clean; center lids on the jars and screw on jar bands. Process for 10 minutes. Turn off heat, remove canner lid, and let jars rest in the water for 5 minutes. Remove jars and set aside for 24 hours. Check seals, then store in a cool, dark place for up to 1 year.

dry (p.71)

infuse (p.68)

can (p.79)

freeze (p.61)

refrigerate (p.59)

→ See page 27 for more about jams and jellies.

Cabbage

Cabbage is a cool-weather crop. In the Northeast, that means we have it in spring and fall. It combines well with carrots and radishes in the early harvests and is a great partner for peppers and green tomatoes as the season comes to a close.

There are a number of varieties available, solid heads of red and green, frilly Savoy, delicate and elongated Napa, and the Chinese cabbages, such as bok choy. All are delicious eaten raw, lightly braised, or tossed in a stir-fry. Most people who don't like cabbage really just don't like overcooked cabbage, which brings out a sulfur smell. These recipes share none of that characteristic.

FRESH STORAGE RECOMMENDATIONS

BECAUSE IT NEEDS COOL TEMPERATURES, cabbage is easy to have on hand. It keeps well in the refrigerator — I've held heads in the crisper for a month — or a root cellar, if you have one. Firm green or red cabbage heads will store for 1 to 3 months in a relatively humid, cool root cellar. Leave their loose outer leaves intact, wrap in newspaper, and store on shelves. Give them a little spritz of water once a week to keep them from drying out.

QUICK CABBAGE PICKLE

Makes about 2 quarts

One of my neighborhood sushi restaurants puts out these pickles to nibble on while diners wait for dinner. I really like their sweetness — it keeps me happy even when I'm famished. This recipe makes a lot; you can halve it or share with your friends.

dry (p.71)

infuse (p.68)

can (p.79)

freeze (p.61)

refrigerate (p.59)

INGREDIENTS

- **2** cups distilled white vinegar
- **2** cups water
- **½** cup sugar
- **2** tablespoons salt
- **1** small head cabbage, cored and chopped into 2-inch pieces
- **2** carrots, peeled and cut into ¼-inch coins
- **1** daikon radish, cut into ¼-inch coins

PREPARE

1. Bring the vinegar, water, sugar, and salt to a boil in a large nonreactive stockpot. Add the cabbage, carrots, and radish, and return to a boil. Turn off the heat and cool to room temperature.

2. Pack the pickles into jars and cover with brine from the stockpot.

PRESERVE

Refrigerate: Cool, cover, and refrigerate for at least 2 days and up to 1 month.

Putting Cabbage to Work

Don't think of fresh cabbage only as the main ingredient in coleslaw. In wintertime cabbage makes a great substitute for out-of-season lettuce when you need a salad fix. Cut it in chiffonade and toss with your favorite dressing.

→ See page 40 for more about vinegar pickles.

GRANNY'S CHOW-CHOW RELISH

Makes about 5 pints

My granny is a Southern woman — the genuine article — who was raised putting up everything the family needed to get them through the winter. We got to talking about her canning, and she said this was one of her favorite recipes. When I asked her what was in it, she said, "Oh, you know, a little of this, a little of that until it tastes right." Typical Granny recipe.

INGREDIENTS

- **4** cups cider vinegar
- **1** cup sugar
- **¼** cup salt
- **2** teaspoons ground allspice
  Red pepper flakes to taste
- **4** cups finely chopped cabbage, from one small head
- **2** pounds green tomatoes, finely chopped
- **1** pound onions, finely chopped
- **2** red bell peppers, finely chopped

PREPARE

Combine the vinegar, sugar, salt, allspice, and red pepper flakes in a large nonreactive stockpot, and bring to a boil. Add the cabbage, tomatoes, onions, and bell peppers, and return to a boil, stirring to ensure that all the ingredients have heated through.

PRESERVE

Refrigerate: Ladle into bowls or jars. Cool, cover, and refrigerate for up to 3 weeks.

Can: Use the boiling-water method. Ladle into clean, hot pint canning jars, covering the relish by ¼ inch with liquid from the stockpot. Leave ¼ inch of headspace between the top of the liquid and the lid. Release trapped air. Wipe the rims clean; center lids on the jars and screw on jar bands. Process for 15 minutes. Turn off heat, remove canner lid, and let jars rest in the water for 5 minutes. Remove jars and set aside for 24 hours. Check seals, then store in a cool, dark place for up to 1 year.

→ See page 52 for more about salsas, chutneys, and relishes.

dry (p.71)

infuse (p.68)

can (p.79)

freeze (p.61)

refrigerate (p.59)

CLASSIC FERMENTED SAUERKRAUT

Makes about 2 quarts

My friend Bekah Wilce is quite a fan of fermenting. If it grows, she can bring it to its festering fruition. This is her recommendation for a basic, fermented kraut.

Note: *Because the high temperatures of the boiling-water method would destroy the beneficial probiotic bacteria that result from the fermentation process, canning is not recommended.*

INGREDIENTS

5 pounds white cabbage (1 large head or 2 small)

5 tablespoons kosher salt

1 tablespoon juniper berries or caraway seed

PREPARE

1. Peel away the outer leaves of the cabbage, and then quarter and core. Shred it finely using a knife, mandoline, or kraut board.* Toss with the salt and juniper berries in a large nonreactive bowl until thoroughly combined. Transfer to a 1-gallon glass jar or ceramic crock and press down. Top the cabbage with a clean plate, just smaller than the opening of the jar. Fill a clean quart jar with water and use it to weight down the plate. Cover with a clean dish towel and remove to a cool place.

2. Check the kraut after 24 hours. With the help of the plate, all the cabbage should be submerged. If it's not, pour enough brine (1 tablespoon of salt to 1 cup of water) over the cabbage to cover it.

3. Check the cabbage daily. Tiny bubbles should be rising through the liquid (easy to see in a glass container). If a scum has formed, don't worry; just ladle it from the top of the liquid and wash and replace the plate and jar. Add more brine, if necessary, to keep the cabbage submerged. The kraut will be fully fermented in 1 to 2 weeks at room temperature or 3 to 4 weeks in a cool basement. You'll know it's done when it stops bubbling and is a pale golden color.

*A kraut board is a traditional tool for shredding cabbage, similar to a wooden mandoline.

PRESERVE

Refrigerate: Store in the refrigerator, covered, for up to 1 month.

→ See page 45 for more about fermented pickles.

KIMCHI

Makes about 2 quarts

For some people, kimchi is a religion — full of mystical, medicinal properties. They hardly let a meal go by without this Korean delicacy. I'm not as fervent a follower, but my friend Chef Michael Young is. He likes the stuff so much he even sneaks it into the specials at his Latin American restaurant, Valencia Luncheria in Norwalk, Connecticut. This recipe is based on one of his.

Note: *Because the high temperatures of the boiling-water method would destroy the beneficial probiotic bacteria that result from the fermentation process, canning is not recommended.*

INGREDIENTS

For the spice paste:

- ¼ cup kosher salt
- 4 scallions
- 2 small chili peppers, stemmed
- 3 garlic cloves
- 1 (2-inch) knob ginger, sliced into coins
- 1 teaspoon anchovy paste

For the kimchi:

- 2 pounds Napa cabbage, chopped
- 1 pound bok choy, chopped
- ½ pound carrots, peeled and cut into ¼-inch coins

PREPARE

1. Combine the salt, scallions, chilies, garlic, ginger, and anchovy paste in a blender or food processor and purée. Put the cabbage, bok choy, and carrots in a large bowl. Add the spice paste and toss. Pack the kimchi tightly into a 1-gallon glass jar or ceramic crock and press down. Let rest for at least 1 hour.

2. Press down the kimchi again so the brine rises up over the vegetables. Top the kimchi with a clean plate, just smaller than the opening of the jar. Fill a clean quart jar with water and use it to weight down the plate. Cover with a clean dish towel and remove to a cool place.

3. Check the kimchi after 24 hours. With the help of the plate, all of the kimchi should be submerged. If it's not, pour enough brine (1 tablespoon of salt to 1 cup of water) over the kimchi to cover it.

4. Check the kimchi daily. Tiny bubbles should be rising through the liquid (easy to see in a glass container). If a scum has formed, don't worry; just ladle it from the top of the liquid and wash and replace the plate and jar. Add more brine, if necessary, to keep the kimchi submerged. The kimchi will be fully fermented in 1 to 2 weeks. You'll know it's done when it stops bubbling and has a pleasantly salty/sour taste.

PRESERVE

Refrigerate: Store in the refrigerator, covered, for up to 1 month.

→ See page 45 for more about fermented pickles.

Cantaloupe

I grew up in Maryland, where sweet melons from the Eastern Shore are still a prize of the summer season. When the good ones hit the farm stands, word quickly spreads. My mother likes her cantaloupe, but she used to work long hours. She would get calls from ladies on their way to her beauty shop, offering to pick them up for her on their way in for their weekly "do." Her customers kept us in fine melons all summer long.

Cantaloupes are related to winter squash, and cooking a melon highlights this similarity. Its sweetness tones down and the squash flavors become more pronounced, turning the cantaloupe into something you would think of more as a savory than a sweet. The Cantaloupe Preserves and Cantaloupe Pickles recipes pair nicely as a spread with a savory sandwich or as a table condiment with a roast dinner where a little warm, autumnal flavor would be welcome.

Cantaloupe skins, with their thickly grooved, porous texture, pick up everything but men and money. To keep that gunk in check, wash melons thoroughly with a little dish soap and rinse well before you cut into them.

FRESH STORAGE RECOMMENDATIONS

"PRESS ON THE STEM END" and "Look for even color" might be good advice for some, but these methods have never worked for me. My suggestions? Give the melon a knock, like you're rapping on a door. Does it sound hollow? Perfect, take that one home. Give that baby a good sniff. Did your mouth water? Then you've found a ripe cantaloupe. Eat it, now! The window of time when a cantaloupe is ripe and ready is fleeting. Get out a spoon or turn it into one of these delectable treats.

CANTALOUPE AGUA FRESCA

Makes about 1 quart

This refreshing beverage is a great way to use up an overripe melon. Or even a perfectly ripe one — it's that good. You can substitute muskmelon, honeydew, or cassava.

INGREDIENTS

- **1** cantaloupe, rind and seeds removed, flesh roughly chopped
- **1** cup water
- **2** tablespoons sugar
  Juice of 1 lime or lemon

PREPARE

1. Set a fine-mesh sieve or colander lined with dampened cheesecloth over a bowl. Purée the melon in a blender or food processor, working in batches if necessary. Transfer the puréed melon to the sieve or colander as you go. Let the purée drain fully for about 30 minutes, pressing on the solids to release as much liquid as possible.

2. Pour the melon juice into a pitcher. Add the water, sugar, and lime juice, and stir to dissolve the sugar. If you're storing it, refrigerate or freeze now. Otherwise, serve over ice, perhaps adding a splash of seltzer and/or a jigger of rum or vodka to each glass.

PRESERVE

Refrigerate: Refrigerate (without ice, seltzer, or alcohol) for up to 3 days.

Freeze: Freeze melon juice in 8-ounce servings for up to 3 months.

→ See page 26 for more about agua fresca and granita.

CANTALOUPE RUM

Makes about 1 quart

I think of cantaloupe as more of a Southern flavor than I do a tropical treat, but it goes really well with island rum. Whip up a batch of this infused rum and it will take you to that summer place, no matter where that is for you. You can also substitute another melon such as a honeydew or a cassava.

INGREDIENTS

- **1** ripe cantaloupe, rind and seeds removed, flesh cut into 2-inch chunks
- **½** cup sugar
- **½** cup water
  Juice of 1 lemon
- **1** (750 ml) bottle white rum

PREPARE AND PRESERVE

Infuse:

1. Purée the melon in a blender with the sugar, water, and lemon juice, working in batches if necessary. You should have about 1 quart of melon purée. Pour the purée and the rum into a large jar, cover, and set aside for 5 to 7 days.

2. Stir daily and check for flavor after the fifth day. Pour the mixture through a fine-mesh strainer and discard the solids. Return the infused rum to a clean jar. Keeps for up to 1 year.

3. Serve chilled, over ice or with a splash of seltzer.

dry (p.71)

infuse (p.68)

can (p.79)

freeze (p.61)

refrigerate (p.59)

CANTALOUPE GRANITA

Makes about 1 quart

Granita is essentially a frozen agua fresca. Sweet enough for kids, sophisticated enough for adults, this dessert is a hit for all ages.

INGREDIENTS

- **1** cup sugar
- **½** cup water
- **1** small cantaloupe

PREPARE

1. Make a simple syrup: Combine the sugar and water in a small saucepan and bring to a boil, stirring to dissolve the sugar. Remove from the heat and cool completely.

2. While the syrup cools, prepare the cantaloupe. Cut away the rind and remove the seeds. Cut the flesh into 2-inch chunks and purée in a blender or food processor until smooth. Stir together the melon purée and the syrup in a shallow baking dish. Freeze for 2 to 3 hours, stirring with a fork every 20 minutes to create a slushy texture.

PRESERVE

Freeze: Will keep in the freezer for 2 weeks. If the granita freezes solid before serving, let it sit at room temperature for 10 to 15 minutes and stir with a fork to regain texture.

Putting Granita to Work

Granita is a really beautiful and refreshing dessert. You can up the ante on its visual appeal by serving it in a pretty glass dish or a classic martini or champagne glass.

dry (p.71)

infuse (p.68)

can (p.79)

freeze (p.61)

refrigerate (p.59)

→ See page 24 for more about agua fresca and granita.

CANTALOUPE PRESERVES

Makes about 4 cups

Don't save this one for toast. These preserves easily make the leap to savory dishes; try them with sautéed pork chops or roasted turkey.

INGREDIENTS

- 1 cantaloupe, rind and seeds removed
- ½ cup water
- 1 cup sugar
- 2 teaspoons Pomona's Universal Pectin
- 2 teaspoons calcium water (included in the Pomona box)
- ½ cup bottled lemon juice
- 1 teaspoon ground cinnamon

PREPARE

Cut the melon into 1-inch chunks; you should have about 4 cups. Combine the melon with the water in a large nonreactive pot and bring to a boil. Stir together the sugar and pectin powder, and then add the mixture to the boiling fruit and stir some more. When the mixture returns to a boil, stir in the calcium water, lemon juice, and cinnamon. Remove from the heat and let rest for 5 minutes, stirring occasionally to enable air bubbles to settle out. Skim off any foam.

PRESERVE

Refrigerate: Ladle preserves into bowls or jars. Cool, cover, and refrigerate for up to 3 weeks.

Can: Use the boiling-water method. Ladle into clean, hot half-pint canning jars, leaving ¼ inch of headspace. Release trapped air. Wipe the rims clean; center lids on the jars and screw on jar bands. Process for 10 minutes. Turn off heat, remove canner lid, and let jars rest in the water for 5 minutes. Remove jars and set aside for 24 hours. Check seals, then store in a cool, dark place for up to 1 year.

→ See page 27 for more about jams and jellies.

dry (p.71)

infuse (p.68)

can (p.79)

freeze (p.61)

refrigerate (p.59)

CANTALOUPE PICKLES

Makes about 4 cups

Who knew? The sweetness of the melon with a spike of vinegar makes for pitch-perfect pickles. Because of the long cooking time, it's best to use a slightly underripe, firm melon.

INGREDIENTS

- **1** cantaloupe, rind and seeds removed
- **2** cups cider vinegar
- **1** cup sugar
- **1** tablespoon freshly grated ginger
- **1** cinnamon stick, broken in half
- **1** bay leaf, torn in half
- **2** whole cloves

PREPARE

1. Cut the melon into 1-inch chunks; you should have about 4 cups. Combine the vinegar, sugar, ginger, cinnamon, bay leaf, and cloves in a large nonreactive saucepan and bring to a boil. Remove from the heat and stir in the melon. Cover and let steep for about 1 hour.

2. Return to a boil, and then reduce the heat and simmer gently for 1 hour, until the fruit is translucent.

PRESERVE

Refrigerate: Ladle into bowls or jars. Cool, cover, and refrigerate for up to 3 weeks.

Can: Use the boiling-water method. Ladle into clean, hot half-pint or pint canning jars, covering the pickles by ½ inch with liquid. Leave ½ inch of headspace between the top of the liquid and the lid. Release trapped air. Wipe the rims clean; center lids on the jars and screw on jar bands. Process for 10 minutes. Turn off heat, remove canner lid, and let jars rest in the water for 5 minutes. Remove jars and set aside for 24 hours. Check seals, then store in a cool, dark place for up to 1 year.

→ See page 40 for more about vinegar pickles.

Carrots

*O*ur grocery stores are overrun with carrots — piles and piles of them, with fronds or without, in 1-pound, 2-pound, and sometimes 20-pound "juicer" bags, or whittled down to digit-sized nubs. You would think something so ubiquitous would be easy to grow. At least that's what I thought until I tended the carrot patch at my local CSA: tweezing out the runts to thin the seedlings, hoeing the weeds without decapitating the vegetable, and then pulling up the bent, arthritic things that suffered from trying to maneuver themselves through Connecticut's notoriously rocky soil — I have learned to appreciate the work that goes into a good carrot.

Carrots come in an array of colors. There's the typical orange, of course, but also yellow, white, and, my favorite, red Dragons' Tongues. You can use any of those varieties in these recipes, and don't hesitate to mix and match. With these carrot recipes, more color equals more joy.

FRESH STORAGE RECOMMENDATIONS

SOMEONE — MAYBE IT'S YOU, MAYBE IT'S A FARMER — has worked hard to grow a good carrot. Store these labors in the root cellar by burying them in buckets of moist sand. Or turn them into one of the following recipes.

FROZEN CARROTS

Frozen carrots are a little on the soft side, fine for throwing into a potpie, stew, or soup.

INGREDIENTS

Any quantity fresh carrots

PREPARE

1. Line several baking sheets with dish towels and set aside. Prepare an ice-water bath in a large bowl or clean sink.

2. Bring a large pot of water to a boil. Wash, peel, and remove the stems from the carrots, and then cut the veggies into chunks or coins. Drop the carrot chunks into the water, no more than 1 pound at a time, and return to a boil. Blanch for 1 minute.

3. Scoop out the carrots and plunge them into the ice-water bath. Remove from the ice bath with a slotted spoon and spread on the towel-covered pans. Blot dry.

PRESERVE

 Freeze: Transfer blanched carrots to freezer bags and press out as much air as possible. Keep frozen for up to 6 months.

→ See page 21 for more about blanching.

dry (p.71)

infuse (p.68)

can (p.79)

freeze (p.61)

refrigerate (p.59)

What Is a CSA?

CSA (community-supported agriculture or commmunity-sponsored agriculture) is an increasingly popular way to purchase local, sustainably raised foods. Similar to a membership or subscription model, eaters pay in advance of the season for "shares" in the farm's harvest. Each week members visit the farm or a satellite pick-up point to collect their portions of what came off the field. By paying in advance, eaters realize substantial savings and farmers get much needed preseason working capital to buy the seeds and equipment to get the farm rolling.

Each CSA is unique. Some are produce only, some are for meat, and others are a combination of many kinds of food. Some farms offer working CSAs that require members to spend at least some time in the field.

To find a CSA that is right for you visit www.localharvest.org/csa.

GINGER-CARROT SLAW

Makes about 2 pints

I could eat ginger all day long — I love its hot, sweet, spicy flavor, and it's a perfect partner for carrots. If you don't share my crush, feel free to use less ginger in this recipe.

INGREDIENTS

- **1** pound carrots, trimmed and peeled
- **½** pound daikon radish, trimmed and peeled, or other radish, trimmed
- **1** red bell pepper, seeds and stem removed
- **¼** cup salt
- **2** cups distilled white vinegar
- **1** cup water
- **1** cup sugar
- **½** cup shredded ginger

PREPARE

1. Cut the carrots, radish, and bell pepper into julienne strips on a mandoline or shred in a food processor or with a box grater. Toss the shredded vegetables with the salt and put in a colander set over a bowl to drain for 2 hours.

2. Rinse the vegetables thoroughly, and then squeeze by the handful to remove as much water as possible.

3. Combine the vinegar, water, sugar, and ginger in a large nonreactive pot and bring to a boil. Stir in the vegetables and return to a boil, stirring to make sure that all ingredients are heated evenly. Remove from the heat.

PRESERVE

Refrigerate: Ladle into bowls or jars. Cool, cover, and refrigerate for up to 3 weeks.

→ See page 40 for more about vinegar pickles.

Putting Carrot Slaw to Work

Serve slaw as is or drained and tossed with 1 tablespoon of flavorless oil (such as organic canola) and 1 teaspoon of sesame oil per cup of slaw.

dry (p.71)

infuse (p.68)

can (p.79)

freeze (p.61)

refrigerate (p.59)

MARDI GRAS DOUBLOONS

Makes about 2 pints

I had the good fortune to live in New Orleans for a summer. When I wasn't eating my way through the city, I was in my little kitchen trying to master the local specialties. The idea for this pickle — and some of my best gumbo recipes — came from Justin Wilson's Homegrown Louisiana Cookin'. *The vegetables here represent the three colors of Mardi Gras: purple, gold, and green. They also taste terrific together.*

INGREDIENTS

- **1** eggplant, cut in half and then in generous ¼-inch half-moons
- **1** pound carrots, peeled and cut into generous ¼-inch coins
- **1** green bell pepper, seeded and chopped
- **¼** cup salt
- **3** cups apple cider vinegar
- **2** garlic cloves, sliced
- **½** teaspoon black peppercorns
- **½** teaspoon, more or less, cayenne pepper
- **½** teaspoon dried oregano
- **½** teaspoon dried thyme
- **1** bay leaf

PREPARE

1. Layer the eggplant, carrots, bell pepper, and salt in a colander set over a large bowl, and let drain for 2 hours.

2. Rinse thoroughly, and then squeeze to remove as much water as possible.

3. Combine the vinegar, garlic, peppercorns, cayenne, oregano, thyme, and bay leaf in a medium nonreactive saucepan, and bring to a boil. Add the vegetables to the brine and return to a boil, stirring to ensure that all ingredients are heated through. Remove from the heat.

PRESERVE

Refrigerate: Ladle into bowls or jars. Cool, cover, and refrigerate for up to 3 weeks.

→ See page 40 for more about vinegar pickles.

DILLED CARROTS

Makes about 3 pints

Dill with cucumber is a classic combo; dill and carrots should be, too. Whether you roast, purée, or eat them raw, carrots benefit from a little of this chopped herb. Pickled carrots are no exception — these taste wonderfully dilly!

Note: *The boiling-water method is necessary to tenderize these cold-pack pickles.*

INGREDIENTS

- **2** pounds carrots, peeled and cut into generous ¼-inch rounds
- **4** garlic cloves, sliced
- **1** onion, chopped
- **1** tablespoon black peppercorns
- **1** large bunch fresh dill or 2 tablespoons dried dill weed and 1 tablespoon dill seed
- **4** cups distilled white vinegar
- **¼** cup sugar
- **2** tablespoons salt

PREPARE

1. Divide the carrots, garlic, onion, peppercorns, and dill among 3 clean, hot pint-size canning jars.

2. Combine the vinegar, sugar, and salt in a medium nonreactive saucepan, and bring to a boil, stirring to dissolve. Pour the brine over the carrots to cover by ½ inch. Leave ½ inch of headspace between the top of the liquid and the lid.

PRESERVE

Can: Use the boiling-water method. Release trapped air. Wipe the rims clean; center lids on the jars and screw on jar bands. Process for 15 minutes. Turn off heat, remove canner lid, and let jars rest in the water for 5 minutes. Remove jars and set aside for 24 hours. Check seals, then store in a cool, dark place for up to 1 year.

→ See page 40 for more about vinegar pickles.

dry (p.71)

infuse (p.68)

can (p.79)

freeze (p.61)

refrigerate (p.59)

SPICY CARROTS

Makes about 3 pints

I like these carrots spicy, so I use a combination of jalapeño peppers and red pepper flakes. You can reduce the heat by adding fewer peppers or omitting the flakes. Make sure to sample your peppers for heat, as their potency varies.

Note: *The boiling-water method is necessary to tenderize these cold-pack pickles.*

INGREDIENTS

- **4–6** garlic cloves, sliced
- **1–2** jalapeño peppers, sliced, with seeds
- **1** teaspoon red pepper flakes (optional)
- **2** pounds carrots
- **4** cups distilled white vinegar
- **1** cup sugar
- **3** tablespoons salt

PREPARE

1. Divide the garlic, sliced jalapeños, and pepper flakes, if using, among three clean, hot, pint canning jars. Trim, peel, and cut the carrots 1 inch shorter than the jars. Pack the carrots into the jars.

2. Bring the vinegar to a boil in a large nonreactive saucepan. Add the sugar and salt and stir to dissolve. Pour the brine over the carrots, covering the vegetables by ½ inch with liquid. Leave ½ inch of headspace between the top of the liquid and the lid.

PRESERVE

Can: Use the boiling-water method. Release trapped air. Wipe the rims clean; center lids on the jars and screw on jar bands. Process for 15 minutes. Turn off heat, remove canner lid, and let jars rest in the water for 5 minutes. Remove jars and set aside for 24 hours. Check seals, then store in a cool, dark place for up to 1 year.

Spicy Carrots

→ **See page 40 for more about vinegar pickles.**

A Sandwich to Go with Your Pickle

My Spicy Carrots (at left) were inspired by a dish I had at the restaurant Tartine in San Francisco. There, the pickles are served alongside seductively rich, open-faced grilled sandwiches (tartines), and the salty/sweet/spicy flavor of the brined vegetables provides a terrific contrast. I've seen a number of blog entries dedicated to the combo and the ritualistic bite of one and then the other that keeps us all coming back for more. If you can't make it to Tartine, serve these spicy pickles alongside a grilled cheese, or make my version, below.

2 tablespoons butter

1–2 tablespoons mayonnaise, preferably organic or homemade

4 slices white sandwich bread

2 teaspoons capers, drained

4 slices Swiss cheese

4 slices roasted turkey

Melt the butter in a medium skillet. Spread the mayo on two slices of bread and sprinkle them with the capers. Layer on the cheese and turkey and top with the remaining slices of bread. Press each sandwich with your hand and then sauté over medium heat until golden and the cheese is melted, about 5 minutes per side. Serve with Spicy Carrots. | **Makes 2 sandwiches**

Cauliflower

A head of cauliflower is a gorgeous vegetable — it's a wonder something so pretty can have such a bad rap. Like any other member of the brassica family (like broccoli), cauliflower will emit a sulfurous reek when overcooked. Lightly cooked — and certainly pickled — cauliflower tastes as good as it looks.

I love, love, love the heirloom varieties of cauliflower. I always give them a little sear in the skillet or let them caramelize in a roasting pan to bring out their nutty flavor. Although any variety will work in these recipes, I recommend sticking to the white heads here — the bright white looks better.

FRESH STORAGE RECOMMENDATIONS

IF YOU'RE SHOPPING AT THE FARMERS' MARKET or growing your own, cauliflower in its natural, protective wrapper of crisp green leaves is a familiar sight. Shrouded in this way, cauliflower heads will keep in the not-so-cold section of the refrigerator or in a cool, humid part of the root cellar for 2 to 3 weeks.

CURRIED CAULIFLOWER

Makes about 3 pints

Cauliflower and Indian flavors are a natural pairing. A little curry powder ... the beautiful florets a bit of spice and splendid color.

INGREDIENTS

- **3** cups distilled white vinegar
- **1** cup water
- **½** cup brown sugar, lightly packed
- **1** tablespoon curry powder, hot or mild
- **1** tablespoon salt
- **1** (2- to 3-pound) head cauliflower, leaves removed, cored, and cut into ½-inch florets
- **1** red bell pepper, diced
- **1** onion, diced

PREPARE

Combine the vinegar, water, brown sugar, curry powder, and salt in a large nonreactive pot, and bring to a boil. Add the cauliflower, bell pepper, and onion and return to a boil. Reduce the heat and simmer until the vegetables just begin to turn tender, 2 to 3 minutes.

PRESERVE

Refrigerate: Ladle into bowls or jars. Cool, cover, and refrigerate for up to 3 weeks.

Can: Use the boiling-water method. Ladle into clean, hot half-pint or pint canning jars, covering the vegetables by ¼ inch with liquid. Leave ¼ inch of headspace between the top of the liquid and the lid. Release trapped air. Wipe the rims clean; center lids on the jars and screw on jar bands. Process for 10 minutes. Turn off heat, remove canner lid, and let jars rest in the water for 5 minutes. Remove jars and set aside for 24 hours. Check seals, then store in a cool, dark place for up to 1 year.

dry (p.71)

infuse (p.68)

can (p.79)

freeze (p.61)

refrigerate (p.59)

→ See page 40 for more about vinegar pickles.

OLIVE SALAD

Makes about 5 pints

I'm sure olive salad enjoys a long tradition, but I have had it only in the Italian delis of New Orleans. This recipe is inspired by those NOLA eateries that use it to top their muffuletta (see the recipe at right).

dry (p.71)

infuse (p.68)

can (p.79)

freeze (p.61)

refrigerate (p.59)

INGREDIENTS

- **4** cups distilled white vinegar
- **1** cup water
- **½** cup sugar
- **1** tablespoon kosher salt
- **1** tablespoon mustard seed
- **1** teaspoon dried oregano
- **¼** teaspoon red pepper flakes (optional)
- **1** small head cauliflower, leaves removed, cored, and cut into ½-inch florets (about 6 cups)
- **4** large carrots, peeled and cut into coins (about 2 cups)
- **1** red bell pepper, chopped (about 1 cup)
- **1** cup pitted sliced black olives
- **1** cup pitted sliced green olives
- **1** cup chopped onion

PREPARE

Combine the vinegar, water, sugar, salt, mustard seed, oregano, and red pepper flakes, if using, in a large nonreactive pot, and bring to a boil. Add the cauliflower, carrots, bell pepper, olives, and onion, and return to a boil. Reduce the heat and simmer until the vegetables just begin to turn tender, 2 to 3 minutes.

PRESERVE

Refrigerate: Ladle into bowls or jars. Cool, cover, and refrigerate for up to 3 weeks.

Can: Use the boiling-water method. Pour into clean, hot half-pint or pint canning jars, covering the solids by ¼ inch with liquid. Leave ¼ inch of headspace between the top of the liquid and the lid. Release trapped air. Wipe the rims clean; center lids on the jars and screw on jar bands. Process for 10 minutes. Turn off heat, remove canner lid, and let jars rest in the water for 5 minutes. Remove jars and set aside for 24 hours. Check seals, then store in a cool, dark place for up to 1 year.

→ See page 52 for more about salsas, chutneys, and relishes.

Muffuletta

When I'm pining for a taste of the Big Easy, I throw together one of these well-stuffed sand-wiches — a culinary gem in the crown of the Crescent City.

- **1** loaf French bread, sliced in half horizontally
- **2** tablespoons olive oil
- **¼** pound ham
- **¼** pound salami
- **¼** pound mortadella or prosciutto
- **¼** pound Swiss or Fontina cheese
- **¼** cup Olive Salad, or more (at left)

On the cut sides, drizzle both pieces of the bread with olive oil. Layer the meats and cheese on one half of the bread, and then top with the olive salad. Cover with the other half of the bread. Press between two cutting boards or large skillets and refrigerate for 2 to 4 hours, to allow the flavors to blend. Enjoy this sandwich as is or toast it in a medium sauté pan. To toast, cut the sandwich in half or in quarters to fit in the pan. Heat the pan over medium-low; add the sandwich pieces and top with another pan or lid to compress the sandwich slightly. Cook until the bread is lightly browned and the cheese is melted, about 5 minutes on each side. | **Makes 2 to 4 servings**

FROZEN CAULIFLOWER

I don't recommend freezing florets you plan to roast, but if you aim to use cauliflower in a cas-serole, soup, or braise, you can freeze it first.

INGREDIENTS

Any quantity cauliflower, leaves removed, cored, and cut into florets

PREPARE

1. Line several baking sheets with dish towels and set aside. Prepare an ice-water bath in a large bowl or clean sink.

2. Bring a large pot of water to a boil. Drop the florets into the water, no more than 1 pound at a time, and return to a boil. Blanch for 2 to 3 minutes.

3. Scoop out the florets with a spider or slotted spoon and plunge them into the ice-water bath. Continue blanching the cauliflower in batches. Remove the cauliflower from the ice bath with a slotted spoon and spread on the towel-covered baking sheets. Blot dry.

PRESERVE

Freeze: Transfer to airtight containers and freeze for up to 4 months.

→ See page 21 for more about blanching.

JARDINIÈRE

Makes about 4 pints

Jardinière is the name of the pickled cauliflower and vegetable salad you often see in Italian groceries. You can use a variety of vegetables in the mix but keep the quantities consistent with those listed here to make sure you have sufficient brine to preserve them.

INGREDIENTS

- **4** cups distilled white vinegar
- **1** cup water
- **1** cup sugar
- **1** tablespoon kosher salt
- **1** tablespoon mustard seed
- **4** large carrots, peeled, trimmed, and cut into coins (about 2 cups)
- **1** small head cauliflower, leaves removed, cored, and cut into ½-inch florets (about 6 cups)
- **1** red bell pepper, seeded and chopped (about 1 cup)

PREPARE

Combine the vinegar, water, sugar, salt, and mustard seed in a large nonreactive pot, and bring to a boil. Add the carrots, cauliflower, and bell pepper, and return to a boil. Reduce the heat and simmer until the vegetables begin to turn tender, 2 to 3 minutes.

PRESERVE

Refrigerate: Ladle into bowls or jars. Cool, cover, and refrigerate for up to 3 weeks.

Can: Use the boiling-water method. Pour into clean, hot half-pint or pint canning jars, covering the solids by ¼ inch with liquid. Leave ¼ inch of headspace between the top of the liquid and the lid. Release trapped air. Wipe the rims clean; center lids on the jars and screw on jar bands. Process for 10 minutes. Turn off heat, remove canner lid, and let jars rest in the water for 5 minutes. Remove jars and set aside for 24 hours. Check seals, then store in a cool, dark place for up to 1 year.

→ **See page 40 for more about vinegar pickles.**

dry (p.71)

infuse (p.68)

can (p.79)

freeze (p.61)

refrigerate (p.59)

Cherries

When I was growing up, my granny Toni had a cherry tree in her backyard. Unlike the peaches she turned into strudel and the apples that became pies, the cherries had a higher calling: they were turned into sweet cherry wine. As a kid I was never permitted to drink the stuff, but I was allowed to dunk a finger into the fermenting crock for a taste. I can still remember the potent sting of the brew — and how its flavor and I seemed to grow more mellow by the time I got to my tenth digit.

You can find a number of kinds of cherries in the market — some best for baking, others good for eating out of hand. They can be basically divided into two types: sweet and sour. Talk to a local grower about what varieties are coming out of his or her orchard. The recipes here note the varieties of cherries that work best in them.

You may need to pit cherries before processing, so it's nice to have a cherry pitter on hand. It's not difficult work, but it's time-consuming. Consider the task an opportunity for daydreaming or contemplation, or pick up a couple of pitters, call some friends, and have a pit-and-gab.

FRESH STORAGE RECOMMENDATIONS

KEEP CHERRIES IN THE REFRIGERATOR CRISPER for up to several days.

dry (p.71)

infuse (p.68)

can (p.79)

freeze (p.61)

refrigerate (p.59)

FROZEN CHERRIES

Cherry season is so brief that it's a shame not to stow away at least a few for later. This quick, easy method makes it a snap to save any variety.

INGREDIENTS

Any quantity cherries

PREPARE

Pit and stem the cherries. Line a baking sheet with parchment paper to keep juicy cherries from sticking to the pan. Arrange the cherries on the lined sheet and freeze overnight, until solid.

PRESERVE

Freeze: Transfer to airtight containers or freezer bags, pressing out as much air as possible. Keep frozen for up to 6 months.

BLACK FOREST SAUCE

Makes about 1 quart

Cherries and chocolate are my favorite fruit-sweet combination. Use sweet, dark cherries, such as Bing, for this recipe. Pour the sauce over ice cream or pound cake or blend it with yogurt and ice for a decadent milkshake.

INGREDIENTS

- **1** cup sugar
- **½** cup water
- **½** cup unsweetened cocoa powder
- **1** pound sweet cherries, stemmed and pitted

PREPARE

Combine the sugar and water in a medium saucepan and bring to a simmer, stirring to dissolve the sugar. Whisk in the cocoa powder. Add the cherries and simmer until the fruit yields its juice and becomes thick and syrupy, about 20 minutes.

PRESERVE

Refrigerate: Ladle into bowls or jars. Cool, cover, and refrigerate for up to 3 weeks.

→ See page 54 for more about butters, sauces, and ketchups.

DRUNKEN CHERRIES

Makes about 1 quart

My Southern family used to "import" a beverage from South Carolina called Cherry Bounce: a half gallon of moonshine with a layer of sweet cherries bobbing around the bottom. It wasn't Kirsch, but it did get one hopping. Reminiscent of that boozy treat, Drunken Cherries is perfect over ice cream. I can't imagine it'd do too badly in a Manhattan, either.

INGREDIENTS

- **1** pound sweet cherries, such as Bing, stemmed but not pitted
- **1½** cups bourbon
- **½** cup brown sugar
- **½** cup water

PREPARE AND PRESERVE

Infuse:

1. Cut a slit in each cherry with a small paring knife to allow the flavors to soak through. Combine the cherries and the bourbon in a quart jar.

2. Bring the sugar and water to a boil in a medium saucepan, stirring to dissolve the sugar. Pour the syrup into the cherry-filled jar. Cover and shake. Let rest for at least 1 week. Keeps at room temperature for up to 1 year.

CHERRY LEATHER

One quart of fruit makes about 1 (17-inch) sheet of leather

You'll say you're making this for the kids, but just wait and see how many nibbles you sneak on the way to their lunch pails.

INGREDIENTS

- **4** cups sweet cherries, stemmed and pitted
- **½** cup sugar

PREPARE

1. Bring the cherries and a splash of water to a boil in a medium saucepan. Simmer until the cherries begin to soften, about 10 minutes. Ladle into a blender and purée, or use a stick blender.

2. Preheat the oven to 170°F. Line a jelly-roll pan or a rimmed baking sheet with parchment paper or a Silpat and set aside.

3. Return the puréed fruit to the pot and simmer over low heat, stirring frequently, until it thickens to the consistency of baby food. Add the sugar and stir to dissolve.

PRESERVE

Dry:

1. Spread the purée on the baking sheet, tilting it to create an even layer about ⅛ inch thick. Dry in the oven until tacky to the touch, about 2 hours.

2. Cool to room temperature. Slide the parchment onto a cutting board and roll the leather into a tube. Slice the tube into 2-inch segments and store in a covered jar for up to 1 month.

DRIED CHERRIES

One quart fresh cherries makes about 1 cup dried cherries

Dried cherries are somewhat like raisins but better. Sweet cherries provide a nice balance of sugar to sour. Their tangy, tart flavor perks up a Waldorf salad, brings pizzazz to a pilaf, and is heaven in a quick red wine reduction.

dry (p.71)

infuse (p.68)

can (p.79)

freeze (p.61)

refrigerate (p.59)

INGREDIENTS

4–8 cups sweet cherries

PREPARE

1. Preheat the oven to 170°F. Line several baking sheets with dish towels and set aside. Prepare an ice-water bath in a large bowl or clean sink.

2. Bring a large pot of water to a boil. Drop the cherries into the water, no more than 1 pound at a time, and return to a boil. Blanch for 1 minute.

3. Scoop out the cherries with a spider or slotted spoon and plunge them into the ice-water bath. Continue blanching the cherries in batches. Remove the cherries from the ice bath with a slotted spoon and spread on the towel-covered baking sheets. Blot dry.

PRESERVE

Dry:

1. Preheat the oven to 170°F. Pit the cherries. Spread the pitted cherries on metal screens or cake cooling racks set over baking sheets. Dry in the oven until the cherries are shriveled and no longer moist in the center, 5 to 7 hours. Cherries are fully dry when you can squeeze a handful and they don't stick together.

2. Set aside the cherries to cool, and then transfer them to a covered container to condition for 1 week or so. This allows the dried fruit to redistribute any trapped moisture. If you notice moisture on the sides of the container, repeat the drying process for another hour. Dried cherries will keep for up to 1 year in an airtight container.

→ See page 21 for more about blanching.

CHERRY-WALNUT RELISH

Makes about 3 cups

The walnuts bring an interesting texture to this relish. It's great with cheese, roast meats, and in place of chutney with Indian dishes.

INGREDIENTS

- **4** cups sweet cherries, stemmed and pitted
- **1** cup sugar
- **1** cup cider vinegar
- **1** onion, finely diced
- **1** cinnamon stick
- **½** cup walnuts, crushed

PREPARE

1. Combine the cherries, sugar, and a splash of water in a medium nonreactive saucepan and bring to a boil. Reduce the heat and simmer for about 5 minutes, stirring and crushing the cherries to release their juices. Add the vinegar, onion, and cinnamon stick, and return to a simmer. Cook until thickened, about 20 minutes, being careful not to boil dry.

2. Add the walnuts and return to a boil for 5 minutes. Remove from the heat and take out the cinnamon stick.

PRESERVE

Refrigerate: Ladle into bowls or jars. Cool, cover, and refrigerate for up to 3 weeks.

Can: Use the boiling-water method. Ladle into clean, hot 4-ounce or half-pint canning jars, covering the solids by ¼ inch with liquid. Leave ¼ inch of headspace between the top of the liquid and the lid. Release trapped air. Wipe the rims clean; center lids on the jars and screw on jar bands. Process for 15 minutes. Turn off heat, remove canner lid, and let jars rest in the water for 5 minutes. Remove jars and set aside for 24 hours. Check seals, then store in a cool, dark place for up to 1 year.

→ See page 52 for more about salsas, chutneys, and relishes.

dry (p.71)

infuse (p.68)

can (p.79)

freeze (p.61)

refrigerate (p.59)

CLASSIC CHERRY PRESERVES

Makes about 3 cups

Cherry preserves are to strawberry jam what a red satin gown is to a puffy pink prom dress. Cherry preserves are that hot little number — sweet, yes, but much more seductive. You can use either sweet or sour cherries in this recipe, depending on how tart you like your preserves. Serve this ruby red spread as you would any other jam or use it to dress a cheese plate or to trick out your favorite sandwich.

INGREDIENTS

3 pounds sweet or sour cherries, stemmed and pitted (about 8 cups)

1 cup sugar

¼ cup bottled lemon juice

PREPARE

1. Combine the cherries with a splash of water in a medium nonreactive saucepan. Bring to a boil, stirring and crushing the fruit to release the juice. Add the sugar and stir to dissolve. Stir in the lemon juice. Continue to cook, stirring frequently, until the preserves reach the desired gel, about 20 minutes.

2. Turn off the heat and let the preserves rest for 5 minutes, stirring occasionally to release air bubbles and to prevent fruit float. Skim any foam from the top.

PRESERVE

Refrigerate: Ladle into bowls or jars. Cool, cover, and refrigerate for up to 3 weeks.

Can: Use the boiling-water method. Ladle into clean, hot 4-ounce or half-pint canning jars, leaving ¼ inch of headspace. Release trapped air. Wipe the rims clean; center lids on the jars and screw on jar bands. Process for 10 minutes. Turn off heat, remove canner lid, and let jars rest in the water for 5 minutes. Remove jars and set aside for 24 hours. Check seals, then store in a cool, dark place for up to 1 year.

→ See page 27 for more about jams and jellies.

Variation: Cherry and Black Pepper Preserves

Prepare the cherry preserves as described above, but add 1 teaspoon of freshly ground black pepper, preferably from Tellicherry peppercorns, along with the lemon juice. Process using the boiling-water method.

Duck with Cherry and Black Pepper Preserves

Make the preserves in the summer and serve them with roasted duck in the fall. You'll never look at the jam pot the same way again.

4 duck breasts
Salt
1 shallot, minced
½ cup fruity red wine, such as Beaujolais

1 cup chicken stock
½ cup Cherry and Black Pepper Preserves (at left)
Freshly ground black pepper

1. Using a very sharp knife, score the duck breasts by lightly cutting shallow slices into the fat, about ½ inch apart, being careful not to cut so deeply that you pierce the meat. Repeat in the opposite direction. Sprinkle lightly with salt.

2. Preheat the oven to 425°F. Heat a large ovenproof skillet over medium heat. Arrange the breasts skin-side down in the hot pan and sauté gently to render the fat, reducing the heat if necessary to prevent burning. When the fat is rendered and the meat begins to cook around the edges, about 15 minutes, turn the breasts and transfer the skillet to the oven to finish cooking the breasts. Duck reaches medium doneness when it registers about 140°F on a meat thermometer, 5 to 10 minutes in the oven.

3. Remove the breasts from the pan and set aside. Pour off all but about 2 tablespoons of the duck fat and return the pan to medium heat. (Save the luscious duck fat for another use.) Add the shallot and sauté until translucent, 2 to 3 minutes. Raise the heat to high and add the wine to deglaze the pan, scraping up all of the browned bits. Cook until the wine is reduced to a syrup, 3 to 5 minutes. Add the chicken stock, bring to a boil, and simmer until reduced by half, about 5 minutes. Whisk in the cherry preserves. Season with salt and pepper.

4. Thinly slice the duck breasts against the grain. Serve with cherry pan sauce on the side. | **Makes 4 to 6 servings**

Chilies

I used to think of chilies simply as hot peppers, but I'm now learning about their myriad flavors: fruit, smoke, citrus, and, of course, spice. Chilies pack a wide range of heat intensity — measured in Scoville units (see the sidebar at right). Use whichever types you like, but keep the quantities consistent so you don't throw off the acid balance of the recipe. Some people have a high tolerance for chili heat, others back away, others run like crazy. Part of this is a matter of preference, but it's also true that one can build up a tolerance to capsaicin, the compound in chilies that burns the tongue. I love habaneros, but a little goes a long way for me. On the other hand, I have a Mexican friend who can nibble on them like candy. If you find that the recipes are just too spicy no matter which variety of chili you use, substitute an equal weight of bell peppers to temper the heat.

FRESH STORAGE RECOMMENDATIONS

ANY CHILIES THAT ARE PICKED BEFORE THEIR PEAK will ripen on a kitchen counter for a few days. Toss ripe peppers into a brown paper bag and stash in the crisper drawer of the fridge. They'll keep for about 2 weeks.

Scoville Units (or how hot is hot?)

When you talk about the heat of peppers, you are really referring to the amount of capsaicin in the produce. This is the chemical compound that stimulates nerve endings in your skin. In 1912, chemist Wilbur Scoville invented the Scoville scale, which measures the amount of capsaicin in peppers. At the bottom of the scale you will find bell peppers with 0 Scoville units, while the habanero weighs in with a searing 350,000 Scoville units.

RED HOT VODKA

Makes about 1 quart

This infused vodka is firewater indeed. Drink it straight, if you dare — icy cold and poured into a glass rimmed with celery salt — or use it in your favorite recipe for a red-hot Bloody Mary. You can also use it to deglaze a pan or to flavor dishes that could use a little heat. No need to use your top-shelf vodka, as its flavors will be overwhelmed by the heat.

INGREDIENTS

- **1** (750 ml) bottle vodka
- **4–6** jalapeño or 3 or 4 habanero peppers

PREPARE AND PRESERVE

Infuse: Pour the vodka into a clean quart jar. Slice the peppers into ¼-inch rings and add them to the vodka. Steep for 2 to 3 days, tasting after the second day for flavor. Pour the vodka through a fine-mesh strainer and then funnel back into the vodka bottle. Keeps for up to 1 year.

dry (p.71)

infuse (p.68)

can (p.79)

freeze (p.61)

refrigerate (p.59)

dry (p.71)

infuse (p.68)

can (p.79)

freeze (p.61)

refrigerate (p.59)

PICKLED CHILI PEPPERS

Makes about 4 pints

The sweet-sour brine mellows the chilies so you can strew them liberally on a pizza, roll them into a burrito, or chop them into your morning eggs for a lot of flavor and a touch of heat.

INGREDIENTS

- **2** pounds chili peppers, any variety, stemmed and sliced
- **3** cups distilled white vinegar
- **2** cups water
- **2** tablespoons salt
- **2** tablespoons sugar

PREPARE

Pack the peppers into 4 clean, hot pint-size canning jars, leaving ½ inch of headspace. Combine the vinegar, water, salt, and sugar in a medium nonreactive saucepan and bring just to a boil. Pour the hot brine over the peppers to cover by ¼ inch. Leave ¼ inch of headspace between the top of the liquid and the lid.

PRESERVE

Refrigerate: Cool, cover, and refrigerate for up to 3 weeks.

Can: Use the boiling-water method. Release trapped air. Wipe the rims clean; center lids on the jars and screw on jar bands. Process for 15 minutes. Turn off heat, remove canner lid, and let jars rest in the water for 5 minutes. Remove jars and set aside for 24 hours. Check seals, then store in a cool, dark place for up to 1 year.

→ **See page 40 for more about vinegar pickles.**

RISTRAS

Ristras, which are strands of dried chilies, are often used as decorations, but they're also a practical way to have a little heat on hand. Just clip off a pepper and toss into soups and stews or a pot of simmering beans, or grind into a powder to flavor any dish. The traditional method calls for braiding the chilies, but I've had great success with this simpler method.

INGREDIENTS

Upholstery thread or fishing line
Upholstery needle
Gloves
Any quantity thin-skinned chilies, such as Anaheim, pequín, or arbol

PREPARE AND PRESERVE

Dry: Thread the needle. Wearing gloves so that the heat of the chilies doesn't scorch your hands, run the needle through the stem of a chili and knot the thread around the stem. This is the bottom chili. Continue to string chilies by running the needle through the bottom of the stems, stacking the chilies as you go and leaving a length of string at the end to hang the ristra. Tie the string to an attic eave or in some other well-ventilated spot. Let chilies dry until they're shriveled and brittle, 1 to 2 weeks.

CHARRED CHILIES

Charring peppers makes them smoky and sweet. Char a number of peppers at once and store them for later use — pantry gold!

INGREDIENTS

Any quantity of any variety chili peppers, such as poblanos or jalapeños
Enough oil to lightly coat peppers (you can use any type of cooking oil you have on hand, such as organic canola, grapeseed, or olive)

PREPARE

1. There are a number of ways to char peppers: on the grill, under the broiler, and skewered and held over an open flame. Lightly coat the peppers with oil and set them close enough to the heat source to hear them sizzle. Char until completely black on all sides, turning as necessary.

2. Put the peppers in a bowl and cover with a lid or plate so the hot peppers can bathe in their own steam. After 5 minutes, remove the lid. When the peppers are cool enough to handle, slip off the skins and take out the seeds and stems

Note: Be sure to protect your hands with gloves when working with chilies.

PRESERVE

⬦ **Refrigerate:** Charred peppers keep in the refrigerator, covered, for 3 to 5 days.

⬢ **Freeze:** Divide the peppers into small containers or ice-cube trays and freeze, covered, for up to about 6 months.

Charred Poblano Potato Salad

2 pounds small, waxy potatoes, left whole
2 tablespoons mustard
¼ cup lime juice

¼ cup extra-virgin olive oil
¼ cup Charred Chilies (above), chopped

Bring a large pot of salted water to a boil. Add the potatoes and boil until tender, about 15 minutes. Drain. Meanwhile, whisk the mustard and lime juice in a large bowl. Slowly drizzle in the olive oil, whisking to emulsify. Add the drained potatoes and chilies and toss to combine. Serve warm or at room temperature. | **Makes 4 to 6 servings**

dry (p.71)

infuse (p.68)

can (p.79)

freeze (p.61)

refrigerate (p.59)

ANY-CHILI HOT SAUCE

Makes about 1 quart

Sprinkle this sauce on rice and beans, your morning eggs, or anything else that could use a little pep. How hot is it? As hot as the peppers you cook up. Talk to growers at the farmers' market to find a spice level that's right for you, or substitute some sweet peppers to tone it down a bit.

INGREDIENTS

- **1** pound mixed chili peppers, green or red
- **2** cups distilled white vinegar
- **1** tablespoon salt

PREPARE

Wearing gloves, stem the chilies and, for a milder sauce, remove the seeds and ribs. Purée the chilies in a blender with the vinegar and salt.

PRESERVE

Refrigerate: Transfer to pint jars. Cover and refrigerate for up to 3 weeks.

→ See page 54 for more about butters, sauces, and ketchups.

CHARRED CHILI SALSA

Makes about 5 pints

Serve with tortilla chips or as a topping for grilled meat or vegetables.

INGREDIENTS

- **2** pounds red or green chili peppers
- **5** pounds tomatoes, peeled, cored, and diced
- **1** pound onions, diced
- **1½** cups distilled white vinegar
- **2** tablespoons salt
- **½** cup chopped fresh cilantro

PREPARE

1. Char the chilies as directed on page 66, and cut into ½-inch dice.

2. Combine the chilies, tomatoes, onions, vinegar, and salt in a medium nonreactive saucepan, and bring to a boil. Reduce the heat and simmer for 15 minutes to thicken. Add the cilantro and remove from the heat.

PRESERVE

Refrigerate: Ladle into bowls or jars. Cool, cover, and refrigerate for up to 1 week.

Can: Use the boiling-water method. Ladle into clean, hot half-pint canning jars, leaving ¼ inch of headspace. Release trapped air. Wipe the rims clean; center lids on the jars and screw on jar bands. Process for 20 minutes. Turn off heat, remove canner lid, and let jars rest in the water for 5 minutes. Remove jars and set aside for 24 hours. Check seals, then store in a cool, dark place for up to 1 year.

→ See page 52 for more about salsas, chutneys, and relishes.

CHARRED CHILI BARBECUE SAUCE

Makes about 4 pints

Try out this homemade condiment and you'll never go back to store-bough[t] chilies you like — mild or intense, red or green. Because this is a blended sauce, I do reco[mmend] that you color-coordinate the ingredients so the purée takes on a pleasing color: with red, yellow, or orange chilies, go with red, yellow, or orange tomatoes. If you plan to use green chilies, green, yellow, or white heirloom tomatoes will make a lovely, pale green sauce.

INGREDIENTS

- **1** pound chili peppers
- **5** pounds tomatoes
- **1** pound yellow onions, chopped
- **2** cups brown sugar, lightly packed
- **1½** cups cider vinegar
- **2** garlic cloves, minced
- **1** tablespoon ground allspice
- **1** tablespoon salt
- **1** teaspoon ground cloves

PREPARE

1. Char the chilies as described on page 66 and roughly chop. Peel, core, and chop the tomatoes.

2. Combine the chilies, tomatoes, onions, brown sugar, vinegar, garlic, allspice, salt, and cloves in a large nonreactive saucepan, cover, and bring to a boil. Remove the cover, reduce the heat, and simmer for 1 to 1½ hours, until sauce is thickened. Purée with a stick blender.

PRESERVE

Refrigerate: Ladle into bowls or jars. Cool, cover, and refrigerate for up to 3 weeks.

Can: Use the boiling-water method. Ladle into clean, hot pint canning jars, leaving ¼ inch of headspace. Release trapped air. Wipe the rims clean, center lids on the jars and screw on jar bands. Process for 20 minutes. Turn off heat, remove canner lid, and let jars rest in the water for 5 minutes. Remove jars and set aside for 24 hours. Check seals, then store in a cool, dark place for up to 1 year.

→ See page 54 for more about butters, sauces, and ketchups.

CHILI RELISH WITH CORIANDER

Makes about 7 cups

This spicy relish will teach that plain old grilled hot dog a new trick. It's also pretty nifty on burgers.

INGREDIENTS

- **2** pounds cucumbers, peeled and diced
- **1** pound green chili peppers, stems, seeds, and ribs removed, diced
- **1** pound yellow onions, diced
- **3** cups distilled white vinegar
- **2** tablespoons salt
- **1** tablespoon whole coriander
- **½** cup chopped fresh cilantro

PREPARE

Combine the cucumbers, chilies, onions, vinegar, salt, and coriander in a large nonreactive saucepan, and bring to a boil. Reduce heat and simmer for 15 minutes. Add the cilantro and remove from the heat.

PRESERVE

Refrigerate: Ladle into bowls or jars. Cool, cover, and refrigerate for up to 3 weeks.

Can: Use the boiling-water method. Ladle into clean, hot 4-ounce or half-pint canning jars, covering the solids by ¼ inch with liquid. Leave ¼ inch of headspace between the top of the liquid and the lid. Release trapped air. Wipe the rims clean; center lids on the jars and screw on jar bands. Process for 15 minutes. Turn off heat, remove canner lid, and let jars rest in the water for 5 minutes. Remove jars and set aside for 24 hours. Check seals, then store in a cool, dark place for up to 1 year.

dry (p.71)

infuse (p.68)

can (p.79)

freeze (p.61)

refrigerate (p.59)

→ See page 52 for more about salsas, chutneys, and relishes.

CHILI-TOMATO JAM

Makes about 3 cups

So many chili and tomato varieties, so little time. This is a quick recipe that uses up that bit of extra produce you couldn't leave the market without. Sweet, tart, and full of late-summer flavor, my favorite way to enjoy this jam is slathered on hot cornbread, fresh from the skillet.

INGREDIENTS

- **2** pounds tomatoes
- **½** pound red chili peppers
- **1¼** cups sugar
- **1** cup distilled white vinegar
- **1** teaspoon calcium water (included in the Pomona box)
- **1** teaspoon Pomona's Universal Pectin

PREPARE

1. Peel, core, and chop the tomatoes. Wearing gloves, remove the stems, seeds, and ribs from the chilies, and dice finely. Combine the tomatoes, chilies, 1 cup of the sugar, and the vinegar in a medium nonreactive saucepan, and bring to a boil. Reduce the heat to medium-low and simmer, stirring frequently, until the vegetables are tender and the water cooks off, about 20 minutes. Add the calcium water.

2. In a small bowl, stir together the pectin and the remaining ¼ cup sugar, and then stir into the jam. Return to a boil and stir to dissolve the sugar.

3. Remove from the heat and let rest for 5 minutes, stirring occasionally to release air bubbles from the mixture. Scoop off any foam.

PRESERVE

Refrigerate: Ladle into bowls or jars. Cool, cover, and refrigerate for up to 3 weeks.

Can: Use the boiling-water method. Ladle into clean, hot 4-ounce canning jars, leaving ¼ inch of headspace. Release trapped air. Wipe the rims clean; center lids on the jars and screw on jar bands. Process for 10 minutes. Turn off heat, remove canner lid, and let jars rest in the water for 5 minutes. Remove jars and set aside for 24 hours. Check seals, then store in a cool, dark place for up to 1 year.

→ **See page 27 for more about jams and jellies.**

Citrus

A confession: I can't grow many things. I once had a lemon tree, however, that I nurtured along (okay, call it benign neglect) until it actually produced fruit — gorgeous, sweet Meyer lemons right in my Connecticut living room. So I know citrus can happen, even in New England.

No matter how you get your vitamin C, these recipes will put it to work. I try to eat and cook with organic fruits to avoid residue from the pesticides used in conventional agriculture. Most citrus is treated with fungicides, waxes, and other topical applications to make the fruits last longer on the shelf. If you buy citrus in the supermarket or even if it comes in a fancy gift box, be sure to scrub all fruits in hot water with unscented dish soap to remove as much of the residue as possible.

FRESH STORAGE RECOMMENDATIONS

BAGS OF WAXED CITRUS FROM THE MARKET seem to keep in the refrigerator almost indefinitely. If you're lucky enough to have access to fresh-from-the-orchard, unwaxed citrus, expect it to tolerate a week or so on the counter or 2 weeks in a cool fridge.

PRESERVED LEMONS

Makes about 1 quart

Preserved lemons are a common ingredient in Moroccan dishes. Thoroughly rinse the fruit, finely dice, and add to tagines, pilafs, and braises for an exotic touch. Some cooks opt to remove the flesh, which drastically reduces the lemon's saltiness.

INGREDIENTS

- ½ cinnamon stick (optional)
- 2–3 whole cloves (optional)
- 1 bay leaf (optional)
- 7–8 lemons
- ½ cup salt

PREPARE

1. Put the cinnamon stick, cloves, and bay leaf, if using, in the bottom of a sterilized wide-mouthed, quart canning jar.

2. Scrub the lemons and pat dry. Cut the ends from six of the lemons and cut each fruit vertically, three-quarters of the way through, into 6 sections, so the sections remain attached at the base of the fruit. Gently separate the sections slightly and pack each cut with 1 teaspoon of the salt. Firmly press the lemons into the jar, one at a time, to release as much juice as possible from the fruit. Continue to add lemons, packing the jar very tightly until it is full; you should be able to fit all 6 lemons. Leave 1 inch of headspace.

3. Cover the lemons by ½ inch with the juice of the remaining lemons. Top with the rest of the salt. Use the rind of the juiced lemons as a wedge between the preserving lemons and the lid to keep the fermenting fruit submerged. Cover with a nonreactive lid.

4. Set in a cool, dark place for 3 weeks, giving the jar a good shake every day or so.

PRESERVE

Refrigerate: Store the lemons in their preserving jar, in the refrigerator, for up to 6 months.

dry (p.71)

infuse (p.68)

can (p.79)

freeze (p.61)

refrigerate (p.59)

Moroccan Rice Pilaf

- 2 tablespoons extra-virgin olive oil
- 2 scallions, diced
- 1 garlic clove, minced
- ½ preserved lemon (above), rinsed, flesh removed, and chopped fine
- 4 cups chicken broth or water
- 2 cups uncooked white rice
- 1–2 cups canned or cooked chickpeas
- ½ cup minced parsley
- 1 cup shelled pistachios (optional)

Warm the olive oil over medium heat in a medium saucepan. Add the scallions and sauté until softened, about 2 minutes. Add the garlic and sauté for an additional minute. Add the preserved lemon and the broth and bring to a boil. Add the rice, return to a boil, then stir once, reduce heat to the lowest setting, and cover. Simmer according to package directions. Fluff the rice and stir in the chickpeas and parsley. Stir in pistachios, if using, and serve. | Makes 6 to 8 side-dish servings

DRIED LIMES

My good friend Cheré, who is half Iranian, shared this Persian method for using up extra limes. She dries them whole, then tosses them into soups and stews for her very own "secret ingredient" touch.

INGREDIENTS

6 limes, or more

PREPARE AND PRESERVE

▦ **Dry:** Scrub limes and dry them well. Place in a wire basket or other container that allows air to circulate freely. Hang in a warm, dry place, out of direct sunlight. Let limes go brown and shrivel until they're completely desiccated. Dried limes will keep at room temperature for up to 4 months.

VIN D'ORANGE

Makes about 2 quarts

This infusion makes a lovely aperitif. Serve it ice cold with a twist of rind or float a star anise in the glass.

INGREDIENTS

2 (750 ml) bottles white wine
1 cup vodka
4 oranges, with the peel, scrubbed and chopped into 1-inch pieces
1 cup sugar
1 cinnamon stick
1 vanilla bean

PREPARE AND PRESERVE

⚗ **Infuse:**

1. Combine the wine, vodka, oranges, sugar, cinnamon stick, and vanilla bean in a large glass bowl or food-grade ceramic crock, and stir to dissolve the sugar. Cover tightly and set in a cool, dark place for 1 week, stirring daily.

2. Strain through a fine-mesh strainer or a single thickness of cheesecloth and taste for sweetness, adding a pinch more sugar if necessary. Decant into bottles, and then cork them. Keeps refrigerated for up to 6 months.

dry (p.71)

infuse (p.68)

can (p.79)

freeze (p.61)

refrigerate (p.59)

ORANGE MARMALADE

Makes about 4 cups

Marmalade: It's so proper and British, but don't be intimidated by the pedigree. _____
spread to make. With the work divided over three days, it's the perfect long-wee____
little effort, big reward, and the house will smell divine! Alter the flavor to suit your fancy by
adding a few cloves or a few tablespoons of grated ginger to the final boil.

INGREDIENTS

- **6** large oranges
- **2½** cups water
- About 3 cups sugar
- **3** whole cloves or 2 tablespoons freshly grated ginger (optional)

PREPARE

1. Scrub the oranges and remove and discard a small slice from each end. Cut the oranges into quarters and remove any seeds, and then slice very thinly and place in a medium nonreactive saucepan. Pour the water over the orange slices and press down on the fruit to release some of its juice. Cover the pan with a tea towel and set aside on your counter overnight.

2. The next day, bring the mixture to a boil, and then simmer until the rinds are tender, about 30 minutes. Cool, cover, and set aside at room temperature again.

3. On the third day, measure the cooled mixture and return it to the saucepan with an equal amount of sugar and the cloves, if using. Bring to a boil and cook, stirring frequently, until the marmalade gels, about 30 minutes. Let cool for about 5 minutes, stirring occasionally to release air bubbles. Skim off any foam and discard cloves.

PRESERVE

Refrigerate: Ladle into bowls or jars. Cool, cover, and refrigerate for up to 3 weeks.

Can: Use the boiling-water method. Ladle into clean, hot 4-ounce or half-pint canning jars, leaving ¼ inch of headspace. Release trapped air. Wipe the rims clean; center lids on the jars and screw on jar bands. Process for 10 minutes. Turn off heat, remove canner lid, and let jars rest in the water for 5 minutes. Remove jars and set aside for 24 hours. Check seals, then store in a cool, dark place for up to 1 year.

→ See page 27 for more about jams and jellies.

LEMON CURD

Makes about 3 cups

Don't let the idea of canning eggs put you off: there's plenty of acid in the fruit juice to keep this curd fresh and lively on the shelf. Try it with different high-acid fruits — lime is luscious and Meyer lemon is particularly delicious.

INGREDIENTS

- **1** tablespoon lemon zest
- **1** cup lemon juice (from 4–5 lemons)
- **1½** cups sugar
- **¾** cup (1½ sticks) butter, cut into pieces
- **4** eggs
- **½** teaspoon salt

PREPARE

Combine the lemon zest, juice, sugar, butter, eggs, and salt in the top of a nonreactive double boiler. Bring the water in the bottom pan to a low boil and whisk the curd constantly until it thickens, about 10 minutes. Strain through a fine-mesh sieve.

PRESERVE

Refrigerate: Ladle into bowls or jars. Cool, cover, and refrigerate for up to 2 weeks.

Can: Use the boiling-water method. Ladle into clean, hot 4-ounce or half-pint canning jars, leaving ¼ inch of headspace. Release trapped air. Wipe the rims clean; center lids on the jars and screw on jar bands. Process for 10 minutes. Turn off heat, remove canner lid, and let jars rest in the water for 5 minutes. Remove jars and set aside for 24 hours. Check seals, then store in a cool, dark place for up to 1 year.

dry (p.71)

infuse (p.68)

can (p.79)

freeze (p.61)

refrigerate (p.59)

→ See page 54 for more about butters, sauces, and ketchups.

CANDIED CITRUS RIND

Makes about 2 pints

This recipe is the ultimate reuse/recycle wonder. It turns something seemingly disposable —
citrus rinds — into a sophisticated treat. Serve as is or dip into melted dark chocolate. Home
economy never looked or tasted so elegant!

INGREDIENTS

Peels, including pith, from 6 oranges or
other thick-skinned citrus fruit

1 cup water, plus more for boiling peels

5 cups sugar

1 vanilla bean

PREPARE

1. Cut the peels into ¼-inch strips. Cover the
   peels with cold water in a large nonreactive saucepan and bring to a boil, stirring
   to ensure that all of the peels are heated
   through. Strain and repeat two more times
   to remove the bitter flavor from the pith and
   to soften the peels. After the third round, set
   aside the peels to drain while you make the
   syrup.

2. Bring 1 cup water to a boil and gradually add
   4 cups of the sugar, stirring to dissolve. Add
   the peels and the vanilla bean. Return to a
   boil, and then reduce to a simmer, cooking
   gently until the peels are translucent and
   tender, about 1 hour.

PRESERVE

Dry: Using tongs, remove the peels to a drying rack placed over a baking sheet and separate them so they don't touch. Let drain, and
then dry for 4 to 5 hours. When quite dry but
still tacky, roll the peels in the remaining 1 cup
sugar to coat. Peels keep, stored in an airtight
container, for up to 1 month.

Putting Leftover Citrus Syrup to Work

Making Candied Citrus Rind will leave you with about a pint of simple syrup flavored
with the citrus peel and vanilla. Don't toss it! The syrup makes a lovely glaze for desserts
or a sweetener for cold drinks.

Corn

Corn is notoriously difficult to grow without a lot of chemical inputs. It pulls nutrients from the soil and, on a good farm, is rotated yearly to give that ground a chance to recover. It's also sweet and tempting to all manner of pests, who like to feast on the plump kernels as much as we do. Many growers resort to sprays to keep invaders at bay. The sprays work really well: you won't see a single bug on sprayed corn. But I wonder, if these sprays are toxic to the pests, how good can they be for me and my family?

That's why I say, if it's not good enough for the worm, it's not good enough for me. When I pull back the corn husk and see a little guy thriving in there, I welcome the worm. I know if it hasn't been sprayed to death, then I won't be either.

My favorite corn is white Shoepeg, which is native to the South, particularly Maryland, where I grew up. It's rarely seen anywhere else, but if you can find it, grab it. It's sweet and flavorful and great for canning. Most farmers grow some version of sweet yellow corn. Yellow or white, it's both good on the cob and great in these recipes.

FRESH STORAGE RECOMMENDATIONS

FRESH CORN ON THE COB STARTS CONVERTING ITS SUGAR into starch the minute it's harvested, so it loses its flavor rapidly. The old country adage holds that for the best-tasting corn, get the water boiling before you harvest the ears. It's no exaggeration. Never refrigerate corn, which speeds the sugar-to-starch conversion. Instead, eat your corn the day it's picked or preserve that summer flavor with one of the following recipes.

OVEN-DRIED SWEET CORN

One full-size baking sheet makes about 4 ounces of dried corn

Drying corn is an ancient way to preserve it. Using the oven makes the process fast and easy.

INGREDIENTS

Any quantity fresh corn on the cob, shucked

PREPARE

1. Bring a large stockpot of water to a boil. Add the corn and boil until just tender, 2 to 3 minutes. Drain.

2. When the corn is cool enough to handle, stand the cobs on end and slice vertically to cut off the kernels using a sharp knife or one of the crafty tools designed specifically for the job, being careful not to cut into the cobs.

PRESERVE

Dry: Preheat the oven to 170°F. Spread the corn, in one layer, on baking sheets and roast, propping open the oven door with a wooden spoon to vent moisture, until the corn is brittle, about 2 hours (time will vary depending on the humidity: the more humid the air, the longer the drying time). Cool and store in airtight containers for up to 1 year.

Dried Sweet-Corn Chowder

This dish is warm and comforting but still brings a little summer sweetness to the table. Top with a few sautéed scallops or shrimp for a heartier version.

2 cups boiling water
1 cup Oven-Dried Sweet Corn (above)
4 cups chicken stock
1 onion, chopped
2 tablespoons butter

2 tablespoons flour
1 pound potatoes, peeled and cubed
Salt
Freshly ground black pepper

1. Pour the water over the corn and set aside for 1 hour to reconstitute.

2. Warm the chicken stock in a small saucepan. Sauté the onion in butter in a soup pot until translucent, 3 to 5 minutes. Whisk in the flour to make a paste. Slowly whisk in the warmed stock. Add the potatoes and the drained, rehydrated corn and simmer until the potatoes are cooked through, about 15 minutes. Season with salt and pepper. | **Makes 4 servings**

dry (p.71)

infuse (p.68)

can (p.79)

freeze (p.61)

refrigerate (p.59)

PICNIC RELISH

Makes about 6 pints

This sweet relish tastes great alongside grilled chicken or shrimp or heaped on top of a juicy burger. It's also delicious spooned onto the middle of a chef's salad for a tangy flavor boost.

INGREDIENTS

- 12 ears corn, shucked
- 3 cups cider vinegar
- 1 cup sugar
- 1 tablespoon mustard powder
- 1 tablespoon salt
- 1 teaspoon ground allspice
- 2 tomatoes, diced
- 1 green bell pepper, diced
- 1 large onion, diced

PREPARE

1. Bring a large nonreactive stockpot of water to a boil. Add the corn and boil for 5 minutes. Drain.

2. When the corn is cool enough to handle, stand the cobs on end and slice vertically to cut off the kernels, being careful not to cut into the cobs. Empty and wipe out the stockpot.

3. Combine the vinegar, sugar, mustard powder, salt, and allspice in the stockpot, and bring to a boil. Add the tomatoes, bell pepper, onion, and corn kernels, and simmer for 5 minutes.

PRESERVE

Refrigerate: Ladle into bowls or jars. Cool, cover, and refrigerate for up to 3 weeks.

Can: Use the boiling-water method. Ladle into clean, hot half-pint or pint canning jars, covering the solids by ¼ inch with liquid. Leave ¼ inch of headspace between the top of the liquid and the lid. Release trapped air. Wipe the rims clean; center lids on the jars and screw on jar bands. Process for 15 minutes. Turn off heat, remove canner lid, and let jars rest in the water for 5 minutes. Remove jars and set aside for 24 hours. Check seals, then store in a cool, dark place for up to 1 year.

→ See page 52 for more about salsas, chutneys, and relishes.

dry (p.71)

infuse (p.68)

can (p.79)

freeze (p.61)

refrigerate (p.59)

CORN SALSA

Makes about 8 pints

Corn adds color and flavor to this party favorite. Scoop it up with tortilla chips or roll it up, burrito-style, with rice, beans, and cheese for a quick meal.

INGREDIENTS

- **12** ears corn, shucked
- **3** cups distilled white vinegar
- **1** cup sugar
- **1** tablespoon ground cumin
- **1** tablespoon salt
- **5** pounds tomatoes, diced
- **1–2** jalapeño peppers, diced
- **1** green bell pepper, diced
- **1** large onion, diced
- **2** garlic cloves, minced
- **½** cup chopped fresh cilantro

PREPARE

1. Bring a large nonreactive stockpot of water to a boil. Add the corn and boil for 5 minutes. Drain.

2. When the corn is cool enough to handle, stand the cobs on end and slice vertically to cut off the kernels, being careful not to cut into the cobs. Empty and wipe out the stockpot.

3. Combine the vinegar, sugar, cumin, and salt in the stockpot, and bring to a boil. Add the tomatoes, jalapeños, bell pepper, onion, garlic, and corn kernels, and return to a boil. Reduce heat and simmer for 5 minutes, to allow flavors to blend. Stir in the cilantro and return to a boil. Remove from the heat.

PRESERVE

Refrigerate: Ladle into bowls or jars. Cool, cover, and refrigerate for up to 3 weeks.

Can: Use the boiling-water method. Ladle into clean, hot half-pint or pint canning jars, leaving ½ inch of headspace. Release trapped air. Wipe the rims clean; center lids on the jars and screw on jar bands. Process for 15 minutes. Turn off heat, remove canner lid, and let jars rest in the water for 5 minutes. Remove jars and set aside for 24 hours. Check seals, then store in a cool, dark place for up to 1 year.

→ **See page 52 for more about salsas, chutneys, and relishes.**

FROZEN CORN

I have a farmer friend who makes freezing corn a group activity — gathering friends and family for an all-day corn shuck. I suggest you do the same. It's simple work, but time-consuming. Juicy gossip makes the hours fly.

INGREDIENTS

Any quantity fresh corn on the cob, shucked

PREPARE

1. Bring a large stockpot of water to a boil. Add the corn and boil until just tender, 2 to 3 minutes. Drain.

2. When the corn is cool enough to handle, stand the cobs on end and slice vertically to cut off the kernels using a sharp knife or one of the crafty tools designed specifically for the job, being careful not to cut into the cobs. (This is messy work; if you can do it outside on a covered picnic table, all the better.)

PRESERVE

Freeze: Transfer the corn kernels into freezer bags, packing them three-quarters full, and pressing out as much air as possible. Divide the bags among all shucker/gossipers. Freeze for up to 6 months.

dry (p.71)

infuse (p.68)

can (p.79)

freeze (p.61)

refrigerate (p.59)

→ See page 93 for more about working in groups.

Cucumbers

*T*he Kirby is the typical pickling cucumber, and the one I recommend. It's sweet and tender and has fewer seeds than do other varieties. Lemon cucumbers, which also lack the bitter flavor present in many other varieties of cukes, are another good choice for pickling.

For the agua fresca and the sake, use any variety of cucumber you have. Making the agua fresca with a different variety each time is an excellent way to taste-test all manner of cucumbers.

FRESH STORAGE RECOMMENDATIONS

MOST OF THE CUKES YOU BUY AT THE GROCERY STORE have been coated with wax to preserve their freshness. Not so the fresh veggies you pick up at the farmers' market. Consequently, some of the food you bring home fresh will begin to wither within a day or two of purchase. Put up cukes quickly, within a day of harvest. Store the rest in a cool fridge, wrapped in a paper bag, for a short time.

dry (p.71)

infuse (p.68)

can (p.79)

freeze (p.61)

refrigerate (p.59)

CUCUMBER AGUA FRESCA

Makes about 1 quart

This is a light breeze of a summer drink (or a terrific base for a Cucumber Martini; see the recipe below). It's also a great way to use up any cucumbers that didn't make it into the canner or crock.

INGREDIENTS

4 cucumbers, peeled, seeded, and roughly chopped

1 cup water

2 tablespoons sugar

Juice of 1 lime

PREPARE

1. Set a fine-mesh sieve or colander lined with dampened cheesecloth over a bowl. Purée the cucumbers in a blender or food processor, working in batches as necessary and transferring the purée to the sieve or colander as you go. Let drain fully, 10 to 15 minutes, pressing on the pulp to release all of the juice. Compost the solids.

2. Pour the cucumber juice into a pitcher. Add the water, sugar, and lime juice, and stir to dissolve the sugar. Serve over ice, adding a splash of seltzer to each glass if you like.

PRESERVE

Refrigerate: Refrigerate, without ice or seltzer, for up to 3 days.

Freeze: Freeze in 8-ounce servings for up to 3 months.

→ See page 24 for more about agua fresca and granita.

Cucumber Martini

Lovely and light. I can't think of a better libation for a summer cocktail party.

3 ounces Cucumber Agua Fresca (above)

1½ ounces vodka

Ice

Cucumber slice, for garnish

Combine the Cucumber Agua Fresca and vodka with the ice in a cocktail shaker and shake to chill. Strain into a martini glass. Garnish with the cucumber slice. | **Makes 1 serving**

CUCUMBER SAKE

Makes about about 3 cups

This infused sake makes a refreshing change from white wine during the summer months — and it's garden fresh!

INGREDIENTS

- **2** cucumbers, peeled and seeded
- **2** cups sake

PREPARE AND PRESERVE

🌡 **Infuse:**

1. Shred the cucumbers with a box grater. Pour the sake into a glass jar, and then add the cucumber. Refrigerate overnight.

2. Strain the sake and pour into a clean, glass jar (with the released juices from the cucumbers, you will have more liquid than your original volume of sake). Enjoy chilled within 1 week.

ASIAN ICEBOX PICKLES

Makes about 2 cups

These quick, delicate pickles are perfect with lamb burgers or Asian fish cakes. The dressing might at first seem heavy on the acid, but the juices from the cucumbers dilute it and make it taste just right.

INGREDIENTS

- **1** cup rice wine vinegar
- **2** tablespoons soy sauce
- **2** teaspoons sugar
- **2** tablespoons toasted sesame oil
  Pinch of red pepper flakes or dash of Asian hot sauce (optional)
- **2** cucumbers, peeled, seeded, and sliced
- **1** small red onion, thinly sliced

PREPARE

Whisk the vinegar, soy sauce, and sugar in a medium nonreactive bowl until the sugar is dissolved. Whisk in the sesame oil and the pepper flakes, if using. Add the cucumbers and onion and toss to combine.

PRESERVE

🍃 **Refrigerate:** Keeps in a covered glass bowl or jar in the fridge for up to 1 week.

→ See page 68 for more about alcohols and vinegars.

→ See page 40 for more about vinegar pickles.

BREAD-AND-BUTTER CHIPS

Makes about 7 pints

Looking for a first pickle to make? Pick this recipe. It's easy and delicious — every year I make a couple of batches, to keep friends and family in supply. Kirby is the go-to cucumber here, and sweet onions such as Vidalia work well if they're local.

INGREDIENTS

- **5** pounds cucumbers, ends removed, sliced into ¼-inch coins
- **1** pound large onions, roughly chopped
- **½** cup plus 1 tablespoon kosher salt
- **2** cups ice cubes
- **4** cups distilled white vinegar
- **2** cups water
- **1** cup sugar
- **2** tablespoons mustard seed
- **1** tablespoon black peppercorns
- **1** tablespoon celery seed
- **1** tablespoon turmeric

PREPARE

1. Layer the cukes and onions with ½ cup of the salt in a large bowl and cover with a layer of ice cubes. Set aside for 2 hours. Drain and rinse in a colander.

2. Combine the vinegar, water, sugar, mustard seed, peppercorns, celery seed, turmeric, and the remaining 1 tablespoon salt in a large nonreactive saucepan and bring to a boil. Add the drained vegetables and return to a boil, stirring to ensure that all of the vegetables are heated through. Remove from the heat.

PRESERVE

⊘ **Refrigerate:** Ladle into bowls or jars. Cool, cover, and refrigerate for up to 3 weeks.

Ⓑ **Can:** Use the boiling-water method. Ladle into clean, hot pint canning jars, covering the pickles by ¼ inch with liquid. Leave ¼ inch of headspace between the top of the liquid and the lid. Release trapped air. Wipe the rims clean; center lids on the jars and screw on jar bands. Process for 10 minutes. Turn off heat, remove canner lid, and let jars rest in the water for 5 minutes. Remove jars and set aside for 24 hours. Check seals, then store in a cool, dark place for up to 1 year.

→ **See page 40 for more about vinegar pickles.**

dry (p.71)

infuse (p.68)

can (p.79)

freeze (p.61)

refrigerate (p.59)

DILL SPEARS

Makes about 6 pints

These pickles have lots of great dill flavor. Keep a bunch to sidle up to a sandwich, or chop them up into preparations such as tartar sauce and Russian dressing.

Note: The boiling-water method is necessary to tenderize these cold-pack pickles.

INGREDIENTS

- **5** pounds cucumbers, ends removed, cut into pint-jar-size spears
- **½** cup salt
- **2** cups ice cubes
- **4** cups distilled white vinegar
- **2** cups water
- **2** tablespoons sugar
- **8** garlic cloves, peeled
- **2** tablespoons dill seed
- **1** teaspoon celery seed
- **1** teaspoon peppercorns

PREPARE

1. Layer the cukes with the salt in a large bowl and cover with a layer of ice cubes. Set aside for 2 hours. Drain, rinse, and pack into clean, hot pint canning jars.

2. Combine the vinegar, water, sugar, garlic, dill seed, celery seed, and peppercorns in a medium nonreactive saucepan, and bring to a boil. Pour the hot brine over the spears to cover by ½ inch. Leave ½ inch of headspace between the top of the liquid and the lid.

PRESERVE

Can: Use the boiling-water method. Release trapped air. Wipe the rims clean; center lids on the jars and screw on jar bands. Process for 10 minutes. Turn off heat, remove canner lid, and let jars rest in the water for 5 minutes. Remove jars and set aside for 24 hours. Check seals, then store in a cool, dark place for up to 1 year.

→ **See page 40 for more about vinegar pickles.**

dry (p.71)

infuse (p.68)

can (p.79)

freeze (p.61)

refrigerate (p.59)

PICKLE RELISH

Makes about 8 cups

This recipe has great relish flavor without any of the super-sweetness you find sometimes in store-bought preparations. Its bright flavor is a super addition to any summer cookout.

INGREDIENTS

- **2** pounds cucumbers, peeled, seeded, and diced
- **1** pound onions, diced
- **1** green bell pepper, diced
- **1** red bell pepper, diced
- **½** cup salt
- **3** cups cider vinegar
- **1½** cups sugar
- **1** cup water
- **2** garlic cloves, minced
- **2** teaspoons ground allspice
- **1** teaspoon black peppercorns
- **1** teaspoon celery seed

PREPARE

1. Toss the cucumbers, onions, green and red peppers, and salt in a large bowl, and set aside for 2 hours. Drain thoroughly.

2. Combine the vinegar, sugar, water, garlic, allspice, peppercorns, and celery seed in a large nonreactive stockpot, and bring to a boil, stirring until the sugar is dissolved. Add the vegetables and return to a boil. Simmer for 5 minutes. Remove from the heat.

PRESERVE

Refrigerate: Ladle into bowls or jars. Cool, cover, and refrigerate for up to 3 weeks.

Can: Use the boiling-water method. Ladle into clean, hot half-pint canning jars, covering the solids by ¼ inch with liquid. Leave ¼ inch of headspace between the top of the liquid and the lid. Release trapped air. Wipe the rims clean; center lids on the jars and screw on jar bands. Process for 15 minutes. Turn off heat, remove canner lid, and let jars rest in the water for 5 minutes. Remove jars and set aside for 24 hours. Check seals, then store in a cool, dark place for up to 1 year.

→ See page 52 for more about salsas, chutneys, and relishes.

INDIAN PICKLE

Makes about 10 cups

This recipe requires a good bit of chopping. You know what that means? Nice project for a good bit of chatting, too. Grab a friend or the phone and time will fly while you socialize.

INGREDIENTS

- **2** pounds cucumbers, peeled, seeded, and diced
- **1** pound onions, diced
- **1** pound cauliflower, diced
- **½** pound carrots, peeled and diced
- **½** cup salt
- **3** cups cider vinegar
- **1** cup water
- **1½** cups sugar
- **2** tablespoons minced fresh ginger
- **2** tablespoons mustard powder
- **1** tablespoon turmeric
- **1** teaspoon curry powder

PREPARE

1. Toss the cucumbers, onions, cauliflower, and carrots with the salt and drain in a colander for 2 hours. Rinse thoroughly.

2. Combine the vinegar, water, sugar, ginger, mustard powder, turmeric, and curry powder in a large nonreactive stockpot and bring to a boil. Add the drained vegetables and return to a boil. Simmer for 5 minutes.

PRESERVE

⊘ **Refrigerate:** Ladle into bowls or jars. Cool, cover, and refrigerate for up to 3 weeks.

⊕ **Can:** Use the boiling-water method. Ladle into clean, hot half-pint canning jars, covering the solids by ¼ inch with liquid. Leave ¼ inch of headspace between the top of the liquid and the lid. Release trapped air. Wipe the rims clean; center lids on the jars and screw on jar bands. Process for 15 minutes. Turn off heat, remove canner lid, and let jars rest in the water for 5 minutes. Remove jars and set aside for 24 hours. Check seals, then store in a cool, dark place for up to 1 year.

→ See page 52 for more about salsas, chutneys, and relishes.

dry (p.71)

infuse (p.68)

can (p.79)

freeze (p.61)

refrigerate (p.59)

CLASSIC CROCK PICKLES

Makes about 1 gallon

Ooohhh, fermentation. So mysterious, so illicit — so easy! Yes, you have to be scrupulously clean. Sure, there are some rules to follow. But the process is time-tested over centuries, and the results are flavors your family will want to pass down for generations. Many traditional cuisines use fermentation to extend the shelf life and enhance the flavor of fresh foods. Additionally, the procedure creates probiotics, the same beneficial bacteria found in yogurt, so fermented foods aid digestion and support good health.

Note: *I don't recommend processing these pickles with the boiling-water method, as the heat would destroy these beneficial probiotic bacteria that result from the fermentation process.*

INGREDIENTS

- **4** pounds pickling cucumbers
- **2** quarts water
- **6** tablespoons kosher salt
- **1** head garlic, cloves separated and peeled
- **2** tablespoons dill seed
- **1** tablespoon mustard seed
- **2** teaspoons celery seed
- **1** handful oak leaves from your backyard or park tree (to preserve crispness) washed well

Oak leaf

PREPARE

1. Have ready a thoroughly washed gallon container,* a plate or cover just smaller than the opening of the container, and a quart jar full of water.

2. Remove the blossom end (the end that doesn't have a stem) from the cukes. Combine the water with the salt, garlic, dill seed, mustard seed, and celery seed in the container, and stir to dissolve. Add the oak leaves and then the cucumbers.

3. Press the plate into the brine to submerge the cucumbers so that they're completely covered with at least 1 inch of liquid. If you need more liquid, mix up a solution of 1 tablespoon of kosher salt to 1 cup of water and add it to the pickling liquid to reach the desired volume. Place the quart jar on top of the plate to keep it submerged. Cover the top of the container with a tea towel and set aside.

4. Check the pickles every day. You will see bubbles rising, sometimes ferrying seeds up and down the pickling liquid. This is a good sign. A scum, or bloom, will form on top of the liquid. This is good, too. Remove the jar, and the plate if necessary, and skim off the bloom every day or so. Rinse the jar and plate and return them to their tasks.

5. When the bubbles stop rising, after a week or two, remove the plate and spear out a pickle. Slice it in half. It should be uniformly pickled to its center. Take a taste. It should be pleasantly sour and salty. If it isn't uniform in texture or sour enough, let it sit for a day or two to complete the ferment.

*Make sure the container is glass, food-grade ceramic, or food-grade plastic. The glaze on imported decorative crockery may contain heavy metals that can leach into food. *Caution:* Industrial plastic buckets used for anything other than food are never safe.

PRESERVE

 **Refrigerate:** When pickles reach the desired flavor, put the whole container in the refrigerator to slow fermentation. Remove any developing scum regularly. They'll keep in the fridge for 4 to 6 months.

→ See page 45 for more about fermented pickles.

Fennel

*F*ennel is one of the great gems of the market, yet it's woefully underused. Its lightly licorice flavor is wonderful shaved raw into a salad or braised until the vegetable becomes meltingly tender. It also adds a nice Mediterranean note to any menu.

Fennel is a cool-weather crop that comes around in the spring, takes a break in summer, and then shows itself again in fall. Most of the plant is edible; even the seeds are prized for their great flavor — in fact, they're offered at the end of rich Indian meals to aid digestion.

FRESH STORAGE RECOMMENDATIONS

FENNEL KEEPS FOR ABOUT A WEEK in a cool refrigerator.

FENNEL CONFIT

Makes about 2 cups

Slow cooking brings out a sweetness in fennel that tones down its licorice bite. Keep a supply on hand and you'll be surprised at the variety of uses you find for it: in soups, as a base for risotto, as a bed for fish, or simply slathered on toast — the list goes on.

INGREDIENTS

- **2** tablespoons butter
- **2** tablespoons extra-virgin olive oil
- **4** cups diced fennel (2–4 bulbs)
- **1** tablespoon salt
  Freshly ground black pepper
- **½** cup white wine or chicken stock

PREPARE

1. Heat the butter and oil in a large skillet. Add the fennel and season with the salt and pepper to taste. Sauté over medium heat, covered, until the fennel is soft. Remove the lid, reduce the heat to low, and continue to sauté until the fennel begins to brown and becomes jammy, 20 to 30 minutes.

2. Add the wine and simmer to deglaze the pan, scraping up any brown bits on the bottom. Remove from the heat.

PRESERVE

Refrigerate: Ladle into bowls or jars. Cool, cover, and refrigerate for up to 5 days.

Freeze: Cool and transfer to ice-cube trays or small freezer containers. Freeze, covered, for up to 6 months.

How to Trim Fennel

If you've never worked with fennel, it can be an intimidating vegetable: Where to start? Which part do you eat? Here's what to do:

1. Chop off the fronds and reserve (these taste like licorice-flavored dill).

2. Slice off the long batons from the bulb; these are a bit tough to sauté but are great slow-cooked in a stew or used as an aromatic in a stock.

3. Peel away any tough outer leaves from the bulb.

4. Slice the bulb in half lengthwise.

5. Cut out the core (the thing that looks like the heart of a head of cabbage) and the root end and discard. You now have a trimmed bulb ready to be chopped, shredded, or sliced into your recipe.

dry (p.71)

infuse (p.68)

can (p.79)

freeze (p.61)

refrigerate (p.59)

dry (p.71)

infuse (p.68)

can (p.79)

freeze (p.61)

refrigerate (p.59)

FENNEL AND ONION JAM

Makes about 4 cups

The onions up the sweetness component of this dish to rival dessert. For sheer bliss, serve on a toasted baguette with goat cheese.

INGREDIENTS

- ¼ cup extra-virgin olive oil
- 2 pounds fennel bulbs, trimmed and chopped
- 2 pounds onions, chopped
- 1 tablespoon salt
- 4 garlic cloves, minced
- 1 teaspoon dried thyme
- ¼ cup cider vinegar
- ½ cup brown sugar, lightly packed
  Freshly ground black pepper

PREPARE

1. Heat the olive oil in a saucepan over medium heat. Add the fennel and onions, and sprinkle with the salt. Sauté, covered, until the vegetables are soft and beginning to brown, 10 to 15 minutes. Remove the lid, lower the heat, and sauté until the mixture is caramelized and jammy, 15 to 20 minutes longer.

2. Add the garlic and thyme and sauté for an additional 1 to 2 minutes. Add the vinegar and sugar and simmer for 10 minutes to combine flavors. Season with pepper.

PRESERVE

Refrigerate: Ladle into bowls or jars. Cool, cover, and refrigerate for up to 5 days.

Freeze: Cool and transfer to ice-cube trays or small freezer containers. Freeze, covered, for up to 6 months.

PICKLED FENNEL

Makes about 7 cups

Fennel and seafood are a marvelous combination. Try this relish on a grilled tuna sandwich or use it to dress up a bagel and lox.

INGREDIENTS

- 3 cups distilled white vinegar
- 1 cup water
- 1 cup sugar
- 3 tablespoons salt
- 1 tablespoon fennel seed
- 2 pounds trimmed fennel bulbs, sliced thin

PREPARE

Combine the vinegar, water, sugar, salt, and fennel seed in a medium nonreactive saucepan, and bring to a boil. Add the fennel, return to a boil, and simmer for 5 minutes, until tender.

PRESERVE

Refrigerate: Ladle into bowls or jars. Cool, cover, and refrigerate for up to 3 weeks.

Can: Use the boiling-water method. Ladle into clean, hot half-pint canning jars, covering the fennel by ¼ inch with liquid. Leave ¼ inch of headspace between the top of the liquid and the lid. Release trapped air. Wipe the rims clean; center lids on the jars and screw on jar bands. Process for 15 minutes. Turn off heat, remove canner lid, and let jars rest in the water for 5 minutes. Remove jars and set aside for 24 hours. Check seals, then store in a cool, dark place for up to 1 year.

→ **See page 40 for more about vinegar pickles.**

Figs

Not everyone has a fig tree in the back-
yard, but for those who do, the annual harvest can create an embarrassment of
riches. The doorman in my old office building brought figs to me by the bagful. He
was a good friend to have.

Figs may be green or black, and either color is fine in these recipes. Figs have
a sweet taste and a unique texture, thanks to a chewy skin that gives way to a succulent interior. When you've had your fill of eating them out of hand, try some of
these recipes.

FRESH STORAGE RECOMMENDATIONS

FIGS, SO PRECIOUS AND FLEETING. They don't ripen once they're picked, so they
have to linger on the tree until they're just right. Figs will keep only a few days
in the fridge; once that perfect ripening moment arrives, it's a quick trip to the
mouth or to star in one of these recipes.

dry (p.71)

infuse (p.68)

can (p.79)

freeze (p.61)

refrigerate (p.59)

FROZEN FIGS

The pure taste of figs, all year-round.

INGREDIENTS

Any quantity figs, stemmed

PREPARE

Spread out the figs on a baking sheet. Pop the pan into the freezer until the figs are solid.

PRESERVE

Freeze: Transfer the frozen figs to an airtight container or bag, pressing out as much air as possible, and return to the freezer. They'll keep frozen for up to 6 months.

DRIED FIGS

Dried figs: More sophisticated than a raisin but just as user friendly. Toss some into your next salad, serve them with a cheese plate — they are transcendent with blue cheese — or pack them into your kids' lunch boxes.

INGREDIENTS

Any quantity figs, stemmed

PREPARE AND PRESERVE

Dry: Preheat the oven to 170°F. Wash and dry the figs. Cut the fruit in half and arrange on cooling racks, cut-side up. Prop open the oven door with the handle of a wooden spoon. Dry for 5 to 6 hours, until squeezing them releases no moisture. Cool and store in an airtight container for up to 1 year.

STICKY FIG JAM

Makes about 4 cups

This is a sexy one. Its sweet but sophisticated flavor and its supple texture make grape and strawberry spreads seem like child's play. Make extra to give as gifts — if you can bring yourself to part with this seductive stuff.

INGREDIENTS

2 pounds figs, stemmed and quartered
1 cup water
1 cup sugar
½ cup balsamic vinegar
¼ cup bottled lemon juice

PREPARE

1. Bring the figs and water to a boil in a large nonreactive pot. Reduce the heat and simmer for 5 minutes to soften the fruit. Using a potato masher, crush the figs.

2. Add the sugar, vinegar, and lemon juice, and return to a boil. Reduce the heat and simmer, stirring frequently, until thick and jammy but not dry, about 20 minutes.

3. Test for gel. Remove from the heat and set aside for 5 minutes, stirring to release air bubbles.

PRESERVE

Refrigerate: Ladle into bowls or jars. Cool, cover, and refrigerate for up to 3 weeks.

Can: Use the boiling-water method. Ladle into clean, hot 4-ounce or half-pint canning jars, leaving ¼ inch of headspace. Release trapped air. Wipe the rims clean; center lids on the jars and screw on jar bands. Process for 10 minutes. Turn off heat, remove canner lid, and let jars rest in the water for 5 minutes. Remove jars and set aside for 24 hours. Check seals, then store in a cool, dark place for up to 1 year.

→ See page 27 for more about jams and jellies.

FIGS PRESERVED IN HONEY SYRUP

Makes about 9 pints

Local honey is utterly delicious, but that's not all. It's reported to support the immune system and to be particularly effective for those with allergies. Delicious and healthful — now that's good medicine. I always use the local products whenever a recipe calls for honey. This recipe takes advantage of the natural affinity between figs and honey.

dry (p.71)

infuse (p.68)

can (p.79)

freeze (p.61)

refrigerate (p.59)

INGREDIENTS

- **10** pounds figs, stemmed
- **6** cups water
- **2** cups honey
- **1** cup sugar
- **9** tablespoons bottled lemon juice (1 tablespoon per pint)

PREPARE

1. In a large saucepan, cover the figs with water by 2 inches and bring to a boil. Simmer for 2 minutes to soften the fruit. Drain.

2. Combine the 6 cups water, honey, and sugar in another large saucepan, and bring to a boil, stirring to dissolve the sugar. Add the figs and gently boil them in the syrup for 5 minutes.

3. Put 1 tablespoon of lemon juice into each clean, hot pint jar. Pack the jars gently but firmly with the figs. Ladle the hot syrup over the figs to cover by ½ inch. Leave ½ inch of headspace between the top of the liquid and the lid. Screw lids on the jars temporarily. Gently swirl each jar to release trapped air bubbles. Remove the lids and add syrup, if necessary, to achieve the proper headspace.

PRESERVE

Can: Use the boiling-water method. Release trapped air. Wipe the rims clean; center lids on the jars and screw on jar bands. Process for 45 minutes. Turn off heat, remove canner lid, and let jars rest in the water for 5 minutes. Remove jars and set aside for 24 hours. Check seals, then store in a cool, dark place for up to 1 year.

Figs and Blue Cheese

Figs and blue cheese are a classic combination. Serve any of these fig recipes alongside a hunk of Stilton, Roquefort, or one of the delectable American blues. Or crumble some blue onto a pizza crust or crostini rounds, add a few dollops of fig jam or slices of preserved figs, and pop in the oven until the cheese melts for an instant appetizer.

Garlic

Ah, the stinking rose. Garlic has sprouted more than its share of food legend, some fact and some fiction. It's well regarded for its medicinal properties and is reported to ward off colds as well as vampires.

Garlic comes in two varieties: hard neck and soft neck. Hard neck is actually the more fragile of the two varieties: it has less white, papery skin covering the cloves to protect them. This family of garlic generates the scapes that are becoming increasingly popular in markets and on restaurant menus. Soft-neck garlic is the one that is grown commercially. It has more but smaller cloves, which are well covered in the white, papery skin. This type of garlic keeps better and is the kind you see braided for storage.

FRESH STORAGE RECOMMENDATIONS

GARLIC HAS TO BE CURED TO BE STORED. Ask at the farmers' market if the vendor is selling bulbs that are meant to be enjoyed fresh or kept. "Keepers" store best in a warm, well-ventilated place to prevent them from sprouting.

GARLIC PURÉE

If you've got an overabundance or you simply feel a big cook coming on, this is a great way to have garlic always ready for action. **Caution:** *Never store puréed garlic at room temperature — it's a low-acid food that can quickly breed botulism toxin if it's not properly refrigerated.*

INGREDIENTS

Garlic heads
Extra-virgin olive oil

PREPARE

1. To peel the cloves, gently crush the bulb with the side of a knife to separate them, and then smash each clove individually to release its paper.

2. Place as many peeled cloves as you like in a small bowl or liquid measuring cup and add about half that volume of oil. Purée with a stick blender, scrape into a small bowl or jar, and pour in oil to cover by ¼ inch to seal out air. This will keep the garlic from oxidizing, so it will taste fresher for a longer period.

PRESERVE

⊘ **Refrigerate:** Store in the refrigerator for 1 to 2 days.

⊛ **Freeze:** Divide into ice-cube trays or small containers and freeze for up to 6 months. (Because of the high oil content in this recipe, it will not freeze solid.)

dry (p.71)

infuse (p.68)

can (p.79)

freeze (p.61)

refrigerate (p.59)

ROASTED GARLIC

Roasted garlic is one of those secret ingredients that — like cinnamon — make everything you put them in taste better. Whip it into potatoes for a special side dish, mix it with goat cheese for a first-rate spread, or purée it with a vinaigrette and toss it with steamed vegetables to jazz them up. Roasted garlic is a workhorse ingredient, and it's easy to have it on hand.

INGREDIENTS

Firm heads of garlic
Extra-virgin olive oil

PREPARE

1. Preheat the oven to 350°F. With a very sharp knife, slice off the top third of each garlic head (you can use the head tops in the Garlic Purée recipe at left). Place each head in the middle of a piece of aluminum foil, roughly 6 inches square. Drizzle lightly with oil, then fold up the foil to wrap tight. Repeat for as many heads as you like.

2. Place the foil packets on a baking sheet and roast until the garlic is softened and caramelized, about 1 hour. Cool, then gently squeeze the flesh out of the skins.

PRESERVE

Refrigerate: Transfer to a small bowl and store in the refrigerator up to 2 days.

Freeze: Transfer to small containers or covered ice-cube trays and freeze for about 6 months.

Roasted Garlic Crostini

This is one of the simplest recipes I know. Great fun as a starter for a casual meal with friends.

1 head Roasted Garlic (above)
4 ounces fresh goat cheese

1 baguette, sliced and toasted

In a small bowl, mash the roasted garlic flesh and the goat cheese with the back of a fork. Spread onto toasted baguette slices and serve | **Makes about ½ cup of spread**

PICKLED GARLIC

Makes about 2 cups

Whether you're a garlic-philiac or a garlic-phobe, this is a great recipe for these versatile bulbs. Pickling mellows the flavor (and the cloves' ability to give you garlic breath), but it may also turn the garlic blue — no worries, it's all good.

INGREDIENTS

- ½ pound garlic (about 6 large heads), separated into cloves
- 1 cup distilled white vinegar
- ¼ cup sugar
-   Pinch of red pepper flakes

PREPARE

1. Lay a dish towel on your work surface. Prepare an ice-water bath in a large bowl or clean sink.

2. Bring a medium pot of water to a boil. Drop the garlic into the water and blanch for 30 seconds.

3. Scoop out the garlic with a spider or slotted spoon and plunge into the ice-water bath. Remove the garlic from the ice bath with a slotted spoon and spread on the towel. Blot dry.

4. Using a small paring knife, remove and discard the skins. If the cloves are large, cut them in half. Divide the cloves among 4 clean, hot 4-ounce canning jars.

5. Combine the vinegar, sugar, and pepper flakes, if using, in a nonreactive saucepan, and bring to a boil. Ladle the hot brine over the garlic to cover by ¼ inch. Leave ¼ inch of headspace between the top of the liquid and the lid.

PRESERVE

⊘ **Refrigerate:** Cool, cover, and refrigerate for up to 3 weeks.

Ⓑ **Can:** Use the boiling-water method. Release trapped air. Wipe the rims clean; center lids on the jars and screw on jar bands. Process for 10 minutes. Turn off heat, remove canner lid, and let jars rest in the water for 5 minutes. Remove jars and set aside for 24 hours. Check seals, then store in a cool, dark place for up to 1 year.

→ See page 21 for more about blanching.
→ See page 40 for more about vinegar pickles.

dry (p.71)

infuse (p.68)

can (p.79)

freeze (p.61)

refrigerate (p.59)

Grapes

I grew up eating grapes. They were in my lunchbox, at picnics, and strewn artfully on a cheese board. But the first time I *tasted* a grape was at the Westport Farmers' Market, where one of my favorite vendors, Elpidio, offered me a Concord. I popped it into my mouth expecting the usual ho-hum, tart-but-nothing-to-sing-about pop between my teeth. He must have gotten the biggest kick out of my expression, and my honest, if not eloquent, response: "It tastes so *grapey*." And it did. The difference between that grape and all others until then was so striking that it changed my view of the fruit. If you have access to fully ripened, flavorful grapes, gobble them up or prepare one of these recipes, but don't let that grapey flavor pass you by.

FRESH STORAGE RECOMMENDATIONS

REMOVE ANY WITHERING GRAPES from the bunch before storing them in the fridge, lightly wrapped in plastic (great use for an old bread bag), for up to a week.

GRAPE SYRUP

Makes about 2 cups

Maple is fine, but grape is sublime! Terrific anywhere you would use maple syrup — on pancakes, waffles, and French toast — it's also good drizzled on grilled duck and game.

INGREDIENTS

- **4** cups grapes (about 1 pound), stemmed
- **1** cup sugar
- **½** cup water

PREPARE

Combine the grapes, sugar, and water in a large saucepan, and bring to a boil. Reduce heat and simmer for 5 minutes. Remove from the heat. Cool the mixture and run through a food mill.

Note: Some sediment will form in the bottom of the cooled syrup. Either decant to another container for storage or simply pour gently when serving.

PRESERVE

Refrigerate: Pour into a jar. Cover and refrigerate for up to 3 weeks.

Freeze: Syrup can be transferred into small freezer containers and frozen for up to 6 months.

→ See page 54 for more about butters, sauces, and ketchups.

HOMEMADE RAISINS

Makes about 1 pint of raisins for every 4 pounds of grapes

Seedless grapes are the way to go here. Any variety will do.

INGREDIENTS

Any quantity grapes, stemmed

PREPARE

1. To soften their skins and aid in drying, blanch the grapes. Line several baking sheets with dish towels and set aside. Prepare an ice-water bath in a large bowl or clean sink.

2. Bring a large pot of water to a boil. Drop the grapes into the water, no more than 1 pound at a time, and blanch for 30 seconds.

3. Scoop out the grapes with a spider or slotted spoon and plunge them into the ice-water bath. Continue blanching the grapes in batches. Remove the grapes from the ice bath with a slotted spoon and spread on the towel-covered baking sheets. Blot dry.

PRESERVE

⊞ **Dry:**

1. Preheat the oven to 170°F. Spread the fruit on metal screens or a baking sheet. Dry in the oven until the grapes are shriveled and no longer moist in the center, 5 to 7 hours. Raisins are fully dry when you can squeeze a handful and they don't stick together.

2. Cool the raisins, and then transfer them to a covered container to condition for 1 week. This allows the dried fruit to redistribute any trapped moisture. If you notice moisture on the sides of the container, repeat the drying process for another hour or so. Keeps in an airtight container for up to 1 year.

→ See page 21 for more about blanching.

Rum Raisin Sauce

Serve this sauce over vanilla ice cream for a simple but grown-up dessert. My brother-in-law, David, serves it with roasted ham. The sweetness of the sauce nicely complements the salty flavor of the ham.

½ cup Homemade Raisins (above)
½ cup white rum
1 cup sugar

1 cup water
½ teaspoon ground cinnamon

Combine the raisins and rum in a small bowl and set aside for at least 4 hours, even overnight. Bring the sugar and water to a boil in a small saucepan, stirring to dissolve the sugar. Continue to boil until the syrup begins to take on a pale golden color, about 5 minutes. Remove from the heat and cool slightly. Whisk in the cinnamon and the raisins. Add the soaking rum, if you like. | **Makes 1 cup**

GRAPE LEATHER

One quart of fruit makes about 1 (17-inch) sheet of leather

I recommend enlisting the kids anytime you make fruit leather. This recipe requires an extra step to seed the grapes, making assistants all the more helpful.

204

INGREDIENTS

- **4** cups grapes
- ¼ cup water
- ½ cup sugar

PREPARE

1. Pinch the grapes to separate the skins from the flesh. Put the flesh in a medium pan as you go, reserving the skins in a separate pan. Add a splash of water to each pan and begin to simmer. When the grape flesh has softened, about 10 minutes, cool and run through a food mill to remove any seeds.

2. Preheat the oven to 170°F. Line a jelly-roll pan or a rimmed baking sheet with parchment paper or a Silpat and set aside.

3. Return the seeded flesh to the pot with the skins. Add the sugar and stir to dissolve. Simmer over low heat, stirring frequently, until the skins are very soft, about 10 minutes. Purée with a stick blender and continue to simmer until the purée thickens to the consistency of baby food.

PRESERVE

▦ Dry:

1. Spread the purée on the baking sheet, tilting it to create an even layer about ⅛ inch thick. Dry in the oven until tacky to the touch, about 2 hours.

2. Cool to room temperature. Slide the parchment onto a cutting board and roll the leather into a tube. Slice the tube into 2-inch segments and store in a covered jar for up to 1 month.

dry (p.71)

infuse (p.68)

can (p.79)

freeze (p.61)

refrigerate (p.59)

QUICK GRAPE JAM

Makes about 3 cups

Locally grown seedless grapes have limited availability, but if there's a grower near you, or some vines in your backyard, use them here for a quick recipe.

INGREDIENTS

- **1** cup sugar
- **2** teaspoons Pomona's Universal Pectin
- **8** cups grapes (about 2 pounds), stemmed
- **½** cup water
- **2** teaspoons calcium water (included in the Pomona box)
- **¼** cup bottled lemon juice

PREPARE

1. Combine the sugar and pectin in a small bowl and set aside.

2. Put the grapes and water in a medium nonreactive saucepan and bring to a boil. Reduce the heat. Simmer, stirring and crushing the grapes, until the fruits are softened and have released their liquid, about 15 minutes.

3. Stir in the calcium water and the lemon juice. Pour in the sugar-pectin mixture and stir to dissolve. Return to a boil. Remove from the heat and let rest for 5 minutes, stirring occasionally to release air bubbles. Skim off any foam.

PRESERVE

Refrigerate: Ladle into bowls or jars. Cool, cover, and refrigerate for up to 3 weeks.

Can: Use the boiling-water method. Ladle into clean, hot half pint canning jars, leaving ¼ inch of headspace. Release trapped air. Wipe the rims clean; center lids on the jars and screw on jar bands. Process for 10 minutes. Turn off heat, remove canner lid, and let jars rest in the water for 5 minutes. Remove jars and set aside for 24 hours. Check seals, then store in a cool, dark place for up to 1 year.

→ See page 27 for more about jams and jellies.

CLASSIC GRAPE JAM

Makes about 4 cups

I use Concord grapes for this jam. They have a delicious, deep grape flavor. Enlist any available children for the first phase of the project, which is separating the grape skins from the pulp — it's the kind of squishy work kids really dig.

INGREDIENTS

- **8** cups grapes (about 2 pounds)
- ½ cup water
- **4** cups sugar
- ¼ cup bottled lemon juice

PREPARE

1. Pinch the grapes to separate the skins from the flesh. Put the skins in a large nonreactive saucepan and the flesh in a medium pan as you go. Add the water to the pot of skins and bring to a boil. Reduce the heat and simmer for 15 to 20 minutes.

2. Meanwhile, bring the grape flesh to a simmer until it loses shape, 5 to 10 minutes. Cool slightly and run through a food mill to remove the seeds.

3. Add the milled grape pulp to the saucepan with the skins and stir in the sugar until it dissolves. Stir in the lemon juice. Bring to a boil and simmer, stirring, until you reach the gel stage, about 10 minutes.

4. Remove from the heat and let rest for 5 minutes, stirring occasionally to release air bubbles. Skim off any foam.

PRESERVE

Refrigerate: Ladle into bowls or jars. Cool, cover, and refrigerate for up to 3 weeks.

Can: Use the boiling-water method. Ladle into clean, hot 4-ounce or half-pint canning jars, leaving ¼ inch of headspace. Release trapped air. Wipe the rims clean; center lids on the jars and screw on jar bands. Process for 10 minutes. Turn off heat, remove canner lid, and let jars rest in the water for 5 minutes. Remove jars and set aside for 24 hours. Check seals, then store in a cool, dark place for up to 1 year.

→ See page 27 for more about jams and jellies.

Variation: Herbed Grape Jam

The addition of herbs makes the Classic Grape Jam savory-friendly. Add 1 tablespoon of fresh thyme leaves when you combine the milled grape pulp with the skins, then process as described above.

dry (p.71)

infuse (p.68)

can (p.79)

freeze (p.61)

refrigerate (p.59)

GRAPE JELLY

Makes about 4 cups

Don't feel like removing the seeds? Here's the answer: jelly. The process leaves them behind.

INGREDIENTS

- **4** pounds grapes, stemmed
- **½** cup water
- **1** cup sugar
- **1** teaspoon Pomona's Universal Pectin
- **1** teaspoon calcium water (included in the Pomona box)

PREPARE

1. Put the grapes and water in a large pot and bring to a boil. Reduce the heat and simmer, crushing the fruit gently with a potato masher and stirring, for about 10 minutes. Cool slightly.

2. Pour the mixture into a dampened jelly bag or colander lined with several layers of damp cheesecloth set over a large bowl. Drain in the refrigerator overnight. Do not press on the solids.

3. Combine the sugar and pectin powder in a small bowl and set aside.

4. Pour off a quart of juice, leaving behind the sediment, and bring to a boil in a medium saucepan. Add the calcium water and return to a boil. Add the sugar-pectin mixture, stirring to dissolve, and return to a boil. Remove from the heat and let sit for 5 minutes, stirring occasionally to release air bubbles. Skim off any foam.

PRESERVE

Refrigerate: Ladle into bowls or jars. Cool, cover, and refrigerate for up to 3 weeks.

Can: Use the boiling-water method. Ladle into clean, hot 4-ounce or half-pint canning jars, leaving ¼ inch of headspace. Release trapped air. Wipe the rims clean; center lids on the jars and screw on jar bands. Process for 10 minutes. Turn off heat, remove canner lid, and let jars rest in the water for 5 minutes. Remove jars and set aside for 24 hours. Check seals, then store in a cool, dark place for up to 1 year.

→ See page 27 for more about jams and jellies.

Herbs

Ancient remedies, mysterious potions, your best meal — what do they have in common? Herbs. There's no better culinary trick than having a stash of a variety of herbs at your disposal. I know that some cooks get in a twist about what to match with what, but really, it doesn't matter that much. Just take them off their stems and chop them up real fine and herbs will make anything taste better. Enjoyed fresh or processed into one of these recipes, herbs bring flavor and personality to every dish. And if they cure what ails you or bring good juju along the way, well, all the better.

FRESH STORAGE RECOMMENDATIONS

TREAT HERBS LIKE FRESH-CUT FLOWERS. Plunk them into a jar of fresh water, lightly wrap the jar in a wet paper towel or old bread bag, and store in the fridge for up to 1 week.

Whether you've picked them up at the farmers' market or grown some on your stoop or a windowsill, don't let extra herbs go to waste. Here are some super-simple ways to use up that half-handful of terrific-smelling herb or squirrel away the tender tasty bits before Jack Frost takes his share.

DRIED HERBS

Okay, here it is: the simplest preserving idea in the book.

INGREDIENTS

Any quantity fresh herbs, such as rosemary, thyme, oregano, dill, basil, or mint

PREPARE

To harvest fresh herbs, clip them close to the ground. Give them a little wash, then dry well.

PRESERVE

Dry: Tie together the root ends with a bit of twine and hang in the attic or other dry place with plenty of air circulation until the greens are crumbly.

Transfer to jars to store if you like. There, you're done.

HERB-SICLES

Here's a quick method to get your herbs put away. Toss these cubes straight from the freezer into soups, stocks, and sauces.

INGREDIENTS

Any quantity fresh herbs, such as rosemary, thyme, chives, savory, or chervil, separately or in combination
An equal amount of water

PREPARE

Wash the herbs and remove any woody stems. Purée with water in a blender, and then pour into an ice-cube tray and freeze.

PRESERVE

Freeze: Transfer cubes to a freezer container. They'll keep frozen for up to 6 months.

dry (p.71)

infuse (p.68)

can (p.79)

freeze (p.61)

refrigerate (p.59)

dry (p.71)

infuse (p.68)

can (p.79)

freeze (p.61)

refrigerate (p.59)

CLASSIC BASIL PESTO

Makes about 3 cups

Just about everybody loves pesto. Make a double batch and freeze some for later.

INGREDIENTS

- **1** cup olive oil
- **1** garlic clove, peeled
- **1** cup grated Parmesan cheese
- **¼** cup pine nuts
- **2** cups fresh basil
  Salt
  Freshly ground black pepper

PREPARE

Pour the oil into a blender or food processor. With the motor running, toss in the garlic and process until the garlic is puréed. Add the Parmesan and pine nuts and process until smooth. Add the basil and process again. Season with the salt and pepper.

PRESERVE

Refrigerate: Transfer to a small bowl or jar and refrigerate for up to 5 days.

Freeze: For single-use cubes, transfer to an ice-cube tray and freeze, and then transfer to a freezer container. They'll keep frozen for up to 6 months.

Pesto Variations

Dill with Feta

Here's a twist on the classic basil pesto. The dill and feta will bring a Mediterranean flavor to the party. Replace the Parmesan with ½ cup of feta cheese, the pine nuts with ½ cup of walnuts, and the basil with 1 cup of fresh dill plus ½ cup of fresh parsley. Process as directed above and store in the refrigerator or freezer.

Cilantro

Here is pesto, Mexican-style. It has a mild taste that is out of sight on grilled fish or a toasted baguette. Replace the Parmesan with ½ cup of queso blanco, the pine nuts with ½ cup of blanched almonds, and the basil with 2 cups of fresh cilantro stems and leaves. Process as directed above and store in the refrigerator or freezer.

Putting Pesto to Work

Pestos bring fresh-from-the-farm flavor when added to pasta, tossed with couscous, or stirred into rice. They're also terrific as an easy sauce for grilled meats, fish, and sausage. Or try them this way, as a quick base for dressings and dips.

Pesto Vinaigrette

Whisk equal amounts of pesto (defrosted if frozen), extra-virgin olive oil, and vinegar in a small bowl to combine. Toss with fresh greens or steamed or grilled vegetables.

Pesto Dip

Whisk equal parts of pesto and strained yogurt or sour cream in a small bowl. Use as a dip for crudités or as a creamy salad dressing.

HERBED VINEGAR

Makes about 1 cup

Use this infused vinegar in vinaigrettes and homemade mayonnaise, or add a splash to soups and stews to add some spark. If you start with a half bottle of vinegar, you'll have plenty of room for the herbs and there's no need to fuss with decanting.

INGREDIENTS

- ½ bottle white wine vinegar or 1 cup distilled white vinegar
- 1 bunch fragrant fresh herbs such as tarragon, rosemary, or thyme
  Pinch salt

PREPARE

Leaving the leaves on the stems, wash the herbs in several changes of water. Dry thoroughly.

PRESERVE

Infuse: Submerge the herbs in the vinegar in the original bottle or in a pint jar. Add the salt. Recap and shake every day for 1 week to develop flavors. Keeps for up to 1 year in a cool, dark place.

dry (p.71)

infuse (p.68)

can (p.79)

freeze (p.61)

refrigerate (p.59)

HERBS IN OIL

Whip up this recipe and pop it in the freezer for worry-free flavor at your fingertips. One of these wondrous cubes is a tasty addition to mashed potatoes, or melt and drizzle over a steak or roast.

Caution: Never store herbs in oil at room temperature — it's a perfect breeding ground for botulism.

INGREDIENTS

Any fresh herbs, such as rosemary, thyme, chives, savory, chervil, parsley, or cilantro
An equal amount of oil, such as olive or organic canola

PREPARE

1. Wash the herbs and remove any woody stems. Dry thoroughly.

2. Purée with the oil in a blender, then pour into an ice-cube tray and freeze.

PRESERVE

Freeze: Transfer cubes to a freezer container. They'll keep frozen for up to 6 months.

COMPOUND BUTTER

Makes about ¾ cup

These little logs transform the mundane into the sublime. Melt a pat on a grilled steak, toss with roasted vegetables, or stir into hot pasta — terrific!

INGREDIENTS

½ cup (1 stick) farm-fresh butter, at room temperature
¼ cup tender fresh herbs, such as chives, tarragon, parsley, chervil, or dill, or a combination, washed, dried, and finely chopped
1 shallot, finely minced
Salt
Freshly ground black pepper

PREPARE

Combine the butter, herbs, shallot, and salt and pepper to taste in a small bowl, and mash with a large fork. Scrape the mixture onto the center of a length of waxed or parchment paper. Fold one side of the paper over the butter and roll to form a log. Wrap tightly in plastic wrap or aluminum foil and freeze. To use, slice coins from the frozen log.

PRESERVE

Freeze: The butter will keep frozen for up to 6 months.

→ **See page 61 for more about Freezing.**

Mushrooms

*W*hen I walk through a forest, there is one thing that makes me believe in magic, and that thing is mushrooms. Perhaps it's the knowledge that some of them are delicious and others will lay you out flat that enhances their mystery. Whatever the reason, when I cook with mushrooms, I feel like I have, in some small way, tamed the wild wood.

A bona fide forager is a treasure. If you know someone who really knows her mushroom stuff, you've won the prize. Wild mushrooms have rich, exotic taste unequaled by any white button. For these recipes you can substitute any kind of mushroom you have on hand, from the precious hen-of-the-woods to the humble button.

Caution: If you haven't a resident mycologist, don't wing it. You can really pick up a case of the nasty, or worse, by playing guess-the-fungus.

FRESH STORAGE RECOMMENDATIONS

MUSHROOMS SLIP SO EASILY INTO SUCH A WIDE RANGE OF DISHES that it makes good sense to keep some on hand. When fresh ones are available, I store them in the refrigerator in a brown paper bag, lightly sprinkled with a few drops of water. They last this way for 5 to 7 days.

MUSHROOM CONFIT

Makes about 1½ cups

Confit is one of those great culinary terms that sound fancy but have practical and rustic roots. It usually refers to meats that are preserved by being cooked in and then covered by their own rendered fat. I'm using the term loosely to describe these silky mushrooms that are one part uptown glamour and one part down-home good eating.

INGREDIENTS

- **1** pound fresh mushrooms, any type
- ¼ cup extra-virgin olive oil, butter, or a combination
- ½ teaspoon dried thyme (optional)
- ¼ teaspoon salt
  Freshly ground black pepper
- ½ cup white wine or chicken stock

PREPARE

1. Brush the mushrooms clean and slice or chop if large (leave whole if they're the size of a quarter or smaller).

2. Heat the oil over medium-high heat in a skillet large enough to hold all the mushrooms in one layer no deeper than 1 inch. Add the mushrooms, thyme if using, salt, and a few grinds of pepper, and sauté, covered, until the mushrooms soften and lose their liquid, 10 to 12 minutes. The mushrooms will initially absorb all of the fat in the pan but will release it with their moisture as they cook.

3. Remove the lid, reduce the heat, and continue to simmer until golden. Deglaze the pan with the wine, scraping up any brown bits from the bottom. Remove from the heat.

PRESERVE

Refrigerate: Transfer to a small bowl or jar. Cool, cover, and refrigerate for up to 1 week.

Freeze: Press into ice-cube trays, cover well, and freeze for up to 6 months. (Transfer frozen mushroom cubes to a reusable freezer bag, press out as much air as possible, and return to the freezer, if you prefer.)

Mushroom Confit and Goat Cheese Tart

This tart is French-country rustic. And because it uses ingredients that keep well in the freezer, it's easy to whip up on the spur of the moment. Serve it in wedges for a light lunch, cut it into bite-sized squares for an easy hors d'oeuvre, or bring it to a potluck.

2 cups all-purpose flour

1 teaspoon kosher salt

¾ cup (1½ sticks) cold unsalted butter, cut into pieces

3 tablespoons ice water

1 (7-ounce) log goat cheese

1 cup Mushroom Confit (at left)

1. To make the tart crust: Combine the flour and salt in a medium bowl. Using your fingers or a pastry cutter, work the butter into the flour until it takes on a sandy texture, leaving some pebbles of butter. Add the water and lightly work it into the flour mixture, until the dough just comes together. Form the dough into a disk, wrap in waxed paper, and refrigerate for 1 hour before proceeding. (You can make this a day ahead or freeze it for up to 6 months. Defrost in the refrigerator before using.)

2. Preheat the oven to 350°F. Roll out the crust to ¼-inch thickness. Transfer it to a baking sheet lined with parchment paper. Spread with the goat cheese. Sprinkle with the Mushroom Confit. Bake until the crust is browned, about 25 minutes. Serve hot or at room temperature. | Makes one 9-inch tart

DRIED MUSHROOMS

Dried mushrooms bring deep flavors to a variety of dishes and are particularly welcome for the savory umami — the so-called fifth flavor, after sweet, salty, sour, and bitter — they lend to vegetarian preparations. Dried mushrooms are easy to make, easy to store, and a cinch to use. Toss them as is into soups, stews, and stocks. Or pour boiling water over them to reconstitute and use the plumped-up fungi and resulting "tea" in risotto, in pasta dishes, or as a base for an off-the-charts cream sauce.

INGREDIENTS

Any quantity fresh-picked mushrooms

PREPARE

Preheat the oven to 170°F, using the convection function if you have it. Brush the mushrooms clean and cut them into ¼-inch slices.

PRESERVE

Dry: Arrange the mushrooms on drying screens and place in the oven. Prop open the oven door with a wooden spoon to vent steam. Dehydrate until leathery, 2 to 3 hours. Store in an airtight jar for up to 1 year.

PICKLED BUTTON MUSHROOMS

Makes about 2 pints

A number of cultures lay claim to mushroom pickles: Italy, Germany, and Poland all have their style with these tasty bites. I've taken the United Nations' approach — this is a mash-up recipe that takes a little bit from each tradition.

INGREDIENTS

- **2** cups cider vinegar
- **½** cup brown sugar, packed
- **2** bay leaves
- **2** tablespoons salt
- **1** teaspoon whole black peppercorns
- **½** teaspoon fennel seed
- **1** pound white button mushrooms, stemmed
- **1** medium onion, chopped
- **1** small red bell pepper, seeded and chopped

PREPARE

Combine the vinegar, brown sugar, bay leaves, salt, peppercorns, and fennel seed in a large nonreactive saucepan, and bring to a boil. Add the mushrooms, onion, and bell pepper and return to a boil. Reduce the heat and simmer for 5 minutes.

PRESERVE

Refrigerate: Transfer to bowls or jars. Cool, cover, and refrigerate for up to 3 weeks.

Can: Use the boiling-water method. Ladle into clean, hot pint canning jars, covering the solids by ¼ inch with liquid. Leave ¼ inch of headspace between the top of the liquid and the lid. Release trapped air. Wipe the rims clean; center lids on the jars and screw on jar bands. Process for 20 minutes. Turn off heat, remove canner lid, and let jars rest in the water for 5 minutes. Remove jars and set aside for 24 hours. Check seals, then store in a cool, dark place for up to 1 year.

→ **See page 40 for more about vinegar pickles.**

dry (p.71)

infuse (p.68)

can (p.79)

freeze (p.61)

refrigerate (p.59)

Onions

*T*he allium family is a large and delicious one. Scallions, shallots, garlic, and yellow, sweet, spring, and red onions — they are all members of this group of edible lilies. Sharp and spicy when they're raw, all varieties turn temptingly sweet when cooked and pickled.

FRESH STORAGE RECOMMENDATIONS

CURED ONIONS CAN BE GOOD KEEPERS. I've seen the panty-hose method mentioned in a lot of preservation books, but truth be told, I haven't worn stockings in ages and it seems a waste to buy them just for onions! I store onions in wicker baskets to allow for good airflow. *Note:* They make good company for garlic, but keep them away from potatoes — they will rot those spuds in a flash.

CARAMELIZED ONION CONFIT

Makes about 2 cups

This spread is the simplest thing to make — as well as inexpensive — but it brings instant elegance to anything it touches. Pair the confit with goat cheese in a sandwich, strew some on a pizza, or simmer with good stock and garnish with a few croutons for a quick onion soup.

INGREDIENTS

- **½** cup (1 stick) butter or 4 tablespoons butter and ¼ cup extra-virgin olive oil
- **2** pounds onions, any variety, chopped
- **⅓** cup chicken or vegetable stock or water
- **1** tablespoon balsamic vinegar
- **1** tablespoon salt
- **1** teaspoon sugar
- **1** teaspoon dried or 1 tablespoon fresh thyme

PREPARE

1. Heat the butter in a Dutch oven or a large, heavy skillet. Add the onions, stock, vinegar, salt, sugar, and thyme. Cover and cook over medium heat until the onions are translucent, 5 to 10 minutes.

2. Remove the lid, reduce the heat to low, and continue to cook until the onions are a rich brown and thick and jammy, about 45 minutes. Add some water or a little more stock and deglaze the pan, scraping up any brown bits and glaze from the bottom.

PRESERVE

Refrigerate: Refrigerate in a covered glass bowl or clean jar for up to 5 days.

Freeze: Cool and transfer to ice-cube trays or small freezer containers. Cover and freeze for up to 6 months.

dry (p.71)

infuse (p.68)

can (p.79)

freeze (p.61)

refrigerate (p.59)

PICKLED RED ONIONS

Makes about 3 pints

These little numbers are sure to put some zing in your swing. Tart, sweet, and zippy, they give a lift to any sandwich. Share these pickles with friends or cut the recipe in half, if you like.

INGREDIENTS

- **2** cups distilled white vinegar
- **1** cup water
- **3** tablespoons sugar
- **1** tablespoon salt
- **2** pounds red onions, sliced

PREPARE

Combine the vinegar, water, sugar, and salt in a large nonreactive bowl, and stir to dissolve the salt and sugar. Add the onions and toss to combine. Let the mixture marinate until the onions wilt, about 1 hour.

→ See page 40 for more about vinegar pickles.

PRESERVE

Refrigerate: Ladle into bowls or jars. Cover and refrigerate for up to 3 weeks.

Pickled Onion and Potato Salad

- **2** pounds boiling potatoes, such as fingerlings or Red Bliss
- **¼** cup pickling liquid from Pickled Red Onions (above)
- **¼** cup extra-virgin olive oil
- **1** cup Pickled Red Onions, chopped
- **2** tablespoons drained capers (optional)
  Salt
  Freshly ground black pepper

Boil the potatoes in a large pot of salted water until just tender, 10 to 15 minutes. Drain and set aside. Whisk together the pickling liquid and olive oil in a medium bowl. When the potatoes are cool enough to handle, cut them into ½-inch slices. Add the potatoes to the bowl with the dressing, along with the onions and capers, if using, and toss to combine. Season with salt and pepper. | **Makes 4 to 6 servings**

SWEET-AND-SOUR PICKLED ONIONS

Makes about 6 pints

I came up with this recipe when I noticed that the onions were disappearing faster than the cucumber slices from my jars of Bread-and-Butter Pickles — my friends liked their sweet taste so much that they were picking them out. Well, they can stop fishing around; here's an onions-only recipe.

dry (p.71)

infuse (p.68)

can (p.79)

freeze (p.61)

refrigerate (p.59)

INGREDIENTS

- **4** cups distilled white vinegar
- **2** cups water
- **1** cup sugar
- **2** tablespoons salt
- **1** tablespoon celery seed
- **1** tablespoon mustard seed
- **1** tablespoon turmeric
- **4** pounds big, sweet onions, chopped
- **6** garlic cloves, sliced

PREPARE

Bring the vinegar, water, sugar, salt, celery seed, mustard seed, and turmeric to a boil in a large nonreactive pot. Add the onions and garlic and return to a boil, stirring to ensure that all ingredients are heated through. Remove from the heat.

PRESERVE

Refrigerate: Ladle the mixture into bowls or jars. Cool, cover, and refrigerate for up to 3 weeks.

Can: Use the boiling-water method. Ladle into clean, hot half-pint canning jars, covering the onions by ¼ inch with liquid. Leave ¼ inch of headspace between the top of the liquid and the lid. Release trapped air. Wipe the rims clean; center lids on the jars and screw on jar bands. Process for 10 minutes. Turn off heat, remove canner lid, and let jars rest in the water for 5 minutes. Remove jars and set aside for 24 hours. Check seals, then store in a cool, dark place for up to 1 year.

→ See page 40 for more about vinegar pickles.

MARTINI ONIONS

Makes about 3 pints

The martini is the little black dress of cocktails — a timeless classic and perfect backdrop for any accessory. Think of these onions as the bling for your next libation or serve them with a charcuterie plate. Stunning!

INGREDIENTS

- **2** pounds pearl onions
- **2** cups distilled white vinegar
- **1** cup water
- **1** tablespoon salt
- **1** tablespoon sugar
- **1** teaspoon fennel seed or caraway seed or a few juniper berries

PREPARE

1. Line several baking sheets with dish towels and set aside. Prepare an ice-water bath in a large bowl or clean sink.

2. Bring a large pot of water to a boil. Drop the onions into the water, no more than 1 pound at a time, and blanch for 1 minute.

3. Scoop out the onions with a spider or slotted spoon and plunge them into the ice-water bath. Continue blanching the onions in batches. Remove the onions from the ice bath with a slotted spoon and spread on the towel-covered baking sheets. Blot dry. Using a small paring knife, peel the papery skins from the onions.

4. Combine the vinegar, water, salt, sugar, and fennel seed in a large nonreactive saucepan, and bring to a boil. Add the onions and boil for 1 minute. Remove from the heat.

PRESERVE

Refrigerate: Ladle into bowls or jars. Cool, cover, and refrigerate for up to 3 weeks.

Can: Use the boiling-water method. Ladle into clean, hot pint canning jars, covering the onions by ½ inch with liquid. Leave ½ inch of headspace between the top of the liquid and the lid. Release trapped air. Wipe the rims clean; center lids on the jars and screw on jar bands. Process for 20 minutes. Turn off heat, remove canner lid, and let jars rest in the water for 5 minutes. Remove jars and set aside for 24 hours. Check seals, then store in a cool, dark place for up to 1 year.

→ See page 21 for more about blanching.

→ See page 40 for more about vinegar pickles.

Peaches

When I was young my grandparents would drive me and my cousins down to South Carolina to get a dose of our roots. We'd always return to Baltimore with bushels of fresh Carolina peaches, their fragrance filling the car as the sun beamed on them through the windows. These trips made me think of peaches as a distinctly Southern fruit, so I was surprised to find them growing so sweetly here in New England.

I enjoy them all season long — from the tart, firm, clingstone peaches in the beginning of the season to the sweet, super-juicy, freestone varieties that come along later in summer. Although I love them equally, you can't use clingstone peaches in the recipes that call for halved fruit, as it's impossible to wrestle the pit out of them without ruining the fruit's shape. You can use freestone peaches in any of the recipes, but save your clingstones for those that call for chopped or crushed fruit.

FRESH STORAGE RECOMMENDATIONS

PEACHES EXPIRE QUICKLY — WITHIN 4 DAYS OF HARVEST. I don't recommend refrigerating them; it won't make them last significantly longer and the chilled fruit is much less succulent. Put them on the kitchen counter with enough room for air to circulate between them and enjoy (soon!).

PEACH BUTTER

Makes about 6 cups

Try peach butter instead of the typical apple butter for your next breakfast spread.

INGREDIENTS

- **2** cups water
- **¼** cup bottled lemon juice
- **8** pounds ripe peaches
- **2** cups sugar
- **1** teaspoon ground cinnamon
- **¼** teaspoon freshly grated nutmeg

PREPARE

1. Combine the water and lemon juice in a large nonreactive pot. Prepare an ice-water bath in a large bowl or clean sink.

2. Bring another large pot of water to a boil. Working in batches of 2 peaches at a time, blanch the fruit in the boiling water for 30 seconds to loosen the skins.

3. Scoop the peaches out of the water and plunge them into the ice-water bath. Repeat with the remaining peaches. Drain.

4. One at a time, peel the peaches, cut them in half, remove the pit, crush the fruit in your hand, and add it to the pot of lemon water. Repeat with the remaining peaches.

5. Bring the peach mixture to a boil. Reduce the heat and simmer until the peaches are soft, about 10 minutes. Cool slightly, and then purée with a stick blender or run through a food mill.

6. Return the purée to the pot and add the sugar, cinnamon, and nutmeg. Simmer over medium-low heat until thickened, about 45 minutes. The butter is ready when a dollop on a plate does not weep juice around its perimeter.

PRESERVE

Refrigerate: Ladle into bowls or jars. Cool, cover, and refrigerate for up to 3 weeks.

Can: Use the boiling-water method. Ladle into clean, hot half-pint canning jars, leaving ¼ inch of headspace. Release trapped air. Wipe the rims clean; center lids on the jars and screw on jar bands. Process for 10 minutes. Turn off heat, remove canner lid, and let jars rest in the water for 5 minutes. Remove jars and set aside for 24 hours. Check seals, then store in a cool, dark place for up to 1 year.

→ See page 21 for more about blanching.

→ See page 54 for more about butters, sauces, and ketchups.

dry (p.71)

infuse (p.68)

can (p.79)

freeze (p.61)

refrigerate (p.59)

PEACHES IN SYRUP

Makes about 6 quarts

These peaches are a sweet taste of summer. The syrup isn't cloyingly sweet, a refreshing change from commercially canned fruits.

INGREDIENTS

- **6** (500 mg) vitamin C tablets, crushed
- **3** quarts cold water
- **4** cups ice
- **10** pounds freestone peaches
- **6¾** cups water
- **1¼** cups sugar
- **½** cup honey (local, if possible)

PREPARE

1. In a large nonreactive bowl, cooler, or your impeccably clean kitchen sink, create an antibrowning ascorbic-acid bath by dissolving the crushed vitamin C tablets in the 3 quarts cold water. Add the ice.

2. Bring a large pot of water to a boil. Working in batches of 2 peaches at a time, blanch the fruit in the boiling water for 30 seconds to loosen the skins.

3. Scoop the peaches out of the water and plunge them into the prepared ice water. Repeat with the remaining peaches. Using a small paring knife, skin, halve, and pit the peaches. Return the halved fruit to the acid/ice bath as you go, to prevent browning.

4. Scoop the peaches from the ice bath and drain. Pack gently but firmly into clean, hot quart jars.

Cut peaches in half around the pit and twist apart the two sections.

dry (p.71)

infuse (p.68)

can (p.79)

freeze (p.61)

refrigerate (p.59)

5. Bring the 6¾ cups water, sugar, and honey to a boil in a medium saucepan, stirring to dissolve the sugar. Remove from the heat and pour the syrup over the peaches to cover by ½ inch. Leave ½ inch of headspace between the top of the liquid and lid. Screw lids on the jars temporarily. Gently swirl each jar to release trapped air bubbles. Remove the lids and add syrup if necessary to achieve the proper headspace.

PRESERVE

Can: Use the boiling-water method. Wipe the rims clean; center lids on the jars and screw on jar bands. Process for 30 minutes. Turn off heat, remove canner lid, and let jars rest in the water for 5 minutes. Remove jars and set aside for 24 hours. Check seals, then store in a cool, dark place for up to 1 year.

Variation: Brandied Peaches

The brandy gives these peaches just a bit of an edge — not so much that they can't make an appearance at the family table, but just enough to add a little sizzle to their sweetness. Prepare peaches as described above. For the syrup, reduce the water to 5 cups and add 2 cups of brandy, 4 cinnamon sticks, and 8 cloves.

→ See page 21 for more about blanching.

dry (p.71)

infuse (p.68)

can (p.79)

freeze (p.61)

refrigerate (p.59)

GINGER PEACH JAM

Makes about 6 cups

I just can't get enough ginger. I use it here to give the peaches a little heat and an exotic back note. Feel free to use less if you're not such a fan.

INGREDIENTS

- **2** cups sugar
- **1** tablespoon Pomona's Universal Pectin
- **1** cup water
- **¼** cup bottled lemon juice
- **4** pounds peaches
- **2** tablespoons freshly grated ginger
- **1** tablespoon calcium water (included in the Pomona box)

PREPARE

1. Stir together the sugar and pectin in a small bowl and set aside. Combine the water and lemon juice in a large nonreactive pot. Prepare an ice-water bath in a large bowl or clean sink.

2. Bring another large pot of water to a boil. Working in batches of 2 peaches at a time, blanch the fruit in the boiling water for 30 seconds to loosen the skins.

3. Scoop the peaches out of the water and plunge them into the ice-water bath. Repeat with the remaining peaches. Drain. Using a small paring knife, peel, pit, and dice the peaches, adding them to the lemon water as you go.

4. Bring the peach mixture to a boil. Add the ginger and simmer for 5 minutes. Lightly mash about one-quarter of the mixture. Stir in the sugar-pectin mixture and return to a boil. Add the calcium water, stir, and remove from the heat.

→ See page 21 for more about blanching.
→ See page 27 for more about jams and jellies.

PRESERVE

Refrigerate: Ladle into bowls or jars. Cool, cover, and refrigerate for up to 3 weeks.

Can: Use the boiling-water method. Ladle into clean, hot half-pint canning jars, leaving ¼ inch of headspace. Release trapped air. Wipe the rims clean; center lids on the jars and screw on jar bands. Process for 10 minutes. Turn off heat, remove canner lid, and let jars rest in the water for 5 minutes. Remove jars and set aside for 24 hours. Check seals, then store in a cool, dark place for up to 1 year.

SPICY PEACH SALSA

Makes about 6 cups

Early clingstone peaches, or even slightly underripe ones, work well in this recipe. Just cut away the flesh from the pits as you peel them.

INGREDIENTS

- **3** pounds peaches
- **1** cup cider vinegar
- **1** cup brown sugar, lightly packed
- **1** tablespoon ground cumin
- **1** tablespoon salt
- **1** pound tomatoes, cored, seeded, and diced
- **1** red bell pepper, diced
- **1** jalapeño pepper, diced
- **1** red onion, diced
- **¼** cup minced fresh cilantro

PREPARE

1. Prepare an ice-water bath in a large bowl or clean sink.

2. Bring a large pot of water to a boil. Working in batches of 2 peaches at a time, blanch the fruit in the boiling water for 30 seconds to loosen the skins.

3. Scoop the peaches out of the water and plunge them into the ice-water bath. Repeat with the remaining peaches. Drain.

4. Combine the vinegar, brown sugar, cumin, and salt in a large nonreactive pot. Using a small paring knife, peel, pit, and dice the peaches, adding them to the pot as you go to prevent browning. Add the tomatoes, bell pepper, jalapeño, and onion, and bring to a boil. Reduce the heat and simmer until thickened, about 15 minutes. Add the cilantro and remove from the heat.

PRESERVE

Refrigerate: Ladle into bowls or jars. Cool, cover, and refrigerate for up to 1 week.

Can: Use the boiling-water method. Ladle into clean, hot half-pint canning jars, leaving ½ inch of headspace. Release trapped air. Wipe the rims clean; center lids on the jars and screw on jar bands. Process for 15 minutes. Turn off heat, remove canner lid, and let jars rest in the water for 5 minutes. Remove jars and set aside for 24 hours. Check seals, then store in a cool, dark place for up to 1 year.

→ See page 21 for more about blanching.
→ See page 52 for more about salsas, chutneys, and relishes.

dry (p.71)

infuse (p.68)

can (p.79)

freeze (p.61)

refrigerate (p.59)

PICKLED GINGER PEACHES

Makes about 2 quarts

There are some dishes so quintessentially Southern that they never make it north of the Mason-Dixon line, and Pickled Ginger Peaches is one of them. The vinegar-and-fruit combo might sound odd to a Yankee, but put up a batch of these and you'll be whistling Dixie no matter where you live. I have adapted this recipe from one in Bon Appétit, Y'all, *a treasure of a book from my dear friend, and an authentic Georgia peach herself, Virginia Willis. For best results, use ripe but firm peaches.*

INGREDIENTS

- **6** (500 mg) vitamin C tablets, crushed
- **2** quarts cold water
- **2** cups ice
- **5** pounds peaches (10–12)
- **4** cups distilled white vinegar
- **4** cups sugar
- **1** (2-inch) knob ginger, sliced into coins
- **2** cinnamon sticks
- **1** teaspoon ground allspice
- **1** teaspoon whole cloves

PREPARE

1. In a large nonreactive bowl, cooler, or your impeccably clean kitchen sink, create an antibrowning ascorbic-acid bath by dissolving the crushed vitamin C tablets in the cold water. Add the ice.

2. Bring a large pot of water to a boil. Working in batches of 2 peaches at a time, blanch the fruit in the boiling water for 30 seconds to loosen the skins.

3. Scoop the peaches out of the water and plunge them into the prepared ice water. Repeat with the remaining peaches. Drain. Using a small paring knife, peel, pit, and halve the peaches, returning them to the ice bath as you go.

4. Bring the vinegar, sugar, ginger, cinnamon, allspice, and cloves to a boil in a large non-reactive saucepan, stirring to dissolve the sugar. Add the drained peaches, return to a boil, and then reduce the heat and simmer until tender, about 10 minutes.

PRESERVE

Refrigerate: Ladle into bowls or jars. Cool, cover, and refrigerate for up to 3 weeks.

Can: Use the boiling-water method. Ladle into clean, hot quart canning jars, covering the peaches by ½ inch with liquid. Leave ½ inch of headspace between the top of the liquid and the lid. Screw lids on the jars temporarily. Gently swirl each jar to release trapped air bubbles. Remove the lids and add syrup, if necessary, to achieve proper headspace. Wipe the rims clean; center lids on the jars and screw on jar bands. Process for 20 minutes. Turn off heat, remove canner lid, and let jars rest in the water for 5 minutes. Remove jars and set aside for 24 hours. Check seals, then store in a cool, dark place for up to 1 year.

→ See page 21 for more about blanching.
→ See page 40 for more about vinegar pickles.

Putting Pickled Ginger Peaches to Work

This is one peach you don't need to save for dessert. Serve them with a holiday meal, as Virginia does, for a little Southern hospitality — and a whiff of summer — in the middle of winter.

PEACH LEATHER

One quart of fruit makes about 1 (17-inch) sheet of leather

Drying peach purée into leather is an easy project to do with kids on a rainy summer day.

INGREDIENTS

- **2** pounds peaches
- **1** cup water
- **2** tablespoons bottled lemon juice
- **¼** cup sugar

PREPARE

1. Prepare an ice-water bath in a large bowl or clean sink.

2. Bring a large pot of water to a boil. Working in batches of 2 peaches at a time, blanch the fruit in the boiling water for 30 seconds to loosen the skins.

3. Scoop the peaches out of the water and plunge them into the ice-water bath. Repeat with the remaining peaches. Drain. Using a small paring knife, peel, pit, and roughly chop the peaches.

4. Bring the peaches and the 1 cup water to a boil in a medium nonreactive saucepan. Simmer until they begin to break down, about 5 minutes. Remove the fruit from the heat, let cool slightly, and purée with a traditional blender or a stick blender, or by running it through a food mill.

5. Preheat the oven to 170°F. Line a jelly-roll pan or a rimmed baking sheet with parchment paper or a Silpat and set aside.

6. Return the purée to the pot and simmer over low heat, stirring frequently, until it thickens to the consistency of baby food. Add the lemon juice and sugar and stir to dissolve.

PRESERVE

▦ Dry:

1. Spread the purée on the baking sheet, tilting it to create an even layer about ⅛ inch thick. Dry in the oven until tacky to the touch, about 2 hours.

2. Cool to room temperature. Slide the parchment onto a cutting board and roll the leather into a tube. Slice the tube into 2-inch segments and store in a covered jar for up to 1 month.

→ See page 21 for more about blanching.

Pears

*T*he poor pear: It doesn't enjoy a fraction of the celebrity of the apple; there is no Johnny Pearseed legend; nobody strives to make it in the Big Pear. It lags behind the apple in annual sales. For me, though, pears are the winning fruit. Surely more succulent than apples, they are equally portable and can be substituted in many recipes. I say: Eat more pears, and start here.

FRESH STORAGE RECOMMENDATIONS

PEARS DO WELL IN THE REFRIGERATOR'S CRISPER or in a root cellar with a cool, moist corner. They will keep in either cool environment for 4 to 6 weeks or longer, depending on their ripeness.

Note: Whether storing in the refrigerator or root cellar, be sure to provide some sort of barrier from other foods — either by distance or by wrapping the fruit in bags or newsprint or, in the cellar, burying it in dry leaves — as the ethylene gas emitted by pears will accelerate the ripening of any neighboring produce.

PEARS IN SYRUP

Makes about 4 quarts

This lightly sweetened syrup is a barely-there preserving liquid, so low in sugar that the pears stay fresh-tasting. You can use any variety of pear that you like, but make sure that you choose fruit that is not overripe. You want it firm enough to withstand the process without falling apart.

INGREDIENTS

- **6** (500 mg) vitamin C tablets, crushed
- **2** quarts cold water
- **6** pounds pears
- **6** cups water
- **1** cup sugar
- **1** cup bottled lemon juice

PREPARE

1. In a large nonreactive bowl, cooler, or your impeccably clean kitchen sink, create an antibrowning ascorbic-acid bath by dissolving the crushed vitamin C tablets in the 2 quarts cold water.

2. Using a small paring knife, peel and halve the pears. Remove the cores with a melon baller or small spoon. Drop the pear halves into the acid bath as you go.

3. Bring the 6 cups water, sugar, and lemon juice to a boil in a medium nonreactive saucepan, stirring to dissolve the sugar. Scoop the pear halves from the acid bath and drain. Add the fruit to the boiling syrup and simmer for 5 minutes.

4. Pack the pears gently but firmly into 4 clean, hot quart jars. Ladle hot syrup over the pears to cover by ½ inch. Leave ½ inch of headspace between the top of the liquid and the lid. Screw lids on the jars temporarily. Gently swirl the jars to release trapped air bubbles. Remove the lids and add syrup, if necessary, to achieve proper headspace.

PRESERVE

🅒 **Can:** Use the boiling-water method. Wipe the rims clean; center lids on the jars and screw on jar bands. Process for 25 minutes. Turn off heat, remove canner lid, and let jars rest in the water for 5 minutes. Remove jars and set aside for 24 hours. Check seals, then store in a cool, dark place for up to 1 year.

dry (p.71)

infuse (p.68)

can (p.79)

freeze (p.61)

refrigerate (p.59)

dry (p.71)

infuse (p.68)

can (p.79)

freeze (p.61)

refrigerate (p.59)

DRIED PEAR CHIPS

Makes about 3 cups

Enjoy these chips as a delicious, wholesome snack or chop them up and incorporate them into your favorite stuffing, trail mix, or granola.

INGREDIENTS

6 (500 mg) vitamin C tablets, crushed

2 cups cold water

6 pears

PREPARE

1. Preheat the oven to 170°F. To prepare an antibrowning ascorbic-acid bath, dissolve the crushed vitamin C tablets in the water in a large nonreactive bowl.

2. Peel and core the pears and cut them into ¼-inch slices. Put the pears in the acid bath as you cut them, and then soak them for 10 minutes.

PRESERVE

⊞ Dry:

1. Pat the slices dry and arrange them on a metal screen or cake cooling rack and set in the oven. Prop open the oven door with a wooden spoon handle to allow moisture to escape. Dry in the oven until leathery, 5 to 7 hours. Slices are fully dry when you can squeeze a handful and they don't stick together.

2. Let the chips cool, and then transfer them to a covered container to condition for 1 week. This allows the dried fruit to redistribute any trapped moisture. If you notice moisture on the sides of the container, repeat the drying process for another hour or so. The chips will keep in an airtight container for up to 1 year.

PEAR CHUTNEY

Makes about 5 pints

This chutney is a natural companion for Indian dishes or "low-and-slow" recipes, such as pot roast or baked ham.

INGREDIENTS

4 cups chopped pears (4–6 pears)

2 cups apple cider vinegar

2 cups brown sugar, lightly packed

1 cup finely chopped onions

1 cup golden raisins

1 tablespoon freshly grated ginger

2 garlic cloves, minced

2 teaspoons ground allspice

1 teaspoon salt

PREPARE

Combine the pears, vinegar, brown sugar, onions, raisins, ginger, garlic, allspice, and salt in a large nonreactive saucepan, and bring to a boil, stirring constantly until the sugar dissolves. Reduce the heat to medium-low and simmer for 30 minutes, stirring occasionally. Remove from the heat.

PRESERVE

Refrigerate: Ladle into bowls or jars. Cool, cover, and refrigerate for up to 3 weeks.

Can: Use the boiling-water method. Ladle into clean, hot pint canning jars, leaving ½ inch of headspace. Release trapped air. Wipe the rims clean; center lids on the jars and screw on jar bands. Process for 15 minutes. Turn off heat, remove canner lid, and let jars rest in the water for 5 minutes. Remove jars and set aside for 24 hours. Check seals, then store in a cool, dark place for up to 1 year.

→ See page 52 for more about salsas, chutneys, and relishes.

HOMEMADE PEAR SAUCE

Makes about 4 cups

This twist on applesauce is a good variation for the kiddies but grown-up enough to make a lovely accompaniment to roast meats such as turkey and pork. Double the recipe if you have a bounty of pears to process.

INGREDIENTS

- **½** cup water
- **1** tablespoon bottled lemon juice
- **3** pounds pears
  Sugar to taste

PREPARE

1. Pour the water and lemon juice into a large nonreactive stockpot.

2. Stem and quarter the pears, tossing them into the lemon water as you go to prevent browning. Bring the mixture to a boil and simmer until the pears are tender, 10 to 20 minutes.

3. Let cool slightly, and then pass through a food mill. Return to the heat and add sugar if you like, 2 tablespoons at a time, until the sauce reaches desired sweetness. Remove from the heat.

PRESERVE

Refrigerate: Ladle into bowls or jars. Cool, cover, and refrigerate for up to 2 weeks.

Freeze: Transfer to freezer containers, cool, then cover and refrigerate until cold. Freeze, covered, for up to 6 months.

Can: Use the boiling-water method. Ladle into clean, hot half-pint canning jars, leaving ¼ inch of headspace. Release trapped air. Wipe the rims clean; center lids on the jars and screw on jar bands. Process for 10 minutes. Turn off heat, remove canner lid, and let jars rest in the water for 5 minutes. Remove jars and set aside for 24 hours. Check seals, then store in a cool, dark place for up to 1 year.

→ See page 54 for more about butters, sauces, and ketchups.

PEAR BUTTER

Makes about 4 cups

Richer and silkier than Homemade Pear Sauce, this variation on apple butter has a delicate, subtle flavor. You can use any variety of pears that you like or a combination if that's what you have on hand. Because you don't need them to retain their shape, this is a great use for very ripe pears that are too soft for other applications.

INGREDIENTS

- **2** cups apple cider or water
- **¼** cup bottled lemon juice
- **8** pounds pears
- **1** cup sugar
- **1** cup honey, preferably local
- **1** tablespoon ground cinnamon
- **¼** teaspoon freshly grated nutmeg

PREPARE

1. Pour the cider and lemon juice into a large nonreactive pot.

2. Stem and quarter the pears, tossing them into the pot as you go to prevent browning. Bring the mixture to a boil. Reduce the heat and simmer until the pears are very soft, 20 to 30 minutes.

3. Let cool slightly, and then run through a food mill to remove the seeds and skins. Return the purée to the pot and add the sugar, honey, cinnamon, and nutmeg. Simmer over medium-low heat until the mixture is thickened, 30 to 40 minutes. The pear butter is ready when a dollop on a plate does not weep juice around its perimeter. Remove from the heat.

PRESERVE

Refrigerate: Ladle into bowls or jars. Cool, cover, and refrigerate for up to 2 weeks.

Can: Use the boiling-water method. Ladle into clean, hot half-pint canning jars, leaving ¼ inch of headspace. Release trapped air. Wipe the rims clean; center lids on the jars and screw on jar bands. Process for 15 minutes. Turn off heat, remove canner lid, and let jars rest in the water for 5 minutes. Remove jars and set aside for 24 hours. Check seals, then store in a cool, dark place for up to 1 year.

dry (p.71)

infuse (p.68)

can (p.79)

freeze (p.61)

refrigerate (p.59)

→ See page 54 for more about butters, sauces, and ketchups.

PICKLED PEARS

Makes about 4 quarts

These whole pears look beautiful in the jar, and they taste terrific too. Pickled fruit is a surprising departure from the more commonplace fruit in syrup — the brine gives it a sophisticated edge and enough of a bite to work as a savory side dish, yet the pears retain enough sweetness to take center stage as dessert.

INGREDIENTS

- **6** (500 mg) vitamin C tablets, crushed
- **2** quarts cold water
- **4** cups apple cider vinegar
- **2** cups water
- **8** cups sugar
- **4** cinnamon sticks, cut into 4-inch pieces
- **1** (2-inch) knob ginger, sliced into coins
- **8** pounds Seckel or other small, firm pears

PREPARE

1. In a large nonreactive bowl, cooler, or your impeccably clean kitchen sink, create an antibrowning ascorbic-acid bath by dissolving the crushed vitamin C tablets in the 2 quarts cold water.

2. Combine the vinegar, 2 cups water, sugar, cinnamon sticks, and ginger in a large nonreactive pot and bring to a boil. Reduce the heat and simmer for 20 minutes.

3. Meanwhile, peel the pears and trim off ¼ inch of the blossom end, adding them to the acid bath as you go. Transfer the peeled pears to the pot of brine and simmer until the pears are tender, 20 to 30 minutes. Remove from the heat.

PRESERVE

Can: Use the boiling-water method. Pack the pears into four clean, hot quart canning jars. Pour the pickling liquid over the pears to cover by ½ inch. Leave ½ inch of headspace between the top of the liquid and the lid. Release trapped air. Wipe the rims clean; center lids on the jars and screw on jar bands. Process for 25 minutes. Turn off heat, remove canner lid, and let jars rest in the water for 5 minutes. Remove jars and set aside for 24 hours. Check seals, then store in a cool, dark place for up to 1 year.

→ See page 40 for more about vinegar pickles.

SPICED PEAR VODKA

Makes about 2 cups

Cooking the pears before you infuse the vodka brings out their sweetness. Ripe pears impart the fullest flavor. Use an inexpensive vodka, as the pear flavor will dominate.

dry (p.71)

infuse (p.68)

can (p.79)

freeze (p.61)

refrigerate (p.59)

INGREDIENTS

- **3** very ripe pears, peeled, cored, and cut into 2-inch chunks
- **¼** cup sugar
- **1** cinnamon stick, broken into pieces
- **1** vanilla bean
- **2** cups vodka

PREPARE

Put the pears, sugar, cinnamon stick, and vanilla bean in a large saucepan, and cook over low heat until the pears break down, about 15 minutes.

PRESERVE

Infuse:

1. Cool and pour into a large jar. Pour in the vodka and stir to combine. Set aside for 5 to 7 days. Stir daily and check for flavor after the fifth day.

2. Pour through a fine-mesh strainer, discarding the solids. Return the infused vodka to a very clean jar or the original vodka bottle. Keeps at room temperature for up to 1 year.

3. Serve chilled, over ice, or with a splash of seltzer.

Spiced Pear-tini

This cocktail makes a lovely prelude to an autumn supper.

- **2** ounces Spiced Pear Vodka (above)
- **1** ounce ginger liqueur, such as Domaine de Canton

Candied ginger (optional)

Combine the vodka and ginger liqueur with ice in a shaker and shake until chilled. Divide between martini glasses and garnish with a sliver of candied ginger, if you like. | **Makes 2 cocktails**

Plums

*F*armers' markets usually provide a wide variety of plums, and some you can't find anywhere else. Japanese plums are clingstone plums (the pit is attached to the flesh) and should be used in recipes in which the fruit will be chopped or diced. European plums are freestone fruits, which means it's easy to remove their pits. Use these in preparations that call for whole or halved fruits.

FRESH STORAGE RECOMMENDATIONS

PLUMS KEEP WELL IN THE REFRIGERATOR for up to 1 week. Let them come to room temperature before eating.

HOMEMADE PRUNES

Makes about 1 pint

These are delectable and far more "plummy" than store-bought prunes. You can dry them fully for a shelf-stable treat, but if you like them juicy, as I do, stop your drying while they are still moist and keep them in the freezer until you're ready to gobble them up. Use freestone plums for easy pit removal.

INGREDIENTS

- **6** (500 mg) vitamin C tablets, crushed
- **2** quarts cold water
- **2** pounds plums

PREPARE

Preheat the oven to 170°F. To prepare an anti-browning ascorbic-acid bath, dissolve the crushed vitamin C tablets in the water in a large nonreactive bowl. Cut the plums in half and pit them, putting them in the acid bath as you go. Soak for 10 minutes.

PRESERVE

Dry:

1. Pat the plums dry and arrange them on a metal screen or cake cooling rack, cut-side up, and set the rack in the oven. Prop open the oven door with a wooden spoon handle to allow moisture to escape. Dry in the oven until the plums are shriveled, about 6 hours. The prunes are fully dry when you can squeeze one and not feel moisture in your hand.

2. Let cool, and then transfer the prunes to a covered container to condition for 1 week. This allows the dried fruit to redistribute any trapped moisture. If you notice moisture on the sides of the container, repeat the drying process for another hour or so. Fully dried prunes keep in an airtight container for up to 1 year.

Freeze: If you take prunes off the heat while they're still moist, you can freeze them for about 6 months.

dry (p.71)

infuse (p.68)

can (p.79)

freeze (p.61)

refrigerate (p.59)

SUGAR PLUMS

Makes about 1 quart

Many of the recipes I've seen for sugar plums are a cookie/cake confection requiring a lot of dried fruit. Authentic sugar plums — recipes for which date back to medieval times — are candied plums. Over the course of 9 days, the plums' moisture is replaced by sugar, which acts as a preservative and makes the fruit as sweet as candy. These are pretty enough to inspire visions to dance in your head.

INGREDIENTS

- **4** cups sugar, plus additional for coating dried plums
- **2** pounds plums, halved and pitted

PREPARE

1. Sprinkle a layer of sugar in the bottom of a large Dutch oven. Follow with a layer of plums, cut-side down, and then another layer of sugar. Repeat until all ingredients are used.

2. Set the pot over the lowest flame and heat, very gently, without stirring. As the sugar dissolves into a syrup, increase the heat slowly to gradually bring the syrup to a boil. Remove from the heat, cool to room temperature, and cover with a dish towel and the lid. Set aside for 3 days.

3. On the third day, return the pot to the stove and slowly bring the syrup and plums to a boil. Cool, cover, and then set aside for another 3 days.

4. On the sixth day, return the pot to the stove and slowly bring the syrup and plums to a boil. Cool, cover, and then set aside for another 3 days.

5. On the ninth day, boil, one last time. Scoop the fruit out of the syrup and drain on a cake cooling rack set over a baking sheet lined with waxed paper.

PRESERVE

Dry: Dry in a well-ventilated place, turning daily, for about 1 week. When nearly dry but still tacky to the touch, toss the plums with sugar to coat. Sugar plums will keep in an airtight container for up to 1 month.

PLUM CHUTNEY

Makes about 9 cups

Sure, chutney is a great accompaniment to Indian food, but don't stop there. This sweet-and-sour condiment will spice up everything from a grilled cheese sandwich to a roast goose.

INGREDIENTS

- 2 cups cider vinegar
- 2 cups sugar
- 4 pounds plums, pitted and diced
- 2 large sweet onions, diced
- ½ cup diced prunes
- 2 tablespoons freshly grated ginger
- 2 tablespoons mustard seed
- 2 teaspoons salt
- Zest of 1 lemon, cut into thin strips
- 2 garlic cloves, minced
- ½ teaspoon ground cloves

PREPARE

Bring the vinegar and sugar to a boil in a large nonreactive pot. Add the plums, onions, prunes, ginger, mustard seed, salt, lemon zest, garlic, and cloves, and return to a boil. Simmer until thickened, about 30 minutes.

PRESERVE

Refrigerate: Ladle into bowls or jars. Cool, cover, and refrigerate for up to 3 weeks.

Can: Use the boiling-water method. Ladle into clean, hot 4-ounce or half-pint canning jars, leaving ½ inch of headspace. Release trapped air. Wipe the rims clean; center lids on the jars and screw on jar bands. Process for 20 minutes. Turn off heat, remove canner lid, and let jars rest in the water for 5 minutes. Remove jars and set aside for 24 hours. Check seals, then store in a cool, dark place for up to 1 year.

dry (p.71)

infuse (p.68)

can (p.79)

freeze (p.61)

refrigerate (p.59)

→ See page 52 for more about salsas, chutneys, and relishes.

CHINESE PLUM SAUCE

Makes about 3 cups

Richly spiced, full of flavor, you won't want to save it just for your moo shu. Be prepared for this condiment to become your new ketchup.

INGREDIENTS

- **2** pounds plums, pitted and chopped
- **½** cup cider vinegar
- **½** cup brown sugar, lightly packed
- **¼** cup soy sauce
- **3** tablespoons freshly grated ginger
- **2** garlic cloves
- **1** star anise

PREPARE

Combine the plums, vinegar, brown sugar, soy sauce, ginger, garlic, and star anise in a large nonreactive pot, and bring to a boil. Reduce the heat and simmer until thickened, 20 to 25 minutes. Fish out the star anise and discard. Purée the sauce with a stick blender.

PRESERVE

Refrigerate: Ladle into bowls or jars. Cool, cover, and refrigerate for up to 3 weeks.

Can: Use the boiling-water method. Ladle into clean, hot 4-ounce or half-pint canning jars, leaving ¼ inch of headspace. Release trapped air. Wipe the rims clean; center lids on the jars and screw on jar bands. Process for 10 minutes. Turn off heat, remove canner lid, and let jars rest in the water for 5 minutes. Remove jars and set aside for 24 hours. Check seals, then store in a cool, dark place for up to 1 year.

→ See page 54 for more about butters, sauces, and ketchups.

Asian Chicken Wrap

- **2** cups diced cooked chicken
- **1** tablespoon soy sauce
- **¼** cup Chinese Plum Sauce (above)
- **2** flour tortillas
- **1** cup shredded lettuce
- **1** cucumber, sliced into ribbons with a vegetable peeler
- Several sprigs fresh cilantro (optional)

Toss the chicken with the soy sauce in a small bowl and set aside. Smear half the Chinese Plum Sauce in the center of each tortilla, being careful to leave at least a 1-inch border all around. Arrange half of the lettuce, cucumber, chicken, and cilantro, if using, on the lower third of each wrap. One at a time, fold up the wraps, first folding the two sides of the tortilla in over the filling, and then, starting with the edge closest to you, rolling the wrap away from you. Turn seam-side down on a plate and serve. | **Makes 2 wraps**

Radishes

*R*adishes are some of the easiest vegetables to grow — even with my black thumb, I'm successful with them. They are also great for loosening compacted soil: throw in a bunch of seeds before you sow summer veggies to help you with the hoeing. However your garden grows, any type of radish works nicely in these recipes: red globe, French breakfast, black, even daikon. The cooking process mellows their heat but won't kill their flavor.

FRESH STORAGE RECOMMENDATIONS

RADISHES WILL WILT ALMOST BEFORE YOUR EYES if left at room temperature. Store them, covered, in the refrigerator for 3 to 4 days.

RADISH RELISH

Makes about 4 cups

The Indian flavors in this relish complement the vegetable's spicy nature. Stir some into curried chicken salad or creamy potato salad to liven up the flavors and add some texture, or drain it and stir it into yogurt for an instant raita.

INGREDIENTS

- **2** cups distilled white vinegar
- **1½** cups sugar
- **1** tablespoon kosher salt
- **1** tablespoon whole coriander
- **1** tablespoon cumin seed
- **1** tablespoon yellow mustard seed
- **2** pounds radishes, shredded
- **1** cup diced onion
- **1** (2-inch) knob ginger, peeled and grated
- **2** garlic cloves, minced

PREPARE

Combine the vinegar, sugar, salt, coriander, cumin seed, and mustard seed in a large non-reactive saucepan, and bring to a boil. Add the radishes, onion, ginger, and garlic, and return to a boil, stirring to ensure that all ingredients are heated through. Remove from the heat.

PRESERVE

Refrigerate: Ladle into bowls or jars. Cool, cover, and refrigerate for up to 3 weeks.

Can: Use the boiling-water method. Ladle into clean, hot half-pint canning jars, covering the solids by ¼ inch with liquid. Leave ¼ inch of headspace between the top of the liquid and the lid. Release trapped air. Wipe the rims clean; center lids on the jars and screw on jar bands. Process for 15 minutes. Turn off heat, remove canner lid, and let jars rest in the water for 5 minutes. Remove jars and set aside for 24 hours. Check seals, then store in a cool, dark place for up to 1 year.

dry (p.71)

infuse (p.68)

can (p.79)

freeze (p.61)

refrigerate (p.59)

→ See page 52 for more about salsas, chutneys, and relishes.

ASIAN PICKLED RADISHES

Makes about 3 cups

I prefer this recipe as a refrigerator pickle — the light flavors complement the crisp texture of an uncooked radish.

INGREDIENTS

- **2** cups thinly sliced radishes
- **1** cup rice or red wine vinegar
- **2** tablespoons fresh cilantro stems, chopped (optional but great!)
- **1** tablespoon mirin (rice wine)
- **1** teaspoon fish sauce
- **1** teaspoon soy sauce
- **1** garlic clove, crushed

PREPARE

Toss the radishes, vinegar, cilantro, if using, mirin, fish sauce, soy sauce, and garlic in a medium nonreactive bowl. Let sit at room temperature for at least 10 minutes to allow the flavors to combine.

PRESERVE

🔖 **Refrigerate:** Ladle into bowls or jars. Cool, cover, and refrigerate for up to 1 week.

→ See page 40 for more about vinegar pickles.

dry (p.71)

infuse (p.68)

can (p.79)

freeze (p.61)

refrigerate (p.59)

Pickled Radishes and Cucumber Salad

For an easy salad, toss Asian Pickled Radishes with sliced cucumbers. The salad is terrific tucked into a falafel or lamb kefta.

- **¼** cup pickling liquid from Asian Pickled Radishes (above)
- **2** tablespoons flavorless oil such as organic canola or safflower
- **1** teaspoon sesame oil
- **½** cup Asian Pickled Radishes
- **2** cucumbers, thinly sliced

Whisk together the pickling liquid, oil, and sesame oil in a medium bowl. Add the Asian Pickled Radishes and the cucumbers and toss to combine. Serve immediately. | **Makes 4 to 6 servings**

Ramps and Scapes

*R*amps, also known as wild leeks, and scapes, the sun-seeking seedpods of planted garlic, are rarely seen in grocery stores, even those selling the most exotic of produce. These seasonal treats are the exclusive territory of CSA members, devotees of farmers' markets, and home gardeners. "Garlic scapes are one of those ingredients that always beg the question, 'What is that?' from farmers' market shoppers," says Janine Meyer, of Fort Hill Farm in New Milford, Connecticut. "The first week I have to explain how to cook them," she says, "and the second week [customers] come back looking for more." If you've never known what to do with them, here's your answer.

FRESH STORAGE RECOMMENDATIONS

RAMPS WILL KEEP, LOOSELY WRAPPED, in the refrigerator for 3 to 4 days. Scapes are much more long-lived — I've had some in the fridge for up to 2 weeks and on the counter for almost as long.

PICKLED SPRING RAMPS

Makes about 1 pint

Ramps are a down-country staple that have worked their way up the culinary ladder to the kitchens of some of the best Manhattan restaurants. This pickled preparation offers a pungent blast of flavor that wakes up the taste buds after a long winter's nap. Serve with Asian noodles or chop the ramps and add them to scrambled eggs.

INGREDIENTS

- **1** pound fresh ramps, washed
- **¾** cup distilled white vinegar
- **¾** cup water
- **1** tablespoon sugar
- **1** tablespoon salt
- **1** teaspoon black peppercorns

PREPARE

1. Coil 3 or 4 ramps at a time over your hand and push them into a clean, widemouthed pint jar. Repeat until you have about an inch of space left at the top of the jar.

2. Combine the vinegar, water, sugar, salt, and peppercorns in a small nonreactive saucepan, and bring to a boil. Pour the preserving liquid over the ramps to cover.

PRESERVE

Refrigerate: Cool, cover, and refrigerate for up to 3 weeks.

dry (p.71)

infuse (p.68)

can (p.79)

freeze (p.61)

refrigerate (p.59)

→ **See page 40 for more about vinegar pickles.**

GARLIC SCAPES IN OIL

Makes about 1 pint

*When the scapes come, they come in droves. Raw, they have the pungent taste of raw garlic —
great in salads or puréed in a pesto. You can tame them with a little heat, however. Sautéed,
they have the taste and texture of asparagus, with just a whiff of garlic. Cooked this way, I can
pack them in the freezer to use whenever the urge hits.*

INGREDIENTS

- ¼ cup olive oil
- 2 cups finely diced scapes
- Pinch of salt

PREPARE

Heat the oil in a skillet over medium heat. Add
the scapes and salt and sauté until softened, 3
to 5 minutes.

PRESERVE

Refrigerate: Transfer to a bowl. Cool, cover,
and refrigerate for up to 3 days.

Freeze: Spoon the scapes into ice-cube
trays, cover, and freeze for up to 6 months.

Garlic Scape Frittata

Garlic Scapes in Oil impart extra zip to simple stir-fries, omelets, quiches, and frittatas, like
this one.

- 8 eggs
- ½ cup milk
- 1 teaspoon salt
- Whole nutmeg
- Freshly ground black pepper

- ¼ cup Garlic Scapes in Oil (above)
- 1 pound potatoes, steamed and cut into
  1-inch pieces

1. Preheat the broiler.

2. In a small bowl, whisk together the eggs and milk. Stir in the salt, grate in one-quarter of
   the nutmeg, and add a few grinds of pepper.

3. In a medium oven-proof skillet, heat the scapes over medium heat. Add the potatoes and
   toss to coat with the oil from the scapes. Add the egg mixture and shake the pan to distrib-
   ute the ingredients. Cook over medium heat until the frittata is done on the bottom and
   the edges begin to solidify, 5 to 10 minutes. Transfer the pan to the broiler and cook until
   lightly browned, 3 to 5 minutes. Serve immediately or at room temperature. | Makes 4 to
   6 servings

Rhubarb

*R*hubarb is related to sorrel and has a lot of the same citrusy notes. Some people, in fact, find it too tart to enjoy straight and mix it with sweet fruits when baking. I say, where's the rhubarb? In for a penny, in for a pound.

Before I met my husband, I had never tasted rhubarb, but his English upbringing brought this wonderful flavor into our home. His family has a long tradition of gathering around rhubarb crumble with custard sauce (like a cobbler with crème anglaise) at every reunion. It's very British, and very delish!

FRESH STORAGE RECOMMENDATIONS

Caution: Rhubarb leaves are toxic — never eat them, use as a garnish, or feed to pets. The stalks should be firm but will vary from pale green to bright fuchsia. Wash them in cold water, wrap in damp paper towels, and store in the refrigerator for 3 to 5 days.

RHUBARB SODA SYRUP

Makes about 2 cups

This soda makes a refreshing alternative to sweet colas and is a great treat for a sunny spring picnic.

INGREDIENTS

- 2 cups water
- 2 cups chopped rhubarb
- ¼ cup sugar
- ½ vanilla bean or ¼ teaspoon vanilla extract
- 1 liter seltzer

PREPARE

Bring the water, rhubarb, sugar, and vanilla bean to a boil in a small saucepan. Reduce the heat and continue to simmer until the liquid is reduced by half and the rhubarb falls apart, about 15 minutes. Strain through a fine-mesh sieve, discarding solids. Cool the syrup. To use, fill a pitcher with ice, pour in seltzer, and add 1 cup of the syrup. Stir to combine, and enjoy.

PRESERVE

⬡ **Refrigerate:** Keeps, covered, in the refrigerator for up to 5 days.

⬡ **Freeze:** Keeps frozen for up to 6 months.

RHUBARB PICKLE

Makes about 2 cups

This refrigerator pickle makes the most of this zingy spring fruit. Its tart flavor pairs well with rich dishes such as roast pork, ham, and goose: a pretty pink addition to the spring holiday table.

INGREDIENTS

- 1 cup distilled white vinegar
- 1 cup water
- ½ cup sugar
- 2–3 cardamom pods
- 8 black peppercorns
- 1 tablespoon kosher salt
- 1 pound rhubarb, cut into ½-inch pieces

PREPARE

Combine the vinegar, water, sugar, cardamom, peppercorns, and salt in a medium nonreactive saucepan and bring to a boil, stirring to dissolve the sugar and salt. Add the rhubarb and return to a boil, stirring to ensure that all ingredients are heated through. Remove from the heat.

PRESERVE

⬡ **Refrigerate:** Ladle into bowls or jars. Cool, cover, and refrigerate for up to 3 weeks.

→ See page 40 for more about vinegar pickles.

RHUBARB CHUTNEY WITH CLOVES

Makes about 4 pints

The cloves here bring a balancing warmth to the citrus flavors of rhubarb. The chutney is festive on the table and brings an exotic touch to even the most conservative Yankee pot roast.

dry (p.71)

infuse (p.68)

can (p.79)

freeze (p.61)

refrigerate (p.59)

INGREDIENTS

- **2** cups sugar
- **1½** cups cider vinegar
- **2** tablespoons freshly grated ginger
- **1** tablespoon minced garlic
- **1** tablespoon salt
- **4** whole cloves
- **4** whole peppercorns
- **2** pounds rhubarb, diced
- **1** cup diced onion
- **1** cup raisins

PREPARE

Combine the sugar, vinegar, ginger, garlic, salt, cloves, and peppercorns in a medium nonreactive saucepan and bring to a boil, stirring until the sugar is dissolved. Lower the heat. Add the rhubarb, onion, and raisins, and stew over low heat until the chutney is thickened, about 15 minutes.

PRESERVE

Refrigerate: Ladle into bowls or jars. Cool, cover, and refrigerate for up to 3 weeks.

Can: Use the boiling-water method. Ladle into clean, hot pint canning jars, leaving ½ inch of headspace. Release trapped air. Wipe the rims clean; center lids on the jars and screw on jar bands. Process for 10 minutes. Turn off heat, remove canner lid, and let jars rest in the water for 5 minutes. Remove jars and set aside for 24 hours. Check seals, then store in a cool, dark place for up to 1 year.

→ See page 52 for more about salsas, chutneys, and relishes.

SPARKLING RHUBARB JELLY

Makes about 2 cups

This is the prettiest jelly you will see on your shelf. It's an elegant addition to the brunch table, or pair it with some breakfast breads for a thoughtful hostess gift.

INGREDIENTS

- **2** pounds rhubarb, trimmed and cut into 1-inch pieces
- **1** cup sugar
- **2** teaspoons Pomona's Universal Pectin
- **2** teaspoons calcium water (included in the Pomona box)

PREPARE

1. Combine the rhubarb and 1 cup of water in a medium saucepan and simmer until the rhubarb falls apart, about 10 minutes.

2. Hang a jelly bag or set a colander lined with several layers of damp cheesecloth over a large bowl. Pour the fruit mixture into the jelly bag and let drain, refrigerated, overnight.

3. Bring 1 cup of water to a boil, and then pour it over the pulp in the jelly bag to release any remaining juice. Drain for an additional 30 minutes. Discard pulp.

4. Combine the sugar and pectin in a small bowl and stir to combine. Set aside.

5. Measure 2 cups of rhubarb juice into a small saucepan and bring to a boil. Add the calcium water. Pour in the sugar-pectin mixture, stirring to dissolve. Return to a boil, and then remove from the heat. Skim off any foam.

PRESERVE

Refrigerate: Ladle into bowls or jars. Cool, cover, and refrigerate for up to 3 weeks.

Can: Use the boiling-water method. Ladle into clean, hot 4-ounce or half-pint canning jars, leaving ¼ inch of headspace. Release trapped air. Wipe the rims clean; center lids on the jars and screw on jar bands. Process for 10 minutes. Turn off heat, remove canner lid, and let jars rest in the water for 5 minutes. Remove jars and set aside for 24 hours. Check seals, then store in a cool, dark place for up to 1 year.

→ See page 27 for more about jams and jellies.

B JAM

to macerate in the sugar
the fruit just enough to
and the heat of the boil and still maintain a bit of "tooth."

INGREDIENTS

2 pounds rhubarb, cut into 1-inch pieces

2 cups sugar

PREPARE

1. Toss the rhubarb and sugar in a medium bowl and let sit, covered with a tea towel, overnight.

2. Transfer the fruit to a medium saucepan and boil vigorously for 5 minutes (do not overcook or the rhubarb will disintegrate). Remove from the heat.

PRESERVE

Refrigerate: Ladle into bowls or jars. Cool, cover, and refrigerate for up to 3 weeks.

Can: Use the boiling-water method. Ladle into clean, hot half-pint canning jars, leaving ¼ inch of headspace. Release trapped air. Wipe the rims clean; center lids on the jars and screw on jar bands. Process for 10 minutes. Turn off heat, remove canner lid, and let jars rest in the water for 5 minutes. Remove jars and set aside for 24 hours. Check seals, then store in a cool, dark place for up to 1 year.

→ **See page 27 for more about jams and jellies.**

FROZEN RHUBARB

I'm crazy about the astringent, floral flavors of rhubarb and use it in both sweet preparations (such as the English crumble with custard) and savory ones (it makes a fantastic sauce for fish). Therefore, I never sweeten rhubarb before I freeze it. I do find that it helps to cut the stalks into the ½-inch pieces that I would use in my recipes. Rhubarb loses its crunchy texture in the deep freeze and isn't easy to chop when it's defrosted.

INGREDIENTS

Any quantity fresh rhubarb

PREPARE

1. Discard the leaves. Wash the stalks and cut away any dry ends. Chop into ½-inch pieces. Line several baking sheets with dish towels and set aside.

2. Bring a large pot of water to a boil. Drop the rhubarb into the water, no more than 1 pound at a time, and return to a boil. Blanch for 30 seconds. Scoop out the rhubarb with a spider or slotted spoon and plunge into a large bowl of ice water. Continue blanching the produce in batches.

3. Remove the rhubarb from the ice bath with a slotted spoon and spread on the towel-covered baking sheets. Blot dry.

4. Spread the pieces on a baking sheet and freeze overnight.

PRESERVE

Freeze: Transfer to freezer containers. Keep frozen for up to 6 months.

→ **See page 21 for more about blanching.**

dry (p.71)

infuse (p.68)

can (p.79)

freeze (p.61)

refrigerate (p.59)

Chandler's Proper Rhubarb Crumble

My sister-in-law, Chandler, makes this wonderful crumble. It's sweet and tart and very English, just like her.

- ¼ cup granulated sugar
- 1 teaspoon cornstarch
- 1 teaspoon ground cinnamon
- 6–8 cups rhubarb, cut into ½-inch chunks, or a combination of rhubarb and strawberries (if you must)

- 1 cup all-purpose flour
- ¾ cup brown sugar, lightly packed
- ½ cup rolled oats
- ½ cup (1 stick) cold unsalted butter, cut into 1-inch pieces

Preheat the oven to 400°F. Butter a 2-quart glass baking dish and set aside. Combine the granulated sugar, cornstarch, and ½ teaspoon of the cinnamon in a large bowl, and toss with the fruit. Pour the mixture into the baking dish. Combine the flour, brown sugar, oats, and the remaining ½ teaspoon of cinnamon in a medium bowl. Using your fingers or a pastry cutter, cut in the butter until the mixture is sandy with some pea-sized lumps of butter intact. Sprinkle the crumble over the fruit and bake until brown and bubbly, about 40 minutes. | **Makes 6 to 8 servings**

Strawberries

My kids wait all year for fresh strawberries. When they finally arrive in the farmers' market, I'm lucky if I can get a quart home — they woodchip right through them. The strawberries we find in the farmers' market are hugely different from those sold in the grocery store. A strawberry is a bright red, smallish fruit with complex flavor but a short shelf life. It's not meant to be as big as your fist (no matter how appealing such a monster would be to dip in chocolate on Valentine's Day) or to last for weeks in the fridge.

Until I started hanging out at farmers' markets, I didn't realize there were so many varieties of strawberries, and with very different flavor profiles. When they come into season in your area, ask the farmers what they're growing and do a taste test to see which ones you like best.

FRESH STORAGE RECOMMENDATIONS

IT'S DIFFICULT FOR ANY FRESH BERRIES TO MAKE IT HOME, but when they do, we don't refrigerate them. We eat them or process them within 24 hours to capture all of that tangy — and eagerly anticipated — flavor.

INDIVIDUALLY FROZEN STRAWBERRIES

Ripe strawberries expire rapidly — sometimes within just a day of picking. Before the clock runs out, pop them in the freezer. Whew! That was a close one!

INGREDIENTS

Any quantity fresh berries, cleaned and hulled

PREPARE

Spread out the berries on a rimmed baking sheet, making sure they don't touch each other. Pop it into the freezer until the berries are solid.

PRESERVE

Freeze: Transfer the frozen berries to an airtight container or bag, pressing out as much air as possible, and return to the freezer. They'll keep frozen for up to 6 months.

BACK-BURNER STRAWBERRY SAUCE

One quart of berries makes about 3 cups sauce

This recipe uses up a surplus of fresh fruit or even those berries that are beginning to look a little rough around the edges. As long as they aren't moldy, toss them into the pot — it will all taste great. Use the sauce to top waffles, pancakes, or ice cream; blend with plain yogurt into a smoothie; or purée with crushed ice and your tipple of choice for a summertime cocktail.

INGREDIENTS

Any quantity fresh strawberries, hulled
Sugar or honey (optional)

PREPARE

Rinse the strawberries and put them, with any clinging water, in a medium saucepan. Crush a few to release their juice. Bring gradually to a boil, stirring occasionally to keep the berries from sticking. Simmer until thickened, 10 to 15 minutes. Add a little sugar or honey, if using, to sweeten the sauce.

PRESERVE

Refrigerate: Transfer to bowls or jars and let cool. Store, covered, in the refrigerator for up to 1 week.

Freeze: Transfer to airtight containers or ice-cube trays and freeze for up to 6 months.

→ See page 54 for more about butters, sauces, and ketchups.

dry (p.71)

infuse (p.68)

can (p.79)

freeze (p.61)

refrigerate (p.59)

QUICK STRAWBERRY JAM

Makes about 4 cups

This recipe is a quick and easy way to keep strawberry jam on hand. Pomona's Universal Pectin gives the jam just enough gel.

INGREDIENTS

- **1** cup sugar
- **1** teaspoon Pomona's Universal Pectin
- **4** cups strawberries, hulled
- **1** teaspoon calcium water (included in the Pomona box)
- **¼** cup bottled lemon juice

PREPARE

1. Combine the sugar and pectin in a small bowl and set aside.

2. Place the berries in a medium nonreactive saucepan and crush with a potato masher. Slowly bring to a boil, stirring frequently to avoid scorching. Stir in the calcium water and lemon juice. Slowly pour in the sugar-pectin mixture and stir to dissolve.

3. Return to a boil, stirring to ensure that the mixture is heated thoroughly. Remove from the heat and let rest for 5 minutes, stirring occasionally to release air bubbles. Skim off any foam.

PRESERVE

Refrigerate: Ladle into bowls or jars. Cool, cover, and refrigerate for up to 3 weeks.

Can: Use the boiling-water method. Ladle into clean, hot half-pint canning jars, leaving ¼ inch of headspace. Release trapped air. Wipe the rims clean; center lids on the jars and screw on jar bands. Process for 10 minutes. Turn off heat, remove canner lid, and let jars rest in the water for 5 minutes. Remove jars and set aside for 24 hours. Check seals, then store in a cool, dark place for up to 1 year.

dry (p.71)

infuse (p.68)

can (p.79)

freeze (p.61)

refrigerate (p.59)

→ See page 27 for more about jams and jellies.

CLASSIC STRAWBERRY JAM

Makes about 3½ cups

This recipe requires a little time and patience, but it will produce one of the best spreads you've ever eaten.

INGREDIENTS

- **8** cups strawberries, hulled and halved if large
- **2** cups sugar
- **¼** cup bottled lemon juice

PREPARE

1. Toss the strawberries and sugar in a large bowl and macerate overnight to coax out the fruit's juice.

2. Transfer the mixture to a large nonreactive saucepan. Bring to a boil, stirring and crushing to release the juice. Stir in the lemon juice. Continue to cook, stirring frequently, until the jam reaches the desired gel, about 20 minutes. Remove from the heat and let the jam rest for 5 minutes, stirring occasionally to release air bubbles. Skim off any foam.

→ See page 27 for more about jams and jellies.

PRESERVE

⊘ **Refrigerate:** Ladle into bowls or jars. Cool, cover, and refrigerate for up to 3 weeks.

Ⓤ **Can:** Use the boiling-water method. Ladle into clean, hot half-pint canning jars, leaving ¼ inch of headspace. Release trapped air. Wipe the rims clean; center lids on the jars and screw on jar bands. Process for 10 minutes. Turn off heat, remove canner lid, and let jars rest in the water for 5 minutes. Remove jars and set aside for 24 hours. Check seals, then store in a cool, dark place for up to 1 year.

Variation: Strawberry-Vanilla Jam

Here's a twist on the classic recipe. Add a vanilla bean and you've got strawberries and cream. Prepare the strawberries as directed above. When the fruit begins to boil, slit the vanilla bean, scrape out the seeds, and add both seeds and pod to the jam mixture along with the lemon juice. Fish out the pod before transferring to jars.

dry (p.71)

infuse (p.68)

can (p.79)

freeze (p.61)

refrigerate (p.59)

STRAWBERRY VINEGAR

Makes about 3 cups

Flavored vinegars make great gifts. Use them to brighten salads or blend in marinades.

INGREDIENTS

- **1** pint strawberries, hulled and sliced
- **2** cups distilled white vinegar

PREPARE AND PRESERVE

Infuse:

1. Combine the berries and vinegar in a quart jar. Set in a cool, dark place for 1 to 2 weeks, checking for flavor after 7 days.

2. Strain the vinegar through a fine-mesh sieve and then a single layer of cheesecloth. Pour into decorative bottles or canning jars. Keeps for 1 year in a cool, dark place.

STRAWBERRY VODKA

Makes about 3 cups

This sweet potion is delicious and decadent — a fine libation to have on hand for warm evenings.

INGREDIENTS

- **2** cups not-your-best vodka
- **1** pint strawberries, hulled

PREPARE AND PRESERVE

Infuse:

1. Pour the vodka into a clean quart jar, and then add the strawberries. Set in a cool, dark place for 1 week, shaking the jar every few days.

2. Strain through a fine-mesh sieve, pressing the berries to release remaining juice, and return the infused vodka to a clean jar or the original vodka bottle. Keeps at room temperature for up to 1 year.

3. Serve chilled or in your favorite cocktail.

Strawberry Blonde

This summertime cocktail is fresh and flirty.

- **3** ounces Strawberry Vodka (above)
- **2** ounces Cointreau or other citrus liqueur

Sugar, to taste

Pour the vodka and Cointreau into a martini shaker with crushed ice. Shake until chilled, then pour into sugar-rimmed martini glasses. | Makes 2 cocktails

Summer Squash and Zucchini

There probably aren't any more prolific vegetables than squash and zucchini. At the peak of the season, the markets are bursting with them, neighbors are giving them away, and if you've got a garden, well, you're probably looking for every culinary nook and cranny in which you can wedge the stuff.

Zephyrs, eight balls, pattypans — squash varieties have great names. I like the array of shapes, and I use the different colors to bring visual interest to my dishes, but frankly, I think they all taste similar enough to be used interchangeably in these recipes. Whichever variety you choose, be sure to select firm, ripe squash. Overgrown specimens can take on a bitter flavor and pithy texture.

FRESH STORAGE RECOMMENDATIONS

SQUASH AND ZUCCHINI KEEP FOR 3 OR 4 DAYS IN THE REFRIGERATOR but tend to dry out and get quite spongy after that.

ZUCCHINI PICKLES

Makes about 4 pints

Pickles, they're not just for cucumbers anymore. Use up some zucchini in a quick fridge pickle; they'll be ready for eating, lickety-split.

dry (p.71)

infuse (p.68)

can (p.79)

freeze (p.61)

refrigerate (p.59)

INGREDIENTS

- 2 pounds zucchini, cut into generous ¼-inch coins
- 1 pound onions, chopped
- 2 cups ice cubes
- ½ cup salt
- 2 cups distilled white vinegar
- 2 cups water
- ½ cup sugar
- 1 tablespoon mustard seed
- 1 teaspoon celery seed
- 1 teaspoon black peppercorns
- 1 teaspoon turmeric

PREPARE

1. Toss the zucchini, onions, ice, and salt in a large bowl, and add enough cold water to cover. Set aside for an hour or two. Drain, rinse, and drain again.

2. Combine the vinegar, water, sugar, mustard seed, celery seed, peppercorns, and turmeric in a medium nonreactive saucepan and bring to a boil. Pour the brine over the vegetables and let cool to room temperature.

PRESERVE

Refrigerate: Ladle into bowls or jars. Cool, cover, and refrigerate for up to 3 weeks.

Putting Zucchini Pickles to Work

These pickles are wonderful in an antipasto platter. Their vinegar zing is a great counterpoint to rich meats. Or just swap them for regular bread-and-butters for a twist on an old favorite.

→ See page 40 for more about vinegar pickles.

ITALIAN-FLAVORED PICKLED ZUCCHINI

Makes about 6 pints

Squash and zucchini were made for Italian flavors. They look top-rate in the jar, too.

Note: *The boiling-water method is necessary to tenderize these cold-pack pickles.*

INGREDIENTS

- **4** pounds summer squash and/or zucchini
- **1** large onion, chopped
- **½** cup salt
- **4** garlic cloves, halved
- **4** cups distilled white vinegar
- **½** cup sugar
- **1** tablespoon dried oregano
- **1** teaspoon black peppercorns
- **1** teaspoon dried rosemary
- **1** teaspoon dried thyme
- **1** bay leaf, crumbled

PRESERVE

Can: Use the boiling-water method. Release trapped air. Wipe the rims clean; center lids on the jars and screw on jar bands. Process for 30 minutes. Turn off heat, remove canner lid, and let jars rest in the water for 5 minutes. Remove jars and set aside for 24 hours. Check seals, then store in a cool, dark place for up to 1 year.

PREPARE

1. Trim the ends from the squash and cut into spears 1 inch shorter than pint jars. Toss the squash and onion with the salt in a large bowl. Cover with cold water and set aside for 2 hours. Drain, rinse thoroughly, and drain again.

2. Pack the squash mixture into clean, hot pint jars and divide the garlic among them.

3. Bring the vinegar, sugar, oregano, peppercorns, rosemary, thyme, and bay leaf to a boil in a large nonreactive saucepan. Pour the hot brine over the vegetables to cover by ½ inch. Leave ½ inch of headspace between the top of the liquid and the lid.

→ See page 40 for more about vinegar pickles.

SQUASH AND ONION RELISH

Makes about 4 pints

Sautéed summer squash and onions is a popular Southern side dish — I grew up on it. This relish has a bit of that sweetness with some pickle tang.

INGREDIENTS

- **2** pounds yellow squash, ends removed, diced
- **2** pounds yellow onions, diced
- **1¼** cups salt
- **3** cups distilled white vinegar
- **1** cup sugar
- **1** teaspoon dried rosemary

PREPARE

1. Toss the squash and onions with the salt in a large bowl. Cover with cold water and set aside for 2 hours. Drain, rinse thoroughly, and drain again.

2. Bring the vinegar, sugar, and rosemary to a boil in a large nonreactive saucepan, stirring to dissolve the sugar. Add the drained vegetables, return to a boil, and simmer for 5 minutes.

PRESERVE

Refrigerate: Ladle into bowls or jars. Cool, cover, and refrigerate for up to 3 weeks.

Can: Use the boiling-water method. Ladle into clean, hot pint canning jars, covering the solids by ¼ inch with liquid. Leave ¼ inch of headspace between the top of the liquid and the lid. Release trapped air. Wipe the rims clean; center lids on the jars and screw on jar bands. Process for 15 minutes. Turn off heat, remove canner lid, and let jars rest in the water for 5 minutes. Remove jars and set aside for 24 hours. Check seals, then store in a cool, dark place for up to 1 year.

dry (p.71)

infuse (p.68)

can (p.79)

freeze (p.61)

refrigerate (p.59)

→ See page 52 for more about salsas, chutneys, and relishes.

Sweet Peppers

When I met my husband, he was a self-proclaimed pepper hater. After more than 15 years of subtle coercion on my part, that's slowly changing — due in no small part to these recipes. When I think of sweet peppers, I think of bells. However, sweet pepper varieties come in all shapes and sizes. Some look similar to chilies but don't pack any heat at all. I always ask growers at the farmers' market to point out the sweet ones. And I always have a taste before I put them in the pot. Better safe than sorry.

FRESH STORAGE RECOMMENDATIONS

MANY SWEET PEPPERS TURN FROM GREEN TO RED AS THEY RIPEN. If you bring yours home in the green stage, leave them on the counter to turn crimson. Store fully ripened peppers in the refrigerator for up to 1 week.

SWEET PEPPER JAM

Makes about 6 cups

Sweet or savory? You decide. Either way, this is heavenly with goat cheese.

dry (p.71)

infuse (p.68)

can (p.79)

freeze (p.61)

refrigerate (p.59)

INGREDIENTS

- **3** cups cider vinegar
- **2** cups sugar
- **2** pounds red bell peppers, diced
- **1** sweet onion, finely diced
- **2** garlic cloves, minced
- **1** tablespoon mustard seed
- **2** teaspoons Pomona's Universal Pectin
- **2** teaspoons calcium water (included in the Pomona box)

PREPARE

1. Combine the vinegar, 1 cup of the sugar, bell peppers, onion, garlic, and mustard seed in a medium nonreactive saucepan, and bring to a boil, stirring to dissolve the sugar. Reduce the heat and simmer for 15 minutes.

2. In a small bowl, combine the remaining 1 cup sugar and the pectin powder and set aside.

3. Add the calcium water to the pot. Pour in the sugar-pectin mixture and return to a boil, stirring to dissolve the sugar and ensure that all ingredients are heated through. Remove from the heat and stir for several minutes to release air bubbles. Skim off any foam.

PRESERVE

Refrigerate: Ladle into bowls or jars. Cool, cover, and refrigerate for up to 3 weeks.

Can: Use the boiling-water method. Ladle into clean, hot 4-ounce or half-pint canning jars, leaving ¼ inch of headspace. Release trapped air. Wipe the rims clean; center lids on the jars and screw on jar bands. Process for 10 minutes. Turn off heat, remove canner lid, and let jars rest in the water for 5 minutes. Remove jars and set aside for 24 hours. Check seals, then store in a cool, dark place for up to 1 year.

→ See page 27 for more about jams and jellies.

ROASTED PEPPER KETCHUP

Makes about 4 cups

This savory spread is such a cut above any condiment sitting on a grocery store shelf that it's almost a sin to call it ketchup. Dollop it on a burger or dunk fries in it, and you'll set a new standard for barbecues.

INGREDIENTS

- **2** pounds tomatoes
- **2** pounds red bell peppers
- **1** medium onion, chopped
- **1** cup cider vinegar
- **1** cup brown sugar, lightly packed
- **1** tablespoon salt
- **2** garlic cloves, sliced
- **1** teaspoon ground allspice
- **½** teaspoon ground cinnamon
- **½** teaspoon ground cloves

PREPARE

1. Prepare an ice-water bath in a large bowl or clean sink.

2. Bring a large pot of water to a boil. Drop the tomatoes into the water, no more than 1 pound at a time, and return to a boil. Blanch for 1 minute.

3. Scoop the tomatoes out of the water with a spider or slotted spoon and plunge them into the ice-water bath. Continue blanching the tomatoes in batches. Remove from the ice bath and drain. Peel, core, and crush the tomatoes.

4. Char the bell peppers as described on page 66 and roughly chop.

5. Combine the tomato pulp, peppers, onion, vinegar, brown sugar, salt, garlic, allspice, cinnamon, and cloves in a large nonreactive saucepan and bring to a boil. Reduce the heat and simmer for about 10 minutes, until the onions are translucent. Remove from the heat and purée with a stick blender. (Be careful of the boiling mixture — hot things are hot.)

6. Return the purée to the heat and simmer over low heat until thickened, 1½ to 2 hours. Remove from the heat.

PRESERVE

Refrigerate: Ladle into bowls or jars. Cool, cover, and refrigerate for up to 3 weeks.

Can: Use the boiling-water method. Ladle into clean, hot 4-ounce or half-pint canning jars, leaving ¼ inch of headspace. Release trapped air. Wipe the rims clean; center lids on the jars and screw on jar bands. Process for 15 minutes. Turn off heat, remove canner lid, and let jars rest in the water for 5 minutes. Remove jars and set aside for 24 hours. Check seals, then store in a cool, dark place for up to 1 year.

→ See page 21 for more about blanching.
→ See page 54 for more about butters, sauces, and ketchups.

SOFRITO

Makes about 1 pint

Sofrito is the thick, rich base of many Spanish and Latin American dishes. Sizzle some in the pan before you boil rice or add a bit to simmering or braising dishes to add depth of flavor.

dry (p.71)

infuse (p.68)

can (p.79)

freeze (p.61)

refrigerate (p.59)

INGREDIENTS

2	pounds tomatoes
½	pound green bell peppers
½	pound red bell peppers
¼	cup olive oil
1	onion, finely chopped
6	garlic cloves, minced
1	teaspoon dried thyme
	Salt and pepper

PREPARE

1. Prepare an ice-water bath in a large bowl or clean sink.

2. Bring a large pot of water to a boil. Drop the tomatoes into the water, no more than 1 pound at a time, and return to a boil. Blanch for 1 minute.

3. Scoop the tomatoes out of the water with a spider or slotted spoon and plunge them into the ice-water bath. Continue blanching the tomatoes in batches. Remove from the ice bath and drain. Core, peel, dice, and set aside. Remove the stems, seeds, and ribs from the peppers, and chop them finely.

4. Heat the oil in a large skillet over medium-high heat. Sauté the peppers and onions until the onions are translucent, 5 to 7 minutes. Add the garlic and thyme and sauté 1 minute. Add the tomatoes, reduce the heat to medium, and sauté until thickened, 20 to 30 minutes. Remove from the heat and purée in a blender or food processor. Season with salt and pepper.

PRESERVE

Refrigerate: Ladle into bowls or jars. Cool, cover, and refrigerate for up to 2 weeks.

Freeze: Divide the sofrito into two ice-cube trays and freeze. Transfer the cubes to a storage container and freeze for up to 6 months.

Sofrito Rice

2	tablespoons olive oil
2	tablespoons Sofrito (above)
4	cups chicken stock or water

2	cups rice
¼	cup chopped fresh cilantro or parsley (optional)

Heat the oil over medium heat in a medium saucepan. Add the Sofrito and sauté for 3 to 4 minutes. Add the stock and bring to a boil. Add the rice, return to a boil, and stir once. Cover the pot, reduce the heat to low, and simmer according to package directions. Remove from the heat, add the cilantro, and fluff. | **Makes 6 to 8 side-dish servings**

PICKLED SWEET PEPPERS

Makes about 4 pints

You can pickle any kind of peppers. These sweet peppers are great on sandwiches or as a pizza topping.

INGREDIENTS

- **4** pounds red or green sweet peppers, or a combination
- **3** cups distilled white vinegar
- **2** cups water
- **¼** cup sugar
- **1** tablespoon salt

PREPARE

Remove the stems, seeds, and ribs from the peppers, and cut into 1-inch strips. Set aside. Bring the vinegar, water, sugar, and salt to a boil in a large nonreactive pot. Add the peppers and return to a boil, stirring to ensure that all of the peppers are heated through. Remove from the heat.

PRESERVE

Refrigerate: Ladle into bowls or jars. Cool, cover, and refrigerate for up to 3 weeks.

Can: Use the boiling-water method. Ladle into clean, hot half-pint or pint canning jars, covering the peppers by ¼ inch with liquid.

Leave ¼ inch of headspace between the top of the liquid and the lid. Release trapped air. Wipe the rims clean; center lids on the jars and screw on jar bands. Process for 10 minutes. Turn off heat, remove canner lid, and let jars rest in the water for 5 minutes. Remove jars and set aside for 24 hours. Check seals, then store in a cool, dark place for up to 1 year.

→ See page 40 for more about vinegar pickles.

CHARRED SWEET PEPPERS

Sometimes it can seem as if I've waited all summer for peppers to turn red. Probably because I have — these are some of the last veggies to ripen in the field. I try to scoop up as many as I can before frost gets them. Layer them on a sandwich, purée them into hummus, strew them on a pizza, or make an addictive yogurt sauce/dip with them: their uses are countless.

INGREDIENTS

Any quantity sweet peppers

Enough oil to lightly coat peppers (you can use any light-flavored oil such as organic canola, grapeseed, or olive)

PREPARE

Have ready a hot grill or preheat the broiler. Rub the peppers with the oil. To grill, arrange the peppers over the hottest part of the flame. To broil, arrange them in a single layer on a baking sheet and broil 2 to 3 inches from the element. Grill or broil the peppers, turning occasionally, until all sides are black. Remove to a bowl or paper bag and cover or seal to trap steam. Let cool until they can be handled. Slip off the charred skins, pull away stems, and remove the seeds.

PRESERVE

Refrigerate: Transfer to bowls or jars. Cool, cover, and refrigerate for up to 5 days.

Freeze: Divide peppers into ¼-cup portions and place in freezer containers or bags. Freeze for up to 6 months.

→ See page 66 for more about roasting.

Addictive Sweet Pepper Yogurt Sauce

This is one of my favorite uses for my stash of Roasted Sweet Peppers. The yogurt keeps it from being too rich. Use as a dip for chips or a sauce for grilled chicken, or drizzle over rice and beans.

2 cups plain whole-milk yogurt
4 ounces cream cheese, at room temperature
¼ cup Roasted Sweet Peppers (above)

1 teaspoon cumin
1 teaspoon salt
Juice of 1 lemon

Line a sieve or colander with a dampened coffee filter. Spoon in the yogurt and set the sieve over a bowl to drain for at least 1 hour and up to 8. (If draining for more than an hour, put the bowl in the refrigerator.) Transfer the drained yogurt to a blender or food processor (reserve the whey for another use). Add the cream cheese and process to blend. Add the Roasted Sweet Peppers, cumin, salt, and lemon juice and purée. Adjust seasoning and serve. | **Makes about 1½ cups**

Tomatillos and Green Tomatoes

Tomatillos are becoming increasingly popular. They have a mildly tart flavor that forms a great background for chili spice, making tomatillos a popular ingredient in Mexican cuisine. Similar to ground-cherries, they come wrapped in their own paper skin that you remove and discard before using. Without this skin, they resemble green tomatoes, which can be substituted in these recipes.

FRESH STORAGE RECOMMENDATIONS

AS WITH TOMATOES, I NEVER REFRIGERATE TOMATILLOS. Chilling turns their sugars into starch and you lose all of their sweetness. They keep, on the counter, for at least a week, maybe up to 12 days.

SALSA VERDE

Makes about 8 cups

This green salsa is great for chips and swell on chicken and fish, too.

INGREDIENTS

- **4** pounds tomatillos, husks removed
- **1** tablespoon lightly flavored oil such as organic canola, grapeseed, or olive
- **1** cup distilled white vinegar or bottled lime juice
- **1** pound yellow onions, chopped
- **½** pound chili peppers, stems and seeds removed
- **2** garlic cloves, peeled
- **¼** cup chopped fresh cilantro
- **1** teaspoon salt

PREPARE

1. Preheat the broiler. Wash and dry the tomatillos. Lightly brush half of the tomatillos with the oil and arrange on a baking sheet, stem-side down. Broil until blackened in spots. Remove and cool to room temperature.

2. Purée the remaining raw tomatillos with the vinegar in a blender or food processor, working in batches if necessary, and remove to a large nonreactive saucepan. Purée the onions, chili peppers, and garlic with the cooked tomatillos and any juice left in the pan, and add to the saucepan. Bring to a boil, reduce heat, and simmer until thickened, about 10 minutes. Stir in the cilantro and salt and remove from the heat.

PRESERVE

Refrigerate: Ladle into bowls or jars. Cool, cover, and refrigerate for up 5 days.

Can: Use the boiling-water method. Ladle into clean, hot half-pint canning jars, leaving ½ inch of headspace. Release trapped air. Wipe the rims clean; center lids on the jars and screw on jar bands. Process for 15 minutes. Turn off heat, remove canner lid, and let jars rest in the water for 5 minutes. Remove jars and set aside for 24 hours. Check seals, then store in a cool, dark place for up to 1 year.

→ See page 52 for more about salsas, chutneys, and relishes.

dry (p.71)

infuse (p.68)

can (p.79)

freeze (p.61)

refrigerate (p.59)

Vegetable Enchiladas

2 tablespoons extra-virgin olive oil

1 onion, diced

1 garlic clove, minced

1 tablespoon ground cumin

2 cups chopped fresh or canned tomatoes

2 cups cooked or canned black beans

1-2 cups leftover, frozen, or steamed
assorted vegetables (optional)

2 cups grated cheddar cheese

1 pint Salsa Verde (at left)

6 large flour or corn tortillas

1. Preheat the oven to 375°F.

2. Make the filling: Heat the oil in a large skillet over medium heat. Add the onion and sauté until translucent, 5 to 7 minutes. Add the garlic and sauté for 1 minute more. Add the cumin and tomatoes and simmer until thickened, about 5 minutes. Add the beans and vegetables, if using, and heat through. Remove from the heat and stir in 1 cup of the cheese.

3. Ladle ½ cup of the salsa verde into a 2-quart baking dish. Lay a tortilla in front of you. Spoon ½ cup of the filling onto the lower third of the tortilla and roll away from you. Place the filled tortilla seam-side down in the pan. Fill the remaining tortillas.

4. Ladle the remaining Salsa Verde over the enchiladas. Top with any remaining filling and the remaining cheese and bake until golden on top, about 20 minutes. | Makes 4 to 6 servings

dry (p.71)

infuse (p.68)

can (p.79)

freeze (p.61)

refrigerate (p.59)

FROZEN TOMATILLOS OR GREEN TOMATOES

If you've got extra tomatillos or want to get in the last of the tomatoes before frost, here's what to do.

INGREDIENTS

Any quantity tomatillos, husks removed, or green tomatoes

PREPARE

Wash, dry, and core the fruit. Arrange on a clean baking sheet and freeze until solid, at least 8 hours or overnight.

PRESERVE

Freeze: Transfer the tomatillos to large freezer bags, pressing out as much air as possible. Keep frozen for up to 6 months.

WHOLE CANNED TOMATILLOS

Makes about 4 quarts

Preserving the tomatillos whole keeps your culinary options open. When you're ready to use them, turn them into salsa, toss them into soups, or chop them into your favorite curry dish for a tart taste of summer.

INGREDIENTS

10 pounds tomatillos, husks removed, washed

8 tablespoons bottled lemon juice

PREPARE

1. Place tomatillos in a large pot with enough water to cover and bring to a boil. Reduce the heat and simmer until tomatillos begin to soften, 5 to 10 minutes.

2. Ladle tomatillos into clean, hot quart jars. Add 2 tablespoons of bottled lemon juice per jar. Pour cooking water over tomatillos to cover by ½ inch. Leave ½ inch of headspace between the top of the liquid and the lid. Screw a lid on each jar temporarily. Gently swirl the jars to release trapped air bubbles. Remove the lids and add liquid, if necessary, to achieve the proper headspace.

PRESERVE

Can: Use the boiling-water method. Wipe the rims clean; center lids on the jars and screw on jar bands. Process for 45 minutes. Turn off heat, remove canner lid, and let jars rest in the water for 5 minutes. Remove jars and set aside for 24 hours. Check seals, then store in a cool, dark place for up to 1 year.

Tomatoes

*L*ocally grown tomatoes taste different from those found in the supermarket. Unlike the fruits in the mega-mart, which are picked while they're still unripe and hard enough to withstand shipping, fresh-grown tomatoes ripen on the vine, so they're full of flavor. Many independent farmers grow heirloom tomato varieties, which can be traced back for generations. Yellow, orange, purple, black, green, and, of course, red heirlooms come in a wide range of shades and varieties. These tomatoes have more complex flavors and are often less acidic than commercially grown tomatoes. Whichever kind of tomatoes you get, their peak season is short, so get them while the getting's good.

FRESH STORAGE RECOMMENDATIONS

NEVER REFRIGERATE TOMATOES — it zaps them of their flavor and texture. Store them on the counter, stem-side down, and enjoy them before they go soft.

FROZEN TOMATO PURÉE

Makes about 6 cups

With this recipe, you'll always have fresh tomato taste on hand. Although the purée must cook for a good bit of time, it's mostly unattended and will leave the house smelling like summer.

INGREDIENTS

10 pounds tomatoes

PREPARE

1. Fill a clean cooler halfway with heavily iced water and bring a large pot of water to a boil. Drop the tomatoes into the boiling water, no more than 1 pound at a time, and return to a boil. Blanch for 1 minute.

2. Scoop the tomatoes out of the water with a spider or slotted spoon and plunge them into the ice water. Continue blanching the tomatoes in batches. Remove from the ice bath and drain. Core the tomatoes, and then peel away the skins with a small paring knife.

3. Crush one-quarter of the tomatoes into a large nonreactive stockpot. Cut the remaining tomatoes in half and add to the pot. Heat over medium-high heat until boiling, and then reduce to a simmer. Cook until the tomatoes begin to break down, 15 to 20 minutes, and then purée them with a stick blender. *Caution:* As always, be very careful when blending hot food.

4. Lower the heat to medium-low and continue to simmer for 2 hours, stirring occasionally. Let cool somewhat, and then ladle the purée into a large baking dish to cool completely in the refrigerator.

PRESERVE

Freeze: Transfer the cold purée to pint jars or freezer bags, leaving a quarter of the volume free for the purée to expand as it freezes. Freeze for up to 6 months.

→ See page 21 for more about blanching.

dry (p.71)

infuse (p.68)

can (p.79)

freeze (p.61)

refrigerate (p.59)

EASY-BAKE TOMATO PASTE

Makes about 4 cups

Tomato paste is so useful to have on hand. Stir it into soup and stew or add it to a slow-simmered curry or sauce; it instantly elevates the flavor of your dish. This recipe makes a nice, thick purée. Too thick, in fact, to process using the boiling-water method, so refrigerate or freeze it until you're ready to use.

INGREDIENTS

10 pounds tomatoes

PREPARE

1. Fill a clean cooler halfway with heavily iced water and bring a large pot of water to a boil. Drop the tomatoes into the boiling water, no more than 1 pound at a time, and return to a boil. Blanch until the skins begin to loosen, 30 to 60 seconds.

2. Scoop the tomatoes out of the water with a spider or slotted spoon and plunge them into the ice water. Continue blanching the tomatoes in batches. Remove from the ice bath and drain. Core the tomatoes, and then peel away the skins with a small paring knife.

3. Preheat the oven to 425°F. Working in batches, purée the tomatoes in a blender, and then pour the purée into a large roasting pan. Roast the purée, stirring occasionally, until it's thick enough to part when you run a spatula through the middle of the pan, about 1½ hours.

PRESERVE

Refrigerate: Ladle into bowls or jars. Cool, cover, and refrigerate for up to 1 week.

Freeze: Transfer to 4-ounce jars, leaving ½ inch of headspace, and freeze, covered, for up to 6 months.

→ See page 21 for more about blanching.

dry (p.71)

infuse (p.68)

can (p.79)

freeze (p.61)

refrigerate (p.59)

ROASTED TOMATO SAUCE

Makes about 1 quart

Well, it's not quite a sauce and it's not quite roasted tomatoes. This is a concoction that I came up with when I had an extra 5 pounds of plum tomatoes gasping their last breath on the kitchen counter and had to do something to use them up — fast. After cooking, you can leave this mixture as it is for a chunky sauce or bruschetta topping or purée it for a smoother consistency.

INGREDIENTS

5 pounds plum tomatoes, cored and chopped

2 tablespoons extra-virgin olive oil

2–4 garlic cloves, sliced
Salt

PREPARE

Preheat the oven to 350°F. Toss the tomatoes, olive oil, garlic to taste, and a pinch of salt in a 4-quart glass baking dish. Roast, turning once or twice, for about 2 hours, until all the juice has cooked off and the tomatoes begin to shrivel and brown.

PRESERVE

Refrigerate: Transfer to bowls or jars. Cool, cover, and refrigerate for up to 5 days.

Freeze: Freeze for up to 6 months.

→ See page 54 for more about butters, sauces, and ketchups.

HEIRLOOM TOMATO SALSA

Makes about 7 cups

Use any variety of heirloom tomato — or a combination. The different colors available make for a gorgeous salsa.

INGREDIENTS

1 cup distilled white vinegar

¼ cup sugar

1 tablespoon salt

3 pounds heirloom tomatoes, seeded and diced

½ pound onions, diced

1–2 jalapeño peppers, finely diced

1 cup chopped fresh cilantro (optional)

PREPARE

Bring the vinegar, sugar, and salt to a boil in a large nonreactive saucepan. Add the tomatoes, onions, and jalapeños, and return to a boil for 5 minutes. Add the cilantro and remove from the heat.

PRESERVE

Refrigerate: Ladle into bowls or jars. Cool, cover, and refrigerate for up to 5 days.

Can: Use the boiling-water method. Ladle into clean, hot half-pint canning jars, leaving ½ inch of headspace. Release trapped air. Wipe the rims clean; center lids on the jars and screw on jar bands. Process for 15 minutes. Turn off heat, remove canner lid, and let jars rest in the water for 5 minutes. Remove jars and set aside for 24 hours. Check seals, then store in a cool, dark place for up to 1 year.

→ See page 52 for more about salsas, chutneys, and relishes.

MY-WAY MARINARA

Makes about 7 quarts

I call this My-Way Marinara because the basic recipe gives me the flexibility to adjust the sauce to fit my needs as I use it. In the middle of winter, when I'm hitting my stash of this canned sauce, I can stir in some of the mushrooms or peppers that I've put by, add dried herbs if that's my mood, or chop in some root-cellared carrots or parsnips. So, you see, it's my way, whatever way that might be.

INGREDIENTS

- **25** pounds plum tomatoes, cut in half
- **1** pound onions, finely diced
- **4** garlic cloves, peeled and minced
- **3** tablespoons bottled lemon juice per quart (about 1¼ cups total)
- **1** teaspoon salt per quart (about 7 teaspoons total)

PREPARE

1. Put 5 pounds of the tomatoes in a large non-reactive saucepan with a splash of water. Cover and bring to a low boil over medium heat, crushing and stirring the tomatoes with a potato masher occasionally to release their juices.

2. Add an additional 5 pounds of tomatoes and repeat, continuing to crush and stir as you go. Repeat with the remaining tomatoes until all are crushed and boiling.

3. Reduce the heat and simmer the tomatoes for 15 minutes. Let cool slightly, and then run the tomatoes through a food mill to remove skins and seeds.

4. Return the tomato purée to the pot. Add the onions and garlic and bring to a simmer. Cook over low heat, stirring occasionally, until the sauce is thick, 1½ to 2 hours.

5. Transfer the sauce to quart containers and add 3 tablespoons of lemon juice and 1 teaspoon of salt to each quart.

PRESERVE

Refrigerate: Cool, cover, and refrigerate for up to 1 week.

Freeze: Freeze for up to 6 months.

Can: Use the boiling-water method. Ladle the sauce (adding the 3 tablespoons of lemon juice and 1 teaspoon of salt to each container) into clean, hot quart jars, leaving ½ inch of headspace. Release trapped air. Wipe the rims clean; center lids on the jars and screw on jar bands. Process for 45 minutes. Turn off heat, remove canner lid, and let jars rest in the water for 5 minutes. Remove jars and set aside for 24 hours. Check seals, then store in a cool, dark place for up to 1 year.

→ See page 54 for more about butters, sauces, and ketchups.

CANNED WHOLE TOMATOES

Canning whole tomatoes is a simple and rewarding process made even more so by good company. The steps involved make for great assembly-line work, so get your friends together, and put 'em up! (See page 93 for tips on working in groups.)

278

dry (p.71)

infuse (p.68)

can (p.79)

freeze (p.61)

refrigerate (p.59)

INGREDIENTS

For each quart of tomatoes:

- **3** pounds plum tomatoes (such as Amish paste or Juliet)
- **2** tablespoons bottled lemon juice or ½ teaspoon citric acid
- **1** teaspoon salt (optional)

PREPARE

1. Fill a clean cooler halfway with heavily iced water and bring a large pot of water to a boil. Drop the tomatoes into the boiling water, no more than 6 tomatoes at a time, and return to a boil. Blanch until the skins begin to loosen, 30 to 60 seconds.

2. Scoop the tomatoes out of the water with a spider or slotted spoon and plunge them into the ice water. Continue blanching the tomatoes in batches. Remove from the ice bath and drain. Core the tomatoes, and then peel away the skins with a small paring knife.

3. Put the lemon juice or citric acid and the salt, if using, into clean, hot quart jars. Pack the tomatoes into the jars one at a time, pressing firmly enough to compress the hollow core and release enough juice to cover the tomato but not so hard that the fruit is crushed. Continue packing tomatoes in this manner, being careful to press out any air pockets. Tomatoes should be covered by ½ inch with their liquid. Leave ½ inch of headspace between the top of the liquid and the lid. Top with a little boiling water, if necessary, to achieve the proper headspace.

Press on the tomatoes to release their juices as you pack them.

→ **See page 21 for more on blanching.**

🅑 **Can:** Use the boiling-water method. Release trapped air. Wipe the rims clean; center lids on the jars and screw on jar bands. Process for 85 minutes. Turn off heat, remove canner lid, and let jars rest in the water for 5 minutes. Remove jars and set aside for 24 hours. Check seals, then store in a cool, dark place for up to 1 year.

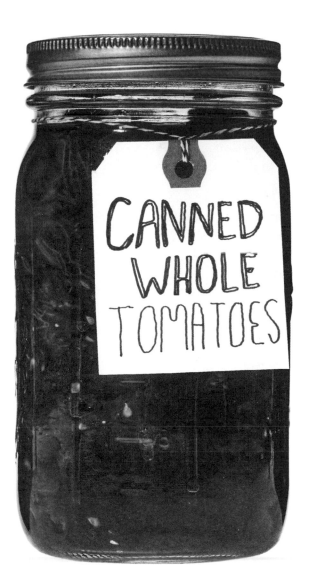

Quick Tomato Sauce

Whole canned tomatoes are so versatile — you'll run out of tomatoes before you run out of ideas for using them. The short simmer of this Quick Tomato Sauce showcases their bright summer flavor.

2 tablespoons extra-virgin olive oil

2 garlic cloves, minced

½ teaspoon salt

1 quart Canned Whole Tomatoes (above)

Heat the oil in a medium saucepan over medium-high heat. Add the garlic and salt and stir. Add the tomatoes one at a time, crushing them in your hand as you go, bring to a boil, and then reduce heat and simmer rapidly for 15 minutes. Do not stir (stirring inhibits the sauce's ability to thicken). If you think the sauce is sticking, give the pan a little shake. Toss with your favorite pasta or pour over grilled chicken or sautéed shrimp. | **Makes about 3 cups**

SPICY TOMATO ASPIC

Makes about 2 cups

Tomato aspic: I know, I know, "aspic" is so 1950s housewife. Let's call it "heirloom tomato gelée" — now we're hip and modern. Either way, it's really tasty on a turkey sandwich or served with some creamy goat cheese or queso fresco.

INGREDIENTS

- **2** pounds ripe tomatoes, cored and chopped
- **1–2** jalapeño peppers, stems and ribs removed, sliced
- **1** teaspoon salt
- **1** cup fresh cilantro stems (optional)
- **½** cup sugar
- **2** teaspoons Pomona's Universal Pectin
- **2** tablespoons distilled white vinegar
- **2** teaspoons calcium water (included in the Pomona box)

PREPARE

1. Bring the tomatoes, jalapeños, and salt to a boil in a large nonreactive saucepan. Reduce the heat and simmer, partially covered, stirring and gently crushing the tomatoes with a potato masher until they release all their juices, about 10 minutes. In the last 5 minutes, add the cilantro, if using. Cool slightly.

2. Transfer the mixture to a jelly bag or a colander lined with cheesecloth and hang, refrigerated, overnight. Do not press on the solids.

3. Combine the sugar and pectin in a small bowl and set aside.

4. Measure 2 cups of the tomato juice into a medium nonreactive saucepan and bring to a boil. Stir in the sugar-pectin mixture and return to a boil. Combine the vinegar and calcium water and stir into the boiling mixture. Remove from the heat and stir for 2 to 3 minutes to release air bubbles. Skim off any foam.

PRESERVE

Refrigerate: Ladle into bowls or jars. Cool, cover, and refrigerate for up to 3 weeks.

Can: Use the boiling-water method. Ladle into clean, hot 4-ounce canning jars, leaving ¼ inch of headspace between top of aspic and lid. Release trapped air. Wipe the rims clean; center lids on the jars and screw on jar bands. Process for 10 minutes. Turn off heat, remove canner lid, and let jars rest in the water for 5 minutes. Remove jars and set aside for 24 hours. Check seals, then store in a cool, dark place for up to 1 year.

→ See page 27 for more about jams and jellies.

Side tab labels:

- dry (p.71)
- infuse (p.68)
- can (p.79)
- freeze (p.61)
- refrigerate (p.59)

TOMATO ASPIC

FROZEN WHOLE TOMATOES

When tomatoes come to the market, or your backyard vines, they can come in spades. If I find my supply getting ahead of my schedule, I use this quick and easy preservation method to put them up before they pass me by.

INGREDIENTS

Any quantity fresh ripe tomatoes

PREPARE

Wash and dry the tomatoes. Arrange on a baking sheet in a single layer and put in the freezer.

PRESERVE

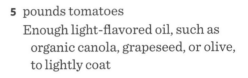 **Freeze:** Transfer the frozen tomatoes to freezer bags. They'll keep frozen for up to 6 months. Skins will slip off frozen tomatoes easily as they begin to thaw or when run briefly under warm water.

OVEN-DRIED TOMATOES

Make 2 cups

These tomatoes have all the flavor of sun-dried with bonus sweetness from little bits of caramelization. With a stash of these on hand, you'll never need to buy expensive sun-dried tomatoes again. Plum tomatoes work especially well.

INGREDIENTS

5 pounds tomatoes
   Enough light-flavored oil, such as organic canola, grapeseed, or olive, to lightly coat

PREPARE

Preheat the oven to 250°F. Cut the tomatoes in half and toss with the oil. Arrange, cut-side up, on two baking sheets. Roast for 5 to 6 hours, depending on size, until the tomatoes are shriveled and browned in spots.

PRESERVE

Freeze: Pack into 4-ounce jars or other containers and freeze for up to 6 months.

Watermelon

Who doesn't love watermelon? It's one of the rewards of a hot summer day. With its juice dripping down your elbows, it's a happy connection to childhood. Seed-spitting contest, anyone? When I was growing up, we had only one kind of watermelon: the oblong 20-pounder. No matter how you grabbed it, it always wanted to slip out of your grip. Now I see all kinds of melons — baby ones, gorgeous deep red ones, bright yellow ones, too — and they'll all work in these recipes.

FRESH STORAGE RECOMMENDATIONS

YOU CAN KEEP A MELON ON THE COUNTER FOR A FEW DAYS, but once you cut it, you have to store it in the fridge. With the cut side covered, it will keep for several days.

WATERMELON GRANITA

Makes about 1 quart

I'll take watermelon any way I can get it, and this is one of the best ways.

INGREDIENTS

- **1** cup sugar
- **½** cup water
- **1** small watermelon (4–5 pounds)

PREPARE

1. To make a simple syrup, bring the sugar and water to a boil in a small saucepan, stirring to dissolve the sugar, about 2 minutes. Set aside to cool completely.

2. While the syrup cools, prepare the watermelon. Wash and dry the fruit. Cut away the rind and remove any large black seeds. Cut into 2-inch chunks and purée in a food processor until smooth.

3. Combine the puréed fruit and the syrup in a shallow baking dish. Freeze for 2 hours, stirring every 20 minutes with a fork to create a slushy texture.

PRESERVE

⬡ **Freeze:** Keeps frozen for 2 weeks. If it freezes solid before serving, let it sit at room temperature for 10–15 minutes and stir with a fork to regain texture.

→ See page 24 for more about agua fresca and granita.

WATERMELON LIQUEUR

Makes about 6 cups

Let's face it, melon liqueur does not have the reputation of being a refined beverage. This concoction, with the fresh flavor of watermelon and just enough sweetness to support the fruit's natural sugar, elevates the category from "tarty barfly" to "cocktails at the club."

INGREDIENTS

- **1** cup sugar
- **1** cup water
- **1** quart puréed watermelon, from a 4- to 5-pound melon
- **1** quart not-your-best vodka
  - Juice of 1 lemon (about 3 tablespoons)

PREPARE

To make a simple syrup, bring the sugar and water to a boil in a small saucepan, stirring to dissolve the sugar, about 2 minutes. Set aside to cool completely.

PRESERVE

🌡 **Infuse:**

1. Combine the syrup, watermelon purée, vodka, and lemon juice in a large jar. Cover and set aside for 5 to 7 days. Stir daily and check for flavor after the fifth day.

2. Pour through a fine-mesh strainer, discarding the solids. Return the liqueur to a clean jar or the original vodka bottle. Keeps for up to 1 year.

3. Serve chilled, over ice or with a splash of seltzer.

→ See page 68 for more about alcohols and vinegars.

Watermelon

283

⊞ dry (p.71)

🌡 infuse (p.68)

⬤ can (p.79)

❄ freeze (p.61)

◈ refrigerate (p.59)

PICKLED WATERMELON RIND

Makes about 4 pints

The ultimate in home economics, this recipe turns trash (watermelon rinds you would usually throw away) into treasure, a beautiful translucent treat.

dry (p.71)

infuse (p.68)

can (p.79)

freeze (p.61)

refrigerate (p.59)

INGREDIENTS

- **3** quarts cold water
- **1** cup salt
- **4** pounds watermelon rind, pink flesh and green skin removed, cut into 1- by 2-inch slices
- **8** cups ice
- **8** cups sugar
- **4** cups cider vinegar
- **4** cups water
- **5** cinnamon sticks
- **1** tablespoon whole cloves
  Zest of 1 lemon, cut into strips

PREPARE

1. Combine the cold water with the salt in a large bowl or impeccably clean cooler and stir to dissolve. Add the watermelon rind and ice and let stand overnight. Drain, rinse, and drain again.

2. Put the rind in a large pot with enough water to cover. Bring to a boil, reduce the heat, and simmer for 10 minutes. Drain and set aside.

3. Combine the sugar, vinegar, water, cinnamon sticks, cloves, and lemon zest in a large nonreactive pot and bring to a boil. Add the melon rind, return to a boil, then reduce the heat and simmer, partially covered, for 1 to 1½ hours, until translucent.

PRESERVE

Refrigerate: Ladle into bowls or jars. Cool, cover, and refrigerate for up to 3 weeks.

Can: Use the boiling-water method. Ladle into clean, hot pint canning jars, covering the solids by ½ inch with liquid. Leave ½ inch of headspace between the top of the liquid and the lid. Release trapped air. Wipe the rims clean; center lids on the jars and screw on jar bands. Process for 10 minutes. Turn off heat, remove canner lid, and let jars rest in the water for 5 minutes. Remove jars and set aside for 24 hours. Check seals, then store in a cool, dark place for up to 1 year.

→ See page 40 for more about vinegar pickles.

HEIRLOOM WATERMELON JELLY

Makes about 4 cups

Okay, you don't have to use an heirloom watermelon, but why not? Whether you choose yellow, red, or orange, this recipe turns all of that tasty watermelon juice into a sparkling spread. Unlike the other jelly recipes in this book, you don't need to heat the watermelon to get it to release its juice.

INGREDIENTS

- **1** small watermelon (4–5 pounds), rind removed
- **1** cup sugar
- **2** tablespoons Pomona's Universal Pectin
- **½** cup bottled lemon juice
- **2** tablespoons calcium water (included in the Pomona box)

PREPARE

1. Cut the melon into chunks, and then purée in a blender or food processor. Don't mind any seeds; you'll strain them out later.

2. Pour the purée into a fine-mesh sieve, a colander lined with dampened cheesecloth, or a jelly bag set over a large bowl. Without pressing on the solids, allow to drip for an hour or so, until all the juice has been released.

3. Combine the sugar and pectin and set aside.

4. Measure 1 quart of melon juice into a medium nonreactive saucepan and bring to a boil. Add the lemon juice and calcium water. Add the sugar-pectin mixture and return to a boil, stirring to dissolve the sugar. Remove from the heat and let sit for 5 minutes, stirring occasionally to release air bubbles. Skim off any foam.

PRESERVE

Refrigerate: Ladle into bowls or jars. Cool, cover, and refrigerate for up to 3 weeks.

Can: Use the boiling-water method. Ladle into clean, hot 4-ounce or half-pint canning jars, leaving ¼ inch of headspace. Release trapped air. Wipe the rims clean; center lids on the jars and screw on jar bands. Process for 10 minutes. Turn off heat, remove canner lid, and let jars rest in the water for 5 minutes. Remove jars and set aside for 24 hours. Check seals, then store in a cool, dark place for up to 1 year.

→ See page 27 for more about jams and jellies.

WATERMELON AGUA FRESCA

Makes about 1 quart

I love, love, love watermelon. But sometimes we have a hard time getting through a whole one before it's past its peak. Here's one way to use up part of a melon.

INGREDIENTS

- **1** small melon or half of a large one, rind removed, fruit cut into large chunks
- **1** cup water
- **2** tablespoons sugar
  Juice of 1 lime

PREPARE

1. Set a fine-mesh sieve or colander lined with dampened cheesecloth over a bowl. Purée the melon in a blender or food processor, working in batches as necessary. Transfer the puréed melon to the sieve as you go. Let drain fully; compost solids.

2. Pour the melon juice into a pitcher. Add the water, sugar, and lime juice and stir to dissolve the sugar. Serve over ice, with a splash of seltzer, if you like.

→ See page 24 for more about aqua gresca and granita.

PRESERVE

⊘ **Refrigerate:** Refrigerate, without ice or seltzer, for up to 3 days.

⊕ **Freeze:** Freeze juice in 8-ounce servings for up to 3 months.

dry (p.71)

infuse (p.68)

can (p.79)

freeze (p.61)

refrigerate (p.59)

Watermelon Martini

Refreshing and pretty, this martini is perfect for a summer evening.

- **4** ounces Watermelon Agua Fresca (above)
- **2** ounces vodka
- **1** ounce Cointreau or other citrus-flavored liqueur

Combine Watermelon Agua Fresca, vodka, and Cointreau in a cocktail shaker full of ice. Shake vigorously and strain into 2 martini glasses. | **Makes 2 cocktails**

Resources

page 209

SWEET & SOUR PICKLED ONION — page 220

Chili Tomato Jam — page 169

CHARRED CHILI BBQ SAUCE — page 167

orange MAR-MA-LADE — page 173

Dilly Beans — page 118

DRIED CORN — page 177

FIGS — page 196

PICKLED CHILI PEPPERS — page 164

GRAPE SYRUP — page 202

Resources

Following are some resources for learning more about local, sustainable agriculture and home food preservation.

FURTHER READING

Fallon, Sally, and Mary G. Enig. *Nourishing Traditions: The Cookbook That Challenges Politically Correct Nutrition and the Diet Dictocrats*. Washington D.C.: NewTrends Publishing, 2001.

Greene, Janet, Ruth Hertzberg, and Beatrice Vaughan. *Putting Food By*. New York: Plume, 1992.

Halweil, Brian. *Eat Here: Reclaiming Homegrown Pleasures in a Global Supermarket*. New York: W.W. Norton, 2004.

Katz, Sandor Ellix. *Wild Fermentation*. White River Junction, VT: Chelsea Green Publishing, 2003.

Kingry, Judi, and Lauren Devine, eds. *Ball Complete Book of Home Preserving*. Richmond Hill, Ontario: Robert Rose, 2006.

McClure, Susan, and the staff of Rodale Food Center, eds. *Preserving Summer's Bounty*. Emmaus, PA: Rodale, 1998.

Nestle, Marion. *Food Politics: How the Food Industry Influences Nutrition and Health*, 2nd ed. Berkeley, CA: University of California Press, 2007.

Pollan, Michael. *The Omnivore's Dilemma: A Natural History of Four Meals*. New York: Penguin, 2007.

Schlosser, Eric. *Fast Food Nation: The Dark Side of the All-American Meal*. New York: Harper Perennial, 2009.

U.S. Department of Agriculture. *Complete Guide to Home Canning and Preserving*, 2nd ed. Mineola, NY: Dover, 1999.

Vinton, Sherri Brooks, and Ann Clark Espuelas. *The Real Food Revival: Aisle by Aisle, Morsel by Morsel*. New York: J.P. Tarcher, 2005.

Ziedrich, Linda. *The Joy of Pickling*, rev. ed. Boston: Harvard Common Press, 2009.

EQUIPMENT

My favorite resource for home canning supplies is my local hardware store. There I can find everything I need — jars, lids, twine, pots, pans, and good company, too. If they don't have it, they'll order it. I can't say enough about supporting your local businesses — it keeps our neighbors working and our communities thriving. You can also find preserving supplies at:

CANNING PANTRY
800-285-9044
www.canningpantry.com

POMONA'S UNIVERSAL PECTIN
www.pomonapectin.com

NATIONAL ORGANIZATIONS

BIONEERS
877-246-6337
www.bioneers.org
I found the most amazing heirloom corn meals and hominy through Bioneers. Log onto this site to help protect biodiversity.

CENTER FOR FOOD SAFETY
202-547-9359
www.centerforfoodsafety.org
The Center for Food Safety works to change public policy through public education and legal action.

CHEFS COLLABORATIVE
617-236-5200
www.chefscollaborative.org
Chefs Collaborative is a national network of more than 1,000 members of the food community who promote sustainable cuisine by celebrating the joys of local, seasonal, and artisanal cooking. Users can search a database of member restaurants that create sustainably produced, delicious meals.

COMMUNITY INVOLVED IN SUSTAINING AGRICULTURE (CISA)
413-665-7100
www.buylocalfood.com
Support CISA and its "Be a Local Hero" campaign by supporting local growers with your grocery dollars, attending events, and donating to the organization.

EDIBLE COMMUNITIES PUBLICATIONS
800-652-4217
www.ediblecommunities.com
Ever wish there was a local guide to all things sustainable and tasty? Now there is. These local guides, the brainchild of Tracey Ryder and Carole Topalian, reflect their local communities and all of the noble, delicious things they have to offer.

ENVIRONMENTAL WORKING GROUP
202-667-6982
www.ewg.org
This group's team of scientists, engineers, policy experts, lawyers, and computer programmers sifts through government data, legal documents, scientific studies, and laboratory tests to expose threats to health and the environment, and to find solutions.

FOODROUTES CONSERVANCY
570-673-3398
www.foodroutes.org
A national nonprofit dedicated to reintroducing Americans to their food, the seeds it grows from, the farmers who produce it, and the routes that carry it from the fields to our tables.

LOCALHARVEST

831-515-5602

www.localharvest.org

LocalHarvest was founded in 1998 and is now the number one informational resource for the "buy local" movement and the top place on the Internet where people find information on direct marketing family farms.

NATIONAL CENTER FOR HOME FOOD PRESERVATION

www.uga.edu/nchfp

This Web site holds a wealth of information.

NATIONAL SUSTAINABLE AGRICULTURE COALITION

202-547-5754

www.sustainableagriculture.net

A source for education and advocacy regarding sustainable agriculture issues.

SLOW FOOD USA

877-756-9366

www.slowfoodusa.org

Slow Food USA envisions a world in which all people can eat food that is good for them, good for the people who grow it, and good for the planet.

SUSTAINABLE AGRICULTURE RESEARCH AND EDUCATION PROGRAM

202-720-5384

www.sare.org

A project of the USDA to support sustainable agriculture through research and grants. Its site provides information about sustainability and searchable listings for farmers' markets and CSAs.

SUSTAINABLE TABLE

212-991-1930

www.sustainabletable.org

Sustainable Table is a consumer program founded to celebrate the sustainable food movement, educate individuals on food-related issues, and build community through sustainable food.

LOCAL SOURCES

Local sources for finding local food and produce seasonability calendars.

ALABAMA
FARMERS MARKET AUTHORITY

www.fma.alabama.gov

ALASKA
ALASKA GROWN

www.alaskagrown.org

ARIZONA
ARIZONA COMMUNITY FARMERS MARKETS

www.arizonafarmersmarkets.com

ARIZONA LOCAL FOOD

www.arizonalocalfood.com

ARKANSAS
ARKANSAS GROWN

www.arkansasgrown.org

CALIFORNIA

BAY AREA

THE CENTER FOR URBAN
EDUCATION ABOUT SUSTAINABLE
AGRICULTURE (CUESA)

www.cuesa.org

NORTHERN CALIFORNIA

CALIFORNIA FEDERATION OF
CERTIFIED FARMERS' MARKETS

www.cafarmersmarkets.com

COLORADO

COLORADO FARMERS' MARKET
ASSOCIATION

www.coloradofarmers.org

CONNECTICUT

CONNECTICUT GROWN

www.buyctgrown.com

DELAWARE

DELAWARE DEPARTMENT
OF AGRICULTURE

http://dda.delaware.gov

DISTRICT OF COLUMBIA

FRESHFARM MARKETS

www.freshfarmmarket.org

FLORIDA

FLORIDA DEPARTMENT OF
AGRICULTURE

www.florida-agriculture.com/consumers.htm

GEORGIA

GEORGIA ORGANICS

www.georgiaorganics.org

HAWAII

AGRICULTURAL DEVELOPMENT
DIVISION

Hawaii Department of Agriculture

http://hawaii.gov/hdoa/add

IDAHO

IDAHO PREFERRED

Idaho State Department of Agriculture

www.idahopreferred.com

ILLINOIS

FARM DIRECT

www.illinoisfarmdirect.org

FARMERS MARKETS

Illinois Department of Agriculture

www.agr.state.il.us/markets/farmers

INDIANA

AGRITOURISM & FARMERS' MARKETS

Indiana State Department of Agriculture

www.in.gov/isda/2342.htm

IOWA

IOWA FARMERS MARKET
ASSOCIATION

www.iafarmersmarkets.org

IOWA NETWORK FOR COMMUNITY
AGRICULTURE

www.growinca.org

KANSAS

KANSAS FARMERS MARKETS

www.ksfarmersmarkets.org

KENTUCKY
OFFICE OF AGRICULTURAL
MARKETING & PRODUCT PROMOTION
Kentucky Department of Agriculture
www.kyagr.com/marketing

LOUISIANA
LOUISIANA DEPARTMENT OF
AGRICULTURE & FORESTRY
www.ldaf.state.la.us

MAINE
GET REAL. GET MAINE!
Maine Department of Agriculture
www.getrealmaine.com

MARYLAND
MARYLAND PRODUCTS
Maryland Department of Agriculture
www.mda.state.md.us/md_products

MASSACHUSETTS
FEDERATION OF MASSACHUSETTS
FARMERS MARKETS
www.massfarmersmarkets.org

MICHIGAN
MICHIGAN FARMERS MARKETS
www.farmersmarkets.msu.edu

MINNESOTA
PRIDE OF THE PRAIRIE
University of Minnesota
http://prideoftheprairie.org

MINNESOTA GROWN
Minnesota Department of Agriculture
www3.mda.state.mn.us/mngrown

MISSISSIPPI
MISSISSIPPI DEPARTMENT OF
AGRICULTURE AND COMMERCE
www.mdac.state.ms.us

MISSOURI
MISSOURI FARMERS' MARKET
DIRECTORY
Agricultural Electronic Bulletin Board
http://agebb.missouri.edu/fmktdir

MONTANA
MONTANA FARMERS' MARKETS
Montana Department of Agriculture
http://agr.mt.gov/farmersmarkets

NEBRASKA
NEBRASKA DEPARTMENT OF
AGRICULTURE
Your Guide to Nebraska Fresh Produce
www.agr.state.ne.us/pub/apd/produce.htm

NEVADA
FARMERS' MARKETS
Nevada Department of Agriculture
http://agri.nv.gov/plant_nursery_farmermkts.htm

NEW HAMPSHIRE
NEW HAMPSHIRE FARMERS' MARKET
ASSOCIATION
www.nhfma.org

NEW JERSEY
NEW JERSEY COUNCIL OF FARMERS
& COMMUNITIES
www.jerseyfarmersmarkets.com

NEW MEXICO
NEW MEXICO FARMERS' MARKETS
http://farmersmarketsnm.org

NEW YORK
FARMERS' MARKET FEDERATION OF NEW YORK
www.nyfarmersmarket.com

NEW YORK CITY
GROWNYC
www.cenyc.org

NORTH CAROLINA
CAROLINA FARM STEWARDSHIP ASSOCIATION
www.carolinafarmstewards.org

NORTH CAROLINA FARM FRESH
www.ncfarmfresh.com

NORTH DAKOTA
NORTH DAKOTA FARMER'S MARKET AND PRODUCERS DIRECTORY
North Dakota Department of Agriculture
www.agdepartment.com/programs/ farmersmarkets.html

OHIO
OHIO PROUD
www.ohioproud.com

OKLAHOMA
OK GROWN
www.okgrown.com

OREGON
AGRICULTURAL DEVELOPMENT AND MARKETING DIVISION
Oregon Department of Agriculture
www.oregon.gov/ODA/ADMD

PENNSYLVANIA
PENNSYLVANIA BUY FRESH BUY LOCAL
Pennsylvania Association for Sustainable Agriculture
www.buylocalpa.org

RHODE ISLAND
FARM FRESH RHODE ISLAND
www.farmfreshri.org

SOUTH CAROLINA
CAROLINA FARM STEWARDSHIP ASSOCIATION
www.carolinafarmstewards.org

SOUTH DAKOTA
SOUTH DAKOTA LOCAL FOODS DIRECTORY
Dakota Rural Action
www.sdlocalfoods.org

TENNESSEE
PICK TENNESSEE PRODUCTS
http://picktnproducts.org

TEXAS
PICK TEXAS
Texas Department of Agriculture
www.picktexas.com

UTAH
UTAH'S OWN
Utah Department of Agriculture and Food
www.utahsown.utah.gov

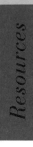

VERMONT
BUY LOCAL, BUY VERMONT
Vermont Agency of Agriculture
www.vermontagriculture.com/buylocal/buy

VIRGINIA
VIRGINIA GROWN
Virginia Department of Agriculture and
Consumer Services
www.vdacs.virginia.gov/vagrown

294

WASHINGTON
**WASHINGTON STATE FARMERS
MARKET ASSOCIATION**
www.wafarmersmarkets.com

WEST VIRGINIA
**WEST VIRGINIA FARMERS MARKET
ASSOCIATION**
www.wvfarmers.org

WISCONSIN
SAVORWISCONSIN.COM
www.savorwisconsin.com

WYOMING
**WYOMING FARMERS MARKETING
ASSOCIATION**
www.wyomingfarmersmarkets.org

Acknowledgments

I would like to thank all of those who were in the kitchen with me, in body and spirit, for this book: my sweet, supportive husband Drew who prepped and cleaned and cheered me through the whole thing, and my kids, Ava and Thayer, for their kitchen company and inexhaustible taste buds. I am deeply grateful to my mother, Nance, for never having a doubt, and to my father, Ray, for his stories about all of the deep cracks and facets. Thank you to Granny Toni, who put the bee in my bonnet in the first place, and to my grandmother Lucille, for giving me a taste of the South. I would like to thank the cooks who shared their recipes and tips, their company and their knife skills: Andrew, Bekah, Cassandra, Chandler, Cheré, David, Ed, Emily, Gabrielle, Irene, Janine, Jennifer, Michael, Nena, Stacia, and Virginia. I would like to thank my agent, Lisa Ekus, for her tireless support of local agriculture and those of us who write about it, and the entire Lisa Ekus Group for their encouragement and skill. Huge thanks also go out to Jane Falla for setting me straight. I would like to thank the Storey team, who have been an absolute treat to work with, particularly editor Margaret Sutherland, publicists Amy Greeman and Michelle Blackley, and designer Dan Williams, for their creative and intelligent work and fresh take on this fun topic. And a thousand gratitudes, always, to all the farmers dedicated to a more sustainable and delicious future — thank you!

Index

Page references in *italics* indicate photos or illustrations.

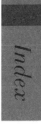

Other Storey Titles You Will Enjoy

The Beginner's Guide to Preserving Food at Home, by Janet Chadwick.
The best and quickest methods for preserving every common vegetable and fruit,
with easy instructions to encourage even first-timers.
240 PAGES. PAPER. ISBN 978-1-60342-145-4.

The Big Book of Preserving the Harvest, by Carol W. Costenbader.
A revised edition of a classic primer on freezing, canning, drying, and pickling
fruits and vegetables.
352 PAGES. PAPER. ISBN 978-1-58017-458-9.

The Herb Gardener, by Susan McClure.
Herb gardening basics for every season, indoors and out.
240 PAGES. PAPER. ISBN 978-0-88266-873-4.

Starter Vegetable Gardens, by Barbara Pleasant.
A great resource for beginning vegetable gardeners: 24 no-fail plans for
small organic gardens.
180 PAGES. PAPER. ISBN 978-1-60342-529-2.

The Vegetable Gardener's Bible, 2nd edition, by Edward C. Smith.
The 10th Anniversary Edition of the vegetable gardening classic, with expanded
coverage of additional vegetables, fruits, and herbs.
352 PAGES. PAPER. ISBN 978-1-60342-475-2. HARDCOVER. ISBN 978-1-60342-476-9.

The Veggie Gardener's Answer Book, by Barbara W. Ellis.
Insider's tips and tricks, practical advice, and organic wisdom for
vegetable growers everywhere.
432 PAGES. FLEXIBIND. ISBN 978-1-60342-024-2.

These and other books from Storey Publishing are available
wherever quality books are sold or by calling 1-800-441-5700.
Visit us at *www.storey.com*.